UNDERSTANDING LANGUAGE ACQUISITION

UNDERSTANDING LANGUAGE ACQUISITION

The Framework of Learning

CHRISTINA E. ERNELING

State University
of New York
Press

Published by
State University of New York Press, Albany

For information, address State University of New York
Press, State University Plaza, Albany, NY 12246

Production by Susan Geraghty
Marketing by Bernadette LaManna

Library of Congress Cataloging-in-Publication Data

Erneling, Christina E.
    Understanding language acquisition : the framework of learning /
by Christina E. Erneling.
        p.   cm. — (SUNY series, literacy, culture, and learning)
    Includes bibliographical references and index.
    ISBN 0-7914-1461-2 — ISBN 0-7914-1462-0 (pbk.)
    1. Language acquisition. 2. Learning, Psychology of. 3. Thought
and thinking. 4. Language and languages—Philosophy.   I. Title.
II. Series.
P118.E76   1993
401'.93—dc20   92-22085
                                                                    CIP

10 9 8 7 6 5 4 3 2 1

For Alf

CONTENTS

ACKNOWLEDGMENTS

This study grew out of my Ph.D. dissertation presented at York University, Toronto, Canada in 1990. I would like to thank Professors F. Cowley, J. H. Hattiangadi, D. Johnson, S. Shanker, and H. T. Wilson for their helpful comments and suggestions. I am especially grateful to my supervisor, Professor J. H. Hattiangadi, whose work on language and ethology has been an important influence. Professor Rom Harré has been a major source of inspiration and I have learned a lot from his teachings; my work owes much to his synthesis of philosophy and psychology. Professor Robert J. Ackermann was the first who introduced me to the writings of Wittgenstein and the possibilities of philosophy, and shaped my development considerably. My thanks also to Professor Judith Buber Agassi and Professor Joseph Agassi for their intellectual stimulation and challenge, and to Dr. Cathy Boyd-Withers for many helpful suggestions on my first draft. The support of my mother, Maij Erneling, has also been invaluable.

My husband, Alf Bång, without whose inspiration, encouragement, intellectual challenges, and support this study would neither have been undertaken nor finished, deserves my greatest thanks.

Neither of them is, of course, committed to any opinions expressed in this book, nor responsible for any mistakes.

INTRODUCTION

During the past thirty years, one of the fastest growing areas in cognitive and developmental psychology has been the study of language acquisition. Central figures in this development have been Noam Chomsky in linguistics and Jean Piaget in psychology. Their theories, although quite different, share some basic assumptions with most theories of language acquisition and learning, namely, individualism and cognitivism. The individualism is expressed in that they both take language to be acquired on the basis of individual mental structures, which are either innate (Chomsky) or acquired (Piaget), and their cognitivism consists in claims to the effect that the language-learning child is a thinker first and a speaker second.

This is in line with the main trend in academic psychology, which studies language acquisition not as a social achievement but as a process internal to the individual, in which the individual learner is on his or her own, interacting with the environment to develop knowledge and language. Other people are seen as aspects of the environment, in principle having the same effects on the child as the physical environment. Academic psychology is here closely connected with a dominant trend in the Western philosophical tradition, in which the epistemological problem is taken to be one that exists for the individual mind in relation to the external world. The interaction with other people is not seen as a condition for knowledge and the individual is not therefore seen as someone who fundamentally shares life, knowledge, and language with other humans. In modern times, Descartes sanctified the "I" and "I think" in his search for ultimate certainty, and he claimed that knowledge begins with the awareness of one's own existence as a thinking being, and knowledge of the world, other minds, and language is founded on this. Influenced by such views, Western philosophy and psychology have centered on humans as isolated subjects set up against the world,

1

and of human beings as thinkers, making individualism as well as cognitivism unquestioned assumptions of rationalism as well as empiricism. In the rationalistic tradition, Leibniz's idea of windowless monads, that is, the idea that the universe consists of totally isolated and independent, intelligent individuals/monads, is an example of this. In the empiricist tradition, Berkeley went further than his predecessor Locke and identified the world with the ideas in the mind of an individual person or thinker. Hume's associationism and Kant's account of knowledge in terms of the synthesizing unity of the individual understanding, although very different in many ways, are also similar in this respect. This kind of individualism and cognitivism has persisted up to the present time and although there have been some attempts to move away from it (e.g., behaviorism, Vygotsky, and to some degree Bruner), it is still dominating. Piaget, although stressing the child's physical activity and interaction with the environment, took individual cognitive development as central to and dominating all other aspects of development, including linguistic development. Chomsky with his view of language acquisition as a process of unfolding of innate grammar triggered by the environment evokes Leibniz's monads. Individuals are seen as isolated independent individuals equipped with complete innate knowledge of language, functioning together and communicating because of a pre-established harmony between them. Both, although disagreeing on the innateness of language, agree that the child acquires language based on individual mental and cognitive structures.

One of the more extreme and conceptually very challenging proponents of individualism and cognitivism applied to the problem of language learning is Jerry Fodor, who has developed and generalized Chomsky's views. In *The Language of Thought* (1979), Fodor agrues that the acquisition of language requires an "innate language of thought," which contains a complete set of representations of anything a person can ever learn, including langauge. The child learns language by forming hypothesizes in the language of thought and tests them against the language spoken around him or her. Thus, learning is seen as a translation from the language of thought to the language of the child's community. This revival of the Platonic innatist conception of learning, which utilizes ideas from cognitive science and Artificial Intelligence, overcomes some problems with cognitivism and individualism, but ultimately fails. The failure is an indication that the two main problems all theories of language acquisition have to solve, namely, the problem of linguistic creativity (i.e., that any competent language user can produce and understand a potentially infinite number of sentences) and the problem that learning presupposes prior knowledge (i.e., the seemingly logical requirement that learning a language presupposes a prior framework of meaning), cannot be solved by theories of this type.

A critique as well an an alternative approach to the whole tradition, and more specifically to Fodor-type theories of language learning, can be found in the philosophy of the later Wittgenstein, especially in his *Philosophical Investigations.* There, in rejecting his own earlier view in the *Tractaus,* Wittgenstein shows what is wrong with Fodor-type conceptions of learning and langauge, and he also provides us with an alternative to the individualistic and cognitivistic assumptions. Although language learning was not a central topic for Wittgenstein, much of what he says addresses the two main problems of learning just mentioned. He shows why the idea that the framework of language learning consists of a language of thought cannot explain learning or the mastery of language, and claims that the framework consists of natural reactions and behaviors as well as the sociolinguistic context in which the child is trained to use language in the same way as other speakers. He furthermore rejects Fodor-type solutions to the problem of productivity, that is, in terms of rule-following, and claims that language is indeterminate in the sense that meaning is not determined by grammatical or other rules, or by past usage, and speaking or communicating is therefore always creative. This means that we do not need to look for an explanation of linguistic creativity, but to what restricts actual language use and what prevents speaking and communication from breaking down into idiosyncratic usages. This is accomplished by social training and one could thus say that the child, according to Wittgenstein, learns language by being domesticated, that is, by having its natural reactions and behaviors shaped in accordance with sociolinguistic activities, and not by translating from an innate language of thought. These claims suggest that the two fundamental problems of learning can be solved without the assumptions of individualism and cognitivism.

The first part of the book is a presentation and discussion of

Fodor's and Wittgenstein's solutions to the two problems of language learning along the lines indicated. The reason I have concentrated on their views is that both are very sophisticated, and that a large part of contemporary psychologists have chosen to develop ideas founded on positions they represent. In the second part, I present a model of my own based on Wittgenstein's reconceptualization of what language learning involves. I have chosen to call it the Domestication Model to emphasize that learning a first language is a matter of social training, when the child's natural behaviors and reactions are shaped by sociolinguistic interaction and training. The framework of learning does not consist of innate or acquired cognitive-linguistic mental structures, but of a combination of the child's natural behavior, sociolinguistic interaction, and the language spoken around him or her, thus involving other things than the individual's mind. As Wittgenstein, I take the child's behavior as well as language to be fundamentally productive, and it is through training or domestication that this productivity is limited, making room for meaningful language and communication. To show this, one does not need to undertake new empirical studies, but rather, look at what we already know about children, their behavior, and the sociolinguistic contexts in which they are raised from a noncognitivistic and nonindividualistic perspective. Children's brains, their perception and production of speech sounds, increasingly complex and structured motor behaviors and activities like imitation and play, all change as a result of maturation, sociolinguistic interaction, and training, and it is around the child's first birthday that they come together resulting in language. It is at this time that the child's indiscriminate babbling has been narrowed and shaped to include only the sounds of the child's mother language, and imitation and play have become complex enough to allow the child to use symbols and engage in conventional play. This has been accomplished by domestication of natural behaviors, by combination and training of different innate and acquired languagelike behaviors to approximate those of a competent language user.

I thus claim that by a reconceptualization of what we already know about children along the line of what Wittgenstein suggests we can identify the framework of learning in languagelike behaviors and sociolinguistic interactions, and that the two problems of learning can be solved in nonindividualistic and noncognitivistic terms.

In sum, the book consists of a philosophical discussion of what language learning involves and a critical analysis of Fodor's and Wittgenstein's views on this. The critique functions as the groundwork for developing a model of my own, the so-called Domestication Model of language learning, which uses already available empirical data to show that learning language is not an individual cognitive process. I hope it will provide impetus for future theoretical and empirical work, which will test its strengths and weaknesses.

CHAPTER 1

Learning: Going Beyond Information Given

THE TWO PROBLEMS OF LEARNING: PRODUCTIVITY AND THE FRAMEWORK

When a newborn human infant confronts its environment for the first time it is a helpless creature which is totally dependent on others to satisfy its needs and cope with dangers from the environment. In many respects the child is more helpless than any other newborn species of animal. Yet, in a few years time and under normal circumstances, it will acquire knowledge and a remarkable ability to deal with its surroundings. And unlike any other animal the child will talk and be talked to, and will have incorporated into its language some of the accumulated social and cultural lore of its elders and its society. The helpless infant transforms into a talking, thinking being, actively involved and contributing in a small way to its cultural and intellectual heritage. The child not only transcends its instincts in a certain sense but also goes beyond its own limited experience, and is able to deal in a culturally and linguistically appropriate way with novel situations and problems personally never encountered before. All this can only happen because a child, having mastered its mother tongue, can understand and produce a potentially unlimited number of new sentences. Instincts, or innate tendencies, and experience are both necessary but not enough for the acquisition of language and knowledge.

How then are we to understand the acquisition of knowledge, and the understanding and the mastery of language? What are the conditions under which individual children learn in order to master the language spoken in their environments, to master concepts and acquire knowledge about the world? What is the relation

7

between the child's initial instincts and later knowledge, and what is the role of experience? The quest to understand the conditions for the acquisition of knowledge, not only in the child but in the adult as well as in science, has a long history in philosophy. More recently, since the emergence of developmental psychology, the same questions are asked in a new framework, and answered in quite different and sometimes mutually exclusive ways by different theoretical approaches. This book is an attempt to show that during this century there has been some progress in both identifying and solving the conceptual problems involved in understanding learning, especially language learning, but much still remains to be done. This chapter aims to present what I take to be the fundamental problem or conceptual dilemma for any theory of learning, and to show how several historical attempts to explain learning have overlooked this or failed to solve it. The recent interest in the learning of language, as especially expressed by N. Chomsky, his follower J. Fodor and the later Wittgenstein, has given us, if not a successful theory of the learning of language, at least a better understanding of what needs to be done.

The issue being addressed concerning learning, especially language learning, is not so much about rote learning or mindless repetition of what experience provides, nor the change in an organism's cognitive abilities due to some chemical or physiological change, though all this must play a part,[1] but concerns concept formation, language acquisition, the growth of knowledge and understanding. Once something is learned in this way, the knowledge can be extended to new situations. Compare, for example, a pupil who has memorized a number of multiplications by heart and is able to solve the problems memorized but is unable to solve new problems, with the pupil who has had the same exposure to examples of multiplications but who is able to cope in addition with new problems. The latter case is a change in the pupil's cognitive ability to deal with certain types of problems, while the former involves merely mechanical repetition. Both use what they have learned through experience, from a teacher or from a book, but one is able to go beyond experience in utilizing it. How this happens, or can happen is, in a nutshell, one of the fundamental problems of learning, no doubt.

Approached in this way learning is a process of change or alteration—as a consequence of relevant experience, but not determined by experience—of the individual's cognitive capabilities. How can we account for this change, its starting point, its character, and so on? How should the cognitive abilities be characterized? Are they instinctual and adaptive behaviors, or are they mental problem-solving strategies? Answering these questions in detail involves much empirical study, but before this can be undertaken the conceptual issues involved have to be clarified. Without conceptual clarification the empirical material will be difficult to interpret and progress in understanding a phenomena slow.

> For in psychology there are experimental methods and *conceptual confusion*.[2]

With this remark Wittgenstein, who himself was deeply interested in language and different psychological problems, wanted to draw attention to the fact psychologists and many other scientists often equalize research with the collecting of facts thus forgetting that research also involves an understanding of which problem(s) the facts are supposed to solve. This cannot be separated from the collection and interpretation of facts. The aim of this book is not to add to the collection of facts about how children learn language, but to lay bare the fundamental logical or conceptual problems that any explanation of learning, especially language learning, has to face. I will show how different way of approaching and making sense of what we already know about language learning have failed partly because the conceptual framework has been inadequate. I will thus argue that one of the most difficult problems, among many to be faced, is to clarify what is entailed by going beyond information given in experience or innate endowments, and how it can be accounted for. To do this I have chosen to discuss two influential but opposed solutions to this problem, the later Wittgenstein's and Jerry Fodor's.[3] This, I hope, will clarify some of the issues involved, and on the basis of this discussion, I will present a sketch of an empirical theory of going beyond information given when learning a language. As I will later show the two thinkers just mentioned are both well aware of some of the conceptual problems involved in understanding the possibility of learning language and have both come up with interesting but ultimately unsatisfactory "new ways of looking at old facts." They both, and especially Wittgenstein, though, can help us find a new understanding of language acquisition.

Before turning to these more theoretical problems it is important to distinguish learning both from growth or maturation and from genuine creativity. Learning involves both maturation and genuine creativity, but understanding these on their own is not enough to understand what going beyond information given in, for example, language acquisition, involves. Growth and maturation are associated primarily with the emergence of the organism's biological or physiological characteristics in a rather fixed and determined order, and not with the acquisition of language and knowledge. This separation has been contested by Noam Chomsky in his book *Rules and Representations* (1980).[4] Here he argues that mechanisms like growth and maturation, which successfully explain changes in physiological systems, can also explain language learning. Theories of learning are only invoked to explain creativity, by which he means acquisition and concept formation in areas of knowledge which are on the border of, or just beyond, our cognitive abilities. I think Chomsky is correct in pointing to creativity as one of the central problems of learning, but mistaken in thinking that creativity in the sense just mentioned can be explained by psychological theories of learning. First, genuine creativity, like radical conceptual innovation or the invention of a new linguistic entity, cannot be explained by any theories, whether they are couched in terms of learning or not. The reason for this is that if we are in the possession of a theory that explains radical conceptual innovation we would already, in one sense, have made the innovation. The innovation may not be explicit in the theory, but it would only be a matter of working something out, not going beyond what we already know. Although innovation in art or science must build on what has already been achieved in the field in question and be a result of human mental/psychological activity, it can not be predicted on basis of previous scientific or artistic achievements, or on the basis of a psychological theory of cognitive functioning. Of course, what is an innovation for the individual learner need not be radical innovation in this sense, but then we are no longer speaking of extending the borders of our cognitive capabilities. If this is correct, and in other writings Chomsky seems to agree, *this* radical creativity is not a problem of learning.[5] The problem involved in learning is more like the creativity that occurs in everyday or mundane situations. For example, a pupil can apply a very simple arithmetic rule beyond the examples he or she has already calculated. Or, as Chomsky himself has pointed out, every normally competent speaker can understand and produce utterances never encountered before. Other skills such as driving a car or operating on a patient's appendix deal with new situations on the basis of acquired knowledge, so explaining these is also the object of learning theories. Hence the problem of how learning or change in knowledge is possible confronts us not so much in the creative artist or the scientist, but in most everyday situations whenever our actions are not mindless repetition or habit. Without question, though, the problem of going beyond information given and learning, gets its sharpest formulation when we consider how a helpless infant who seemingly knows nothing becomes a speaking, knowing being. How is it to be accounted for? How are we to understand the framework of prior knowledge or ability, of experience and social interaction which makes this possible?[6]

There are two fundamental puzzles that any learning theory has to confront, namely the problem of creativity or productivity, which has already been mentioned, and the problem of the basic framework, namely the problem of the starting point or basis of learning, which acts to define the boundaries of what can be learned in a given area. These problems create a puzzle or a dilemma because they pull in different directions. The first problem deals with the way all learning involves moving *beyond* the limits of what was previously known, while the second problem seems to imply that any moving beyond is impossible. The problem of creativity refers to the ability of language users or thinkers to produce or understand sentences or thoughts which are new to their experiences,[7] and the tendency to go beyond particular experiences to general knowledge, that is, to go beyond information given. Once something is learned or acquired this knowledge can be extended to new situations or contexts. For example, as already mentioned, one can learn the multiplication tables by heart, and be able to give correct answers to all cases of multiplication one has learned. Or, one can learn the tables in such a way that one is able to deal with, not only the cases one has been confronted with in the learning situation, but also with cases of multiplication never encountered before. The last indicates a change in the pupil's ability to deal with certain types of new situations, not only a passive repetition of a finite set of cases. On the basis of practicing a finite set of examples of multiplications a pupil can do a potentially infinite set of nontrivial multiplications. Experiencing a few instances of a certain object or event the learner generalizes to all objects or event of the relevant kind. Even more fundamentally, using words and concepts necessarily involve going beyond individual experiences.

> when we want to describe them we must necessarily make use of words; and these words and the propositions they form must by the nature of the case have a meaning of a more general nature than the single and individual experiences they refer to.[8]

The problematic hinted at here, namely that all our experiences are unique events, yet are subsumed under the same concepts, is not unique to the problem of learning but is a special case of the problem of induction, namely the generalization from a finite set of instances to a potentially infinite set. One example of this is the generalization "All swans are white" based on the observation of a large, but not indefinite number of swans; another is applying the word "table" to a new instance of a piece of furniture similar to what one earlier has called table. Yet another is the assumption that just because lightening has been followed in the past by thunder, this will happen the next time one is observing lightning in close vicinity. In all reasoning, everyday, scientific and even in using language, the principle of induction, or going beyond information given, is utilized.[9] Any theory of learning has thus to confront one of the perennial problems of philosophy.

Not any occurrence of a new sentence, thought, or generalization counts as an instance of learning. The new instance cannot be a random utterance or action, but has to meet certain standards or criteria. Depending on what is learned, it has to be justifiable in light of a body of knowledge, or of a grammar and so forth. It has to be intelligible, understood, or meaningful, and it has to be connected in a nonarbitrary way both with experience and with what is already known, that is, it has to fit into an already established framework of knowledge or experience. It also has to be applied or used in a systematic way when confronted with new experiences or knowledge. Furthermore, a framework of knowledge or at least a mechanisms for sorting, incooperating or even rejecting what is encountered is needed for learning from experience. To benefit from experience the learner has to sort relevant experiences (e.g., speech sounds) from irrelevant experiences (e.g., other sounds), and connect these with other relevant experience or information already possessed. But to do this the learner already has to have some idea of what is relevant and what is not, that is, the learner must already have some basic grasp of what is to be learned. This brings us to the second puzzle—the problem of the basic framework, namely that unless one already knows something, or has some basic knowledge or set of assumptions, it is impossible to learn something new. Just as the puzzle of productivity can be understood as a special case of the problem of induction, the idea of the necessity of an underlying framework is exploited by proponents of relativism. The relativist claims that mutual understanding is impossible between different cultures, different historical times, or between different scientific theories unless there is a framework of shared assumptions. Someone claiming that it is impossible for someone who does not have children (i.e., lacks the relevant first hand experience or knowledge) to understand the worries involved in raising children, or someone claiming that it is impossible for men to understand women, is a relativist in the sense of saying that it is impossible to understand or learn something new unless on already has the relevant knowledge. Historians or anthropologists claiming that it is impossible to use Western concepts and ideas to understand other cultures are making the same assumption. Other well known examples of the same idea can be found in contemporary philosophy of science. For example, to use Kuhn's terminology,[10] unless two scientists share a paradigm or set of shared assumptions, definitions, and procedures, which serve to delimit their scientific field, communication and understanding is impossible. This implies that scientists from different paradigms cannot understand the problems and their solutions in that of the other, and hence can not learn from it, unless they translate it into their own conceptual scheme. But this translation is always incomplete because the concepts have no counterparts in the other system. Newton's physics, for example, was not an extension and improvement of Aristotle's theory, but introduced a radically new way of conceptualizing the phenomena studied. Newton's theory was incommensurable with

Aristotle's and physicists schooled in Aristotelian physics are unable to use their knowledge to understand and learn from Newtonian physics. In adopting Newtonian physics, physicists had to give up their old way of understanding physics and "convert," perhaps even to some extent, uncritically or irrationally to the new theory. It is impossible to learn an alien paradigm that is incommensurable with the paradigm one is operating within. It follows that communication, discussion and learning is only possible within a paradigm or shared framework of assumptions and beliefs related to the area in question. Does this mean that all learning involves prior knowledge of the type one is learning? Does this imply that an infant learning its native language also has to know what it is learning, that is, that it already possesses a body of relevant knowledge? Does it mean that one already has to possess the knowledge one is learning, hence learning is really a myth? This problem is not new and was already stated by Plato in *Meno*:

> a man cannot search either for what he knows or for what he does not know? He cannot search for what he knows since he knows it, there is no need to search—nor for what he does not know, for he does not know what to look for.[11]

Given this should we conclude that learning is impossible and that productivity or the ability to generalize is only appearance, or even a myth? The paradox seems to imply the impossibility of learning something new, yet acquiring something new is at the heart of learning. Can both these poles—the going beyond information given, and the necessity of already knowing what one is learning be reconciled? Is it possible to go beyond information given, and if so how? This is the fundamental dilemma that has to be faced in understanding learning; is a trade off between productivity and the framework possible? If so, how?

All learning theories have to deal with this problem and in doing so they are forced to make explicit *firstly* the nature and characteristics of the framework or basic assumptions, or more generally the unlearned givens from which learning has to start. To avoid infinite regress of new knowledge building on old knowledge there has to be something unlearned, but given the puzzle of the framework discussed above, this seems to have to be fundamentally the same as that which is learned.[12] *Secondly,* the nature of the relationship between what is known and what is learned has to be specified along with the nature of the process or mechanism which makes this possible, that is, in what ways new knowledge connect with what is already known. *Thirdly*, since we defined learning as a change in knowledge due to, but not determined by experience, the role of experience has to be accounted for. *Finally*, since not anything new counts as an instance of learning, the standards or limits of the change in learning have to be made explicit.

To further illustrate the problems of learning, especially the tension between productivity and the framework, I will briefly analyze some paradigmatic historical attempts, found in the already mentioned dialogue by Plato, and the English eighteenth-century philosopher David Hume, arguing that they are unsuccessful. I will then state what I see as important improvements over these traditional solutions.

HISTORICAL ATTEMPTS
TO SOLVE THE PROBLEMS OF LEARNING

Historically the problem of learning and the issue of productivity and the framework were seen as part of epistemology or the theory of knowledge, and the two main traditions of rationalism and empiricism provide two different and mutually incompatible attempts to account for the possibility of learning. Rationalism characterized learning in terms of inherent or inbuilt reason, which functions independent of experience. Although experience could have a role of triggering or activating the inherent reason it could never change its fundamental structure or content. Empiricists, on the other hand, saw learning as a result of the association of ideas given to the mind by experience. This associationistic approach was taken over by nearly all learning theories which emerged as psychology established itself as an independent discipline in the late nineteenth and early twentieth century. Opposition to this approach came first from Gestalt psychology and later from information processing theories, cognitive and ecological theories.[13, 14]

One way to characterize their disagreement is to say that they disagreed about the nature of the framework, with the associationsits saying that the individual mental framework is relatively poor. The mind only contains mechanisms for association and all else is provided by experience. Protesting this the Gestalt psychologists, information processing and cognitive theories claimed that the mental framework necessary for learning contains much more, either in the form of actual knowledge or at least elaborate structures for analyzing experience. They also differed on the issue of productivity, or the learner's ability to go beyond information given. The associationistic theories characterized this in terms of new material from experience and a process trial and error in contrast to the rationalists' view that productivity amounts to working out or making explicit something already in the mind. The dilemma created by the tension between the framework and productivity was never addressed explicitly by these early learning theories and mirrored the failure of traditional philosophies to adequately solve the two fundamental problems of learning (i.e., productivity and the basic framework). I think this failure is best illustrated by brief sketches of two paradigmatic solutions, namely Plato's theory of innate ideas as an example of rationalism and Hume's empiricism. This also serves as a discussion and illustration of the difficulties involved in the two problems of learning.

The natural starting point for such a discussion or inquiry is Plato's dialogue *Meno*. In this dialogue a young Athenian, Meno, asks Socrates to answer the question: "Can virtue be taught?" This leads to a discussion of what virtue is because Socrates insists that we cannot claim to know if something is teachable unless we know what it is. Socrates and Meno, though, fail in their joint attempt to define virtue and this leads to the conclusion that unless one already knows what virtue is one cannot learn it, hence their whole discussion is fruitless. Here the fundamental problem, already mentioned, is stated in terms of a paradox. If one already knows what one is learning there is no need to to learn it, and if one does not know what one is learning one does not know where to find the new knowledge. Does this mean that the quest for new knowledge is hopeless and just a myth both in the individual and for human beings as a collective, in science? No, not even Plato thought so, and immediately after stating the paradox he attempts to show how new knowledge is possible, arguing that knowledge which is new to the individual, or new on particular occasions, even if not new in a fundamental sense, is possible.

Socrates, in answering the paradox claims that the soul is immortal, it has at one time seen and known all things. Learning is really a recollection of what was known before.

> As the whole of nature is akin, and the soul has learned everything, nothing prevents man, after recalling one thing only—a process man calls learning—discovering everything else for himself.[15]

As Socrates illustrates in questioning a slave boy, the boy recollects or recalls geometrical truths simply by being presented with verbal or visual examples of the truths involved.

This account depends on a distinction between latent or implicit knowledge and actual or explicit knowledge. The new knowledge is knowledge one already possesses latently. Through "learning" it becomes actually present to the mind. The slave boy under the questioning of Socrates, not only gets rid of false beliefs, but becomes aware of knowledge latent in his mind. Once some of this knowledge has been made actual, he is also able to work out further consequences of what he already knew, but had forgotten. The slave boy has learned something, acquired knowledge which is new to him on this occasion. But what has changed is not the content of what is in the boy's mind, or the content or structure of the knowledge itself,[16] but the slave boy's relation or attitude to it because he has become aware of, or knows, something he didn't know before. So that which the pupil has to know in order to learn something is *the same* as that which he learns.

Hence the claim of the paradox, that one has to have knowledge to learn something, that learning always involves prior knowledge, has not been violated, yet there is room for productivity of sorts. At least particular individuals on particular occasions can go beyond knowledge already given, in the sense of making knowledge that is latent actual to the mind. What was once known but forgotten is re-presented to the mind. In this sense it is new, but since it was already known before in a fundamental sense it is not new.

The possession of latent or old knowledge is, though, not in itself enough for learning or going beyond information given. Learning is not spontaneous, not generated by the mind alone, but something is needed to get the process going. The slave boy is asked leading questions and is confronted with examples to which he either assents or dissents. Here experience clearly plays a role in learning because without it recollection or learning does not take place. But what role does experience play according to Plato? In *Meno* experience seems to trigger or release latent knowledge, which then independently of experience is extended or further developed by the mind. But in another of Plato's dialogues *Phaedo*[17] this fundamentally causal role of experience is questioned since to be reminded of something, to recollect something we have to see similarities or the relevant connection between what experience provides and what is already known. Experience has to be acknowledged as relevant and only then can it aid in recollection. Again, one has already to know what one is learning. Once experience has played its role the process of learning seems to be a process of deduction, that is, of working out or deducing consequences of what one already knows:

> nothing prevents man after recalling one thing only—a process which man calls learning—discovering everything else for himself.[18]

In this model further learning clearly is a matter of deductive reasoning, that is, reasoning where the conclusions follow necessarily from the premises and hence can be said to be already contained in the premises. This is not implausible given Plato's example of geometrical knowledge which is a prime example of a deductive system. But what about learning empirical truths, for example whether or not a particular plant is poisonous? Or who won a particular battle? Or what about color terms, where there seems to be no deductive relation between them? Knowing what red is like does not help one deduce what green is like, just like knowing about a particular battle in the First World War does not help one to deduce or learn about what happened during the Second World War. Some knowledge is not related in a straightforward way to what one already knows. This is a challenge to Plato because this seems to be a case of learning something genuinely new, something not entailed in one's innate knowledge. The question remains—if not all knowledge is like geometrical knowledge, how are these other things learned? Is it possible to go beyond information given?

With this in mind Plato's theory leaves us with the feeling that not much is gained, because the end result of learning is just a representation of what one already knew. The learner has not gained new knowledge, but only changed his or her attitude to something that has not changed. So, are we left with the paradox unresolved, are we left with a static framework and unexplained creativity?

Not necessarily, because what the paradox implies, I think, is not that to learn something one has to know exactly and fully the thing one is learning. To use Plato's metaphor, it is clear that we can search and recognize something which we haven't encountered before, or even had a full description of. It is true that if we have no idea of what we are looking for, we cannot recognize it, but it does not follow that we have to know everything about it to recognize it, or for that matter where to search for it. If this is correct the new knowledge has to be intelligible to the learner, that is, it has to fit with something the learner already knows, but it does not have to be a replica of what is already known. Hence something is needed, but it is not necessary that one has to have a permanent, unchanging preexistent structure of knowledge. It is not even (logically) possible that new knowledge builds on old knowledge, because it is possible, (although extremely unlikely), that without learning we acquire a new framework every five minutes or so, for no cause at all, or for a cause that would not count as learning.[19]

A version of the last is what the empiricists have assumed in their account of learning. What is known without learning or "given," that is, the framework which new knowledge builds on or is developed out of, is sense experience. They see learning as a function of experience. The individual learner notices or rather receives certain experiences or images, which when repeated in a certain sequence become associated with one another. Different images of sense experiences get combined or changed to yield new compound ideas. In this way what is given in experience together with the combinatorial tendencies of the mind gives rise to new knowledge. In David Hume's words:

> and that all this creative power of the mind amounts to no more than the faculty of compounding, transposing, augmenting, or diminishing the materials afforded us by the senses and experience.[20]

Does creativity here, as well as in Plato's account, only amount to the rearrangement or re-presentation of what is given? Let us consider Hume's account of causation as an example of going beyond information given to see if he can account for productivity. The causation of one event by another is not directly given in experience, it cannot be simply observed or experienced. We only see a set of separate events or actions, for example, one moving billiard ball touching another and the second moving, not the causal relation between them. But he argues that repeated observations of events occurring together result in the habit of expecting the events in question to occur together.[21] In this case the human mind is able to go beyond what is given in experience to new knowledge, by utilizing an internal response or habit to link certain things together. According to this view, the mind is not an instrument for the passive re-presentation of what is given (in experience), but actively creates something new. New knowledge is possible in two ways—experience constantly provides new building blocks and the mind is combining and recombining these. No latent knowledge is necessary, only experiential input and the mechanisms of the mind for combining knowledge.

But already Plato had seen some obvious problems with any such approach. The mere enumeration of examples of virtue, shape, or color cannot teach us what virtue, shape, or color is because if we do not know what the examples are examples of, we cannot look for relevant features, and the like, and then we, of course, cannot learn that all cases of a particular thing or characteristic have something in common. For example, someone pointing to pictures of the Sears Building in Chicago, the CN Tower in Toronto and the Empire State Building in New York City could be trying to teach me what a high rise is, but unless I already know this I could just as well take the pictures to be examples of ugly buildings, or expensive buildings, or North American buildings and so forth. Some prior knowledge is clearly required to learn from the enumeration of examples or other experiences. In the case of causation, to observe a sequence of events as similar presupposes that they are recognized as similar. In that case one already has acquired the relevant generalizations, or the relevant habit. In other words, one has to know what one is learning.

But there is an additional related problem with the empiricistic account. Because all knowledge transcends experience, the empiricists' account of learning quickly runs into an extremely difficult and persistent problem, namely the problem of induction and/or the problem of the underdetermination of theories based on experience. The problem of induction has been formulated in many different ways, but basically it is the problem of the justification of inference from particular instances of a certain kind to all instances of the kind in question. For example, from having experienced the sun to rise every day of our life we conclude that it will always rise, but of course nothing in our past experiences guarantee that the future is going to be the same. Saying that our past expectations have always been fulfilled in the past and thus will be so in the future is only another example of making an inference from particular instances (past experiences) to all instances of fulfilling one's expectations.

The problem of induction can be formulated or approached in another way which is equally challenging to the empiricist account of learning. The so-called 'new riddle of induction' was formulated by the American philosopher Nelson Goodman (1972).[22] It deals with the problem of if and how we, from a finite set of experiences of a particular kind, are justified in drawing one conclusion rather than another. For example, suppose that all emeralds we have observed up to a point *t* have been green. This would support equally well the generalization that "All emeralds are green" as the generalization "All emeralds are grue," if 'grue' stands for the property of being green up to point *t* and blue thereafter.

If experience is underdetermined in this way, that is, indefinitely many conclusions or generalizations can be drawn from experience, how is learning or new knowledge ever possible unless the mind is equipped with a set of hypothesis limiting which conclusions are justified? We seem to be back at Plato's paradox. If these problems are at the heart of learning, how is the acquisition of knowledge possible unless we already possess the relevant knowledge in question? Moreover, how is it possible to learn something new, to go beyond information given by experience or the mind? How is it possible to go from something finite to something universal or potentially infinite? Let me turn to some more contemporary attempts to deal with this problem.

CONTEMPORARY SOLUTIONS: SKINNER, CHOMSKY, FODOR, AND WITTGENSTEIN

During this century one of the most influential developments of empiricist theories of learning was behaviorism, especially in its formulation by B. F. Skinner.[23] Like earlier empiricists, he takes learning to be a function of experience. Skinner developed a theory of reinforcement to account for the development in the individual animal or human being of certain ways of responding. A rat, for instance, learns to run a certain way through a maze if there is food at the relevant turns. In the case of learning about the physical environment the reinforcement is the positive feedback, analogous to the food in the case of the rat in the maze. In the case of learning social behaviors, like speaking a language, the reinforcement is other people's approval or disapproval of what the child or learner utters. In all learning the starting point is randomly emitted behavior which through reinforcement is shaped and selected to become appropriate to the relevant environment.

In order to account for language and language learning Skinner sought to identify the variables in the environment that control and determine verbal behavior. He argued that the verbal behavior of a person could be predicted and controlled by manipulating the environment of the speaker. This manipulation of the environment is the "essence" of learning. Thus, the child's random babbling would gradually become like the language spoken in its surroundings, because only the sounds and sound combinations similar to that language would be rewarded by the parents and other speakers. In this way the verbal community sets up reinforcements schedules which select and shape the child's verbal behavior. The child comes to utter the correct things in the correct situation; for example, say "the door is open" when the door is open. The child's future use of language is determined by past responses and reinforcement schedules and can be predicted if these are known. To understand learning, on this account, one does not have to assume or take into account any internal structure of the learner's mind, nor assume anything about how it processes information or organizes behavior.

I do not think Skinner saw his behaviorism as an attempt to solve Meno's dilemma that we already have to know what we are learning, but it is an improvement over more traditional empiricist theories, like Hume's, in this respect. This is so because the individual does not "need" to recognize what is a relevant response, or what stimuli are relevantly similar, because the physical and social environment does this by rewarding only certain responses relative to certain stimuli. The child does not have to know or recognize that certain responses are appropriate to certain stimuli, or even recognize stimuli and/or behavior as similar, because this is taken care of by external "forces" like rewards and punishments. Although this suggests a solution to Meno's paradox, Skinner's view that past experience and behavior determine future behavior is problematic, that is, it cannot account for productivity. It has difficulty explaining such a common occurrence as "over-regularization," where children make grammatical mistakes by using a grammatical construction just learned in an inappropriate context. It even has more difficulty in explaining that all normal speakers constantly understand and utter sentences never heard before.[24]

The most forceful criticism of Skinner's project has come from the linguist Noam Chomsky, who in his well-known criticism of Skinner's behaviorism and in numerous other writings has pointed out that our language is creative, or productive.[25] We are not limited in understanding or speaking to what we have earlier heard but can, and do as a matter of fact, say and understand linguistic utterances never encountered before. The language we have actually encountered is often faulty, but more importantly is only a limited set of examples of particular language use. Thus, experience and reinforcement cannot account for the ability to understand and produce novel utterances. How then, can this creative ability that all competent language users possess be picked up or learned on the basis of limited experience? Chomsky's solution to this problem is to propose that human language is possible because we possess a special intellectual ability, namely an innate universal grammar which contains generative as well as transformative rules, that is, it is itself creative. We all speak different languages, but our ability to speak as the people around us is grounded in a grammar which is inherent in the human mind and the same for every one. The rules of this grammar enable us to construct the grammar of our native language and also to understand and produce new meaningful sentences because the rules can be used in a recursive way. This universal grammar has to be innate because it can never be picked up from the limited and often faulty experience we have of language. The language the child hears as it learns to speak cannot be utilized unless the child already has innate grammatical hypotheses with which the child can interpret and analyze the heard language, and thereby gains access to the rules governing a natural language. Nothing new is really learned, but experience triggers what is already inherent in the mind. Speaking creatively is only a reflection or expression of a creative intellectual ability inherent in our minds. Thus, the behavioristic claim that anything can be learned (and that all intellectual abilities are learned) is turned into its opposite—one can only learn what one already knows, so there is really no such thing as learning. Chomsky's solution to the problems of learning has been taken up and developed by J. Fodor in his theories of a computational language of thought underlying all learning.[26] He has developed and made explicit a theory of learning inspired by Chomsky and henceforth I will focus on his theory. Fodor agrees with Plato and Chomsky that there really is no learning because the acquisition of new knowledge requires that we already know what we are learning.[27] His conception of a computational language of thought with recursive rules is, though, an improvement over Plato's and similar theories, because the innate framework, the language of thought, is itself productive, enabling the learner to go beyond the information given in the language of thought. The language of thought is productive but it also functions as a limiting framework. The child uses the language of thought to form and test hypotheses about language use in its linguistic community. Just as Skinner's reinforcement schedules limit and guide what the child learns from experience, so does the innate language of thought.

What makes Fodor's theory particularly interesting is that he has attempted to characterize the structure and functioning of the innate productive language in terms of recent ideas of the mind as a computer program. That is, he is not just as Chomsky describing the innate linguistic rules but sets forth a theory or mechanism of how the mind actually work, that is, he provides us with an empirical theory of learning, not only of language, but in general.

THE PROBLEM OF THE MEANINGFULNESS OF THE FRAMEWORK: WITTGENSTEIN

The same problem that Chomsky saw in syntax was seen by the philosopher Ludwig Wittgenstein, later in his life, in semantics:

how can our language be rule governed and productive at the same time?[28] How can the meaning be governed by specific and determinate rules and yet apply to new instances of what the word refers to? His discussion of this problem in terms of family resemblance (to illustrate productivity) and skill, technique or custom (to illustrate problems with rule following) is radically different from Chomsky's and Fodor's account, and was developed as a critical reaction to a Chomsky/Fodor-like conception of language. Wittgenstein tried to show that the questions this kind of approach asks are misconceived, but his discussion addresses the same fundamental problem because for him, as for Chomsky, language is inherently productive, yet determinate. But neither this nor the fact that children learn to speak productively and meaningfully needs to be explained in terms of an innate rational ability. Indeed Wittgenstein thought such explanations or accounts were empty or circular—they presuppose what they set out to explain. Hence Wittgenstein shows that the problem of productivity, or the problem of induction, arises not only in the context of connecting old knowledge with new knowledge as in the case of understanding a sentence never encountered before, but also in connecting one's representations with the world. How can the child master certain semantic rules? And how is the child able to apply them to new situations? Learning a language is going beyond information in two senses; to go beyond signs to what they represent and to go beyond past uses to new uses.

But the problem of the framework arises here as well. The issue here is best illustrated by considering language learning. In learning a language the child has to master semantic rules. In order to learn how words are connected with nonlinguistic items or events, the child, according to the paradox of Meno, either already knows the semantic relationship or does not. In the first case no learning is necessary and in the second learning is impossible. Neither overhearing language nor getting the semantic relationship explained can help the child learn unless it already knows what it is.

> one cannot meaningfully and significantly say in a language what these meaning relations are, for in any attempt to do so one must already presuppose them.[29]

This is one of the main problems that Wittgenstein tries to illuminate in his later writings.

So the problems of productivity and of the framework appear twice or on two different levels in accounts of learning, on the level of transformation of knowledge and on the semantic level. They also reappear on the level of communication, of going beyond one's own private language and interacting with others.

COMMUNICATION

Language involves not only describing the world but also communicating with fellow speakers. The child has to learn to communicate and make sense to other speakers and here we encounter again the two problems of learning: productivity contra a limiting framework. Communicating requires something beyond the speaker's subjective, private mental state, namely an objective and intersubjective framework, which the speakers share. Two speakers do not only have to share the same framework, but there has to be something outside each private mental sphere which backs it up or insures that they mean more or less the same thing. In this sense the language learning child has to move from its own private experience to something beyond. The framework (socio-linguistic conventions) is itself limited yet allows the speaker to create new conventions of linguistic use. Does this mean that the child has to know the socio-linguistic conventions in order to communicate, and hence cannot learn them? If this is the case we are faced with the problem of productivity again: how can the child cope with new situations?

I will attempt to answer all these related questions, by critically discussing both Fodor's and Wittgenstein's contributions to our understanding of learning, specifically language learning. I will argue that although they both have increased our understanding of what a theory of learning has to involve, they both fall short of providing such a theory. Fodor's theory of an innate language of thought does not explain what it attempts to explain. Wittgenstein never attempted to develop a theory of learning or productivity but to clear the way for such a theory by exposing conceptual confusion. His criticism and scattered remarks on learning can, though, be taken as the basis for a model of learning. This model uses his basic conceptual clarifications and adds empirical and theoretical developments in contemporary psychology, biology, and neurophysiology to it. The critical discussion of Fodor and Wittgenstein will, thus, function both as a "tool" to lay bare the conceptual or logical problems involved in understanding learning and as a source for a new way of looking at old facts.

THE DOMESTICATION MODEL
OF LEARNING AND PRODUCTIVITY

This model is an attempt to show that it is possible to reconcile or make a trade off between productivity and a framework for learning. The model I would like to propose is, as was just mentioned, a development of the later Wittgenstein's approach, and takes as evident that (1) language like skills (e.g., they, like language, entail representations of the environment) are required as a staring point for learning language and acquiring conceptual thought. (2) Actual language heard or conceptual experience is limited and (3) language and concepts are learned and used in a communicative context. Both the starting point of learning (a set of skills and behaviors) and the context in which learning takes place function to limit what can be learned. They impose limits and structure on language and thought which are inherently underdetermined; that is, open to different interpretations and use, and therefore also inherently productive.

I suggest that we can begin to understand the learning of language and begin developing a tenable theory, if we use the lessons learned from Chomsky, Fodor, and Wittgenstein. Such a theory has to take into account that experience is limited and that language itself is productive, and recognize that human beings are limited creatures.

The Domestication Model of learning, which I am proposing, presupposes Wittgenstein's account of productivity, that is, a version of finitism.[30] Language and thought are seen as inherently underdetermined and open-ended, and can be developed or used in an indefinite number of ways. This poses two problems for a theory of learning, namely how can the underdetermined experience be limited and how are communication, objectivity, and constancy in meaning acquired? I agree with Wittgenstein that it is not necessary to assume an innate language of thought, but that the limiting framework is found in the child's natural behaviors and, equally important, social interactions. Furthermore I claim that the "learning mechanism" is not a rational process based on the language of thought, but a process of training based on certain similarities between innate nonrational skills and behaviors.[31]

The Domestication Model of learning sees the newborn infant as a purely natural or biological being which possesses specific behaviors or skills, but lacks typically human features like language. The behaviors can be called skills, because they are structured in order to accomplish specific tasks, for example, sucking or grasping. The skills have an innate basis, but develop to become functional as a result of experience. These and other skills, although not entailing explicit knowledge or language, nevertheless are language-like. For example orofacial movements like chewing a piece of bread is a sequence of steps and sub-steps which must be executed in a specific way and order. The same holds for the utterance of a sentence. Because of this similarity they can be the basis of, or rather the ingredients in, the mastery of language (e.g., syntactic speech). The child can incorporate these changing skills into the demands or restrictions set by the socio-linguistic environment. In this way something individual, when combined or structured by the social environment, emerges as something public and shared by others.

The Domestication Model of learning, thus, splits the framework into two components—on the one hand we have the innate and individual specific behaviors and skills, and on the other the external and public socio-linguistic environment. The socio-linguistic environment provides both language heard in a specific social context and the mechanisms to limit the interpretation or generalizations which are socially acceptable. The individual contributes the behavior or skills which are shaped and changed by this experience. Although the individual contributions are necessary for learning, the way they develop and eventually come to be replaced by social characteristics are not predetermined but depend on the extra-individual aspects of the framework. In this sense learning a language is a negotiated social construction.

This approach shares the view of innate theories that something like that which is to be learned has to be innate, but does not take the innate to be a language of thought. Instead it takes specific behaviors and skills to be part of the framework and in these respects is similar to Piaget. The Domestication Model sees, just like Piaget, the skills as structured and not as random behavior as the behaviorists like Skinner assumed. It differs, though, from Piaget in that the acquisition of language is not based on the acquisition of thought, nor is it the result of interaction between the individual and its physical environment, but necessarily involves the social environment as well. Furthermore, language is not seen as only a continuation of mental constructions following a set pattern. In stressing the importance of other people in learning language it is similar to behaviorism, but due to finitism (i.e., the idea that language is underdetermined or that future uses of language are not determined by previously established habits of language use) it escapes the failure of behaviorism to account for productivity. The Domestication Model owes much to such philosophers as the later Wittgenstein, Harré, Hattiangadi; psychologists like Vygotsky and Bruner; and draws from areas such as neurophysiology and evolutionary biology.[32]

The Domestication Model sees the learning of language as a result of the combination and interaction of different skills in the context of increasingly complex social interaction. Much is given to the child, like innate structures of perceptual organs and reactions, ways of manipulating objects, and just as important examples of language, correction, and help by adults. The child is able to transcend this and go beyond what is given. The Domestication Model divides the relevant skills into two groups: (1) linguistic skills and (2) communicative-semantic skills. Linguistic skills involve such things as speech perception and speech production. Both of these have an innate foundation but are modified in interaction with a linguistic community. Linguistic skills also involve syntactic skills, which, it is argued, are based in different motor skills. Lieberman (1985) suggested, for example, that behaviors like chewing or swallowing are the basis of sentence construction. Psychologists of Piaget's school also operate with a similar hypothesis.[33] The communicate-semantic skills consist, as the name indicates, of semantic skills which are developed in the context of imitation and play. Both these skills involve symbolism and the ability to relate to something not immediately present to the mind. For example, the child plays with a stick as a horse, and can imitate behaviors like the closing of the eyes which are appropriate to another situations like going to sleep. Social skills also develop in play such as "Peekaboo," but are also important in the close interaction between the child and its care giver. These two often function in a symbiotic relationship, where the adult complements the child and ascribes to the child desires and beliefs on the basis of which the child is treated in specific ways.

A presupposition for all this is an undeveloped and flexible brain, cross-model transfer of skills (e.g., orafacial to speech), and a long childhood. Many of the skills involved in language are found in other species as well, but it is only their unique combination that is found in man. This approach to language acquisition in the individual can be applied to the problem of the evolution of language, since it sees language learning as a case of biological flexibility or redundancy of biological functions. As already Darwin pointed out in the Origin of Species, one and the same biological structure can perform many different functions and two different organs can perform the same function, thus enabling the emergence of new structures and functions. In the purely biological as well as in the linguistic world it is possible to go beyond structures and information given.

SUMMARY OF THE BOOK

In what follows I focus my critical discussion on Fodor's and Wittgenstein's solutions to the problems of productivity and learning. Their approaches are paradigmatic in that one (Fodor) represents a revival of of some of Plato's ideas and the other (Wittgenstein) is closer to empiricist accounts of learning.[34] In addition to having carefully argued approaches to the issues discussed above, their approaches can also be seen as representative of the two main, and conflicting, theoretical approaches taken in psychology. Ideas like Fodor's have been influential not only for theories in linguistics but also in cognitive science, especially in the area of Artificial Intelligence. Wittgenstein-like ideas are found in Vygotsky and explicitly in J. Bruner's work. Piaget,[35] perhaps the most influential of developmental psychologists in this century, developed a theory of cognitive growth which in many aspects is an attempt to bridge the gap between empiricists and rationalists. The Domestication Model of learning owes some things to Piaget (especially his empirical studies), but takes his approach to be lacking in an important respect, namely in not making social interaction an integral part of any learning process. Learning is not individual construction, it is social construction.

The problem of learning has both a philosophical and an empirical side to it. Without a clear understanding of what learning involves, of which conceptual and meta-theoretical problems have to be solved, empirical data are difficult to make sense of and use in giving a coherent picture of learning. But meta-theoretical and conceptual clarifications are only the first and incomplete steps. Such considerations are the focus of the first part of this book, where I discuss Fodor's and the later Wittgenstein's arguments in detail. Here Fodor's theory is rejected in favor of a reconstruction of a Wittgensteinian account of learning. The second part consists of an attempt to develop an empirical theory based on the conclusions from the theoretical discussion. The Domestication Model of learning can, since it is a development of some of Wittgenstein's remarks, be seen as a test of his ideas. Also, do these ideas provide a better alternative to the theory Fodor suggests?

Fodor, as mentioned, relies on Chomsky, but has generalized and developed Chomsky's ideas on learning in his theory of an innate language of thought. In chapter 2, I present Fodor's conception of mind focusing on his conception of the language of thought. This view entails that an individual's cognitive performance and learning can be accounted for in terms of the deductive relations that hold between propositions the learner already knows, and that one can not learn a conceptual system richer than the conceptual system one already has. In chapter 3, I discuss the shortcomings of Fodor's theory, arguing that his hypothesis of an innate language of thought does not explain what it sets out to explain, cannot be empirically tested, and, even if this criticism is disregarded and one takes the hypothesis as empirically testable, it clashes with a better established theory, namely the theory of evolution.

This is followed up in chapter 4, where I present the later Wittgenstein's criticism of his own earlier views, which I interpret as a criticism of Fodor-type theories. In chapters 5 and 6, I reconstruct a Wittgensteinian account of learning showing that it is more viable than Fodor's, hence arguing that a theory of learning resolving the dilemma of the framework and productivity is possible.

Chapter 7 is devoted to a sketch of such a theory of learning—the Domestication Model of learning. It supplements Wittgenstein's basic insights with empirical and theoretical results in contemporary biology, neurophysiology, and psychology. Quite a lot is already understood about the learning of language, and the Domestication Model of learning provides a way to draw this together. In chapter 8, the Domestication Model is evaluated in light of the questions raised in this chapter as well as in the discussion of Fodor and Wittgenstein.

Throughout the book I focus more or less exclusively on language learning. This has long been the center of the debate and research both in philosophy and psychology, and language is crucial to all cognitive and so-called higher learning. Furthermore the philosophy of mind has become more and more intertwined with the philosophy of language. Also, in language the contrast between the productivity and the framework is especially acute. This will be seen even more clearly in the presentation of both Fodor and Wittgenstein, who from different or even opposed starting points confronted these questions.

This is one reason why I have chosen focus my attention exclusively on Fodor and Wittgenstein. Another is that they represent two opposing strategies in the philosophy of mind, yet both see language as crucial to understanding the mind and its function. Furthermore Fodor's philosophy of mind—his representational theory of mind, his language of thought hypothesis, and his account of learning—grew out of an explicit rejection of the philosophy of mind that Wittgenstein and the behaviorists shared. Wittgenstein, although he of course could not have anticipated Fodor's theory of mind, criticizes theories very much like Fodor's. Thus, by juxtaposing the two theories I hope to show what the problems of learning and especially productivity are, and what a viable theory of learning can look like. I will devote more space to Wittgenstein, but I justify this with the fact that his views can be used both as a critique of Fodor and as a basis for a more viable theory, which have left behind both the idea that learning is a structured and in fundamental sense predetermined process, and the idea that learning is some thing the individual is engaged all by him- or herself. The view that learning primarily is a matter of an individual mind confronting and making sense of experience is mistaken; learning involves a complex interaction of individual and social factors. The myth of learning is not that it is impossible, but that it is something an individual accomplishes by him or herself. The old English meaning (and also contemporary Swedish and German meanings) of learning as including both teaching and learning, as well as the etymological roots of learning as "following in the footsteps of" betray an important insight. Learning is the adaptation of natural abilities to the path that has been laid by others speaking language and engaging in related human activities. It requires both the participation of the individual as well as the guiding of others. In this sense learning and teaching cannot be separated.

CHAPTER 2

Fodor's Theory of Learning

THE PROBLEM SITUATION

One of the best elaborated among contemporary examples of the conception of learning which is first found in Plato's *Meno* is to be found in Jerry Fodor's writings. Both claim that learning presupposes an innately structured body of knowledge, or more specifically that an individual's cognitive learning and performance can be explained with reference to the deductive relations that hold between propositions or ideas already possessed by the individual. As already mentioned Fodor's views and arguments are interesting for several reasons. They are attempts to explicate and solve the problem of productivity, and he deserves credit, together with Chomsky, for showing both the importance and difficulty of this problem. The solution Fodor proposes in terms of an innate language of thought is a modern version of an idea that has been prevalent throughout the Western intellectual tradition.[1] As such it has been influential in contemporary philosophy of mind and psychology, and especially in the cognitive sciences. Fodor's argument, although less well-known than Chomsky's, is spelling out the content and consequences of this approach in detail and is also very clear and well-developed and throws light on the problems at hand.

Inspired by Noam Chomsky's work in linguistics and by current developments in cognitive science,[2] in *The Language of Thought* (1979),[3] Fodor sets out to develop what he calls "computational cognitivism." The cognitive or psychological processes that underlie and explain complex human behavior and learning are computational or the manipulation of symbols according to rules, that is, transformations of linguistic-conceptual representations which the mind is innately equipped with.

This view, reminiscent of Plato's, sees new knowledge in the individual as well as in science only as an explication or transformation of what is already known. Hence, learning is at most recollection or re-presentation of what is already inherent in the mind, and the ability to go beyond information given is explained in terms of the characteristics of the framework.

Although some of the ideas of *The Language of Thought* derive from Plato, as a whole they are a response to a very modern problem situation, namely, the failure of behaviorism. In the late 1950s and early 1960s psychology was still dominated by behavioristic theories of learning and perception (e.g., Skinner). Replacing the introspectionist psychology of the first decades of this century they were, if not a paradigm,[4] at least the dominating school or research program in academic psychology. Also, in the philosophy of mind logical behaviorism, the view that mentalistic terms really describe behavior, was in vogue. It was by many, including Fodor, ascribed to philosophers such as Ryle and to some extent the later Wittgenstein.[5]

At the same time, however, there was a growing discontent and awareness of serious problems in the behavioristic research program. Most notable was the failure to satisfactorily explain higher mental processes like language and concept acquisition. The failure was felt in all areas of learning and perception, the core of behaviorism. The insistence that stimuli and response should be defined in physically specifiable terms severely limited the scope of behaviors that could be studied, the reduction of mental states to behavioral dispositions did not quite succeed,[6] but the most serious problem was the failure to account for genuine novelty in behavior. In spite of gross variations in the physical rendering of a tune any normal listener can recognize it. For example, a listener can recognize a performance of "Lillibullero" in which acoustic characteristics are very different from anything heard before. One can recognize it if it is played as a march, as a waltz or in different pitch, volume and tempo. On the level of skills one can type words or combinations of letters never done before. Furthermore we can communicate creatively with language, thus understanding, uttering or writing a potentially infinite number of sentences. The last fact was the center of Chomsky's review of Skinner's *Verbal Behavior* (1959).[7] In response to behaviorism's impotence to explain this Chomsky proposed his transformational universal grammar. With this he not only claimed to have solved the problem of creativity, but also the problem of language learning. The innate universal grammar functions as a linguistic acquisition device helping the child learn the language spoken around him or her.

Fodor's conception of mental processes and learning is basically a development and a generalization of Chomsky's ideas. In the book *Psychological Explanation* Fodor says:

> Readers who are familiar with the work of Professor Noam Chomsky on linguistic theory and metatheory will hardly fail to detect its influence on the general approach to psychological explanations taken here. Indeed, this book is in part an attempt to make explicit some aspects of a view of psychological explanation that comports naturally with the generative approach to language.[8]

This book does present an alternative to behaviorism, but the main part of the book is an extension of Chomsky's critique in that it is an attack on the philosophical basis of behaviorism.

Fodor's rejection of behaviorism has two strands. The *first* is an investigation and rejection of a priori or philosophical arguments. He first turns to such philosophers as Ryle and (although seldom referred to directly) the later Wittgenstein, whose arguments, according to Fodor, claim that an explanation of psychological phenomena in terms of the mental and private are problematic and should be avoided.[9] Behaviorism can not be supported by these, as it were, negative arguments, and Fodor rejects all their arguments claiming that all philosophical or conceptual analysis can provide us with are necessary or grammatical truths, hence they can say something about how we use language but very little or nothing about psychological phenomena. Another way to explicate Fodor's criticism is to say that these philosophers have confused the description with what it describes. The analysis of how we talk about or describe mental states is not the same as an analysis of the phenomena themselves.

The *second* line of argument in *Psychological Explanation* is to show that certain psychological phenomena such as perception and speech recognition can not be explained by behaviorism. In short, Fodor's argument is that mental processes, like choosing and recognizing, must be postulated in order to explain these activities and how we can recognize a potentially infinite set of different renderings of a tune, a new sentence, and so on.

Our behavior, both in perceiving or speaking is, in an important sense, productive and we can go beyond what is given in experience, training, or learning to deal with new stimuli or responses.

> Indeed, it is in large part because infinitely many hypotheticals are true of the behavior of any organism that psychological theories are necessary; otherwise, the behavioral repertoire of an organism could in principle be represented by a list.[10]

Here Fodor's argument parallels Chomsky's but is extended to areas other than language and it is this argument which is the basis for the theory of mind and learning presented in *The Language of Thought*. What Fodor does can be characterized as an attempt to explain productivity and thereby learning by proposing a theory or hypothesis about the framework, namely that the framework itself, or in his terms the mental processes, are productive.

THE NATURE OF THE FRAMEWORK:
FODOR'S THEORY OF MIND

In *The Language of Thought* the central claim is that cognition, or for that matter all mental processes, are computational, or the manipulation of symbols according to rules, and that there is an internal or mental code of representation, or, as Fodor calls it, a language of thought. This is a direct response to behaviorism's failure to deal with productivity.

In chapter 2 of his book the basic argument is that any psychological theory or explanation has to account for productivity or the ability to go beyond information given by experience, and hence has to give an account of the transformation of information which occurs. Productivity is thus not only a problem in accounting for learning, but is central to all psychology.

Fodor's argument here is Kantian or transcendental. Starting from the uncontested fact that we can understand or produce sentences, thoughts, and so on, never encountered before, he argues what has to be the case for this to be possible.

Schematically Fodor's argument can be summarized as follows:

1. Psychological processes are productive.[11]
2. Productivity consists in the organism's ability to grasp and

produce a potentially infinite set of sentences, actions, and the like.

3. Experience as well as the mind's structure is finite, that is, the actual input and the cognitive structures are finite.

4. Psychological processes are computational processes, that is, the generative use of rules or operations, defining the succession of mental states. The rules or instructions are finite in number but are used recursively.

5. Computation requires a medium of representation.

6. The medium of representation is a language of thought.

This is not intended as a strict argument but it seems that Fodor takes premise (4) to be the conclusion of (1)+(2)+(3) and (5), and (6) to follow from (4).

What does this mean, or rather how does Fodor substantiate these claims?

The Productivity of Mental Processes

To support the first premise, that is, the productivity of psychological functioning, which as we have seen is the core of Fodor's whole project, three cases are considered: conceptual learning, action or rather deliberate choice, and perception.[12]

It seems clear that certain kinds of learning involve more than the change of what the individual knows as a result of experience. Taking a blue pill to learn Latin or learning a hymn by heart are both certainly changes in a person's knowledge as a result of experience, but only the last is considered a case of learning. In this case, what is remembered, the hymn word for word, exhausts what is learned. Learning enables one to repeat it, but nothing more. If behaviorism is correct, this is all there is to learning. But a little consideration shows that learning a language or forming concepts is not like this. It is not just being able to repeat literally what one has heard but involves going beyond the information given. The child mastering language or a particular concept can and will apply it not only in situations identical to the learning situation, but to new situations as well. This can be illustrated by the example of learning multiplication tables discussed in chapter 1, and by the fact that children normally can apply the word "table" to a round table, although they have never seen such a thing or heard anyone call it a table. If this is correct, and Fodor rightly takes it to be self-evident, it implies that some manipulation and transformation of what was given by experience takes place.

To further support the productivity of psychological functioning Fodor considers acting and deliberating to act. In explaining actions, in ordinary life as well as in psychology, we typically refer to the beliefs the individual has about the situation, his or her own behavior, the likely outcomes of different behaviors and the individual's preferences. For example, an explanation of why someone did not show up for an job interview refers to such things as the applicant's belief that he or she would not get the job, that the job interview would be too difficult, that another and better job has come up, that showing up at the interview would lead to missing a wedding, and so forth. According to this picture at least some actions seem to be the result of choices among a range of options contemplated by the actor. The action is a response to possible outcomes and not a response to the actual input (stimuli present in the situation), and in this sense goes beyond information given.

Furthermore productivity is central in perception as well:

> For though the information provided by causal interactions between the environment and the organism is information about physical properties in the *first* instance, in the *last* instance it may (of course) be information about any property the organism can perceive the environment to have.[13]

By this Fodor means that although it is possible to view the output of the perceptual mechanisms as physical descriptions, perceptual judgments are typically not articulated in terms of such descriptions. For example "I hear Lillibullero," or "I see a robin" are not physical descriptions but go beyond the physical input to our sense organs. "Robin" is not a physical description of a feathered, roundish and moving object. Furthermore we can recognize a tune, a bird or a speech sound even if we have not heard or seen a particular physical rendering or token of it before.

So, to sum up, Fodor's point in the cases considered, shows that although experience is limited, it is possible to go beyond it by various transformations of the input. How can this be explained? Fodor answers by proposing a computational theory of the mind, which also provides a productive framework for learning.

The Computational Nature of the Mind

For Fodor the mind is a theoretical entity only accessible indirectly via behavioral data. We cannot study other people's thought processes directly, only their result in action and speech. We know something about our own mental processes through introspection, but this knowledge is very limited and unreliable. As soon as one tries to focus on one's own thinking, for example, the very thought seems to escape. Given this the processes or operations we ascribe to the mind are inferred either from behavior, biology, neurophysiology, theoretical assumptions or all of these, not something that is directly directly known by introspection or observation.[14]

What then can we infer about mental processes from the productivity of behavior, perception, and language? Clearly, as we have seen, there must be some transformation of the information or experience since the output is something more than the input. Deciding on a course of action is not a mere response to the actual stimuli input, but a response to possible outcomes; perception is not mere physical stimulation; speaking a language is not mere repetition of what one has heard. The transformation of information in all these cases is not arbitrary but rule governed, and the most obvious example of this is language. In learning a language one learns, among other things, grammatical rules and it is on the basis of these rules that one is able to combine and recombine a finite vocabulary in potentially endless different grammatical sentences. But given that the brain is not limitless and that the rules no less than the vocabulary are finite in their extent, the outcome, which in principle, is infinite, must be accomplished by the finite means at one's disposal,[15] that is, infinite outcome has to be accomplished by finite means. In proposing his transformational grammar, where a recursive use of a limited set of generative rules applied to a limited vocabulary can produce an infinite number of new grammatical sentences, Chomsky provides a striking and simple solution and Fodor is following in his footsteps.

The idea of generative rules used recursively and of language as constituent (i.e., consisting of parts that can be recombined) is, I take it, the heart of Fodor's claim that mental processes are computational. In *The Language of Thought* he is not explicit about what the thesis that mental processes are computational entails, but it is quite clear from his numerous references to Chomsky that he has something like this in mind. Indeed, I think, the idea of generative use of rules not only is compatible with his other views but central to his answer to the failure of behaviorism.

Another impetus for Fodor's computational theory of the mind is coming from cognitive science, Artificial Intelligence and the idea that the mind works like, or at least, can be simulated by a computer program. This commits him to a very specific version of the computational nature of the mind. Given the failure of behavioral and neurophysiological reductionism,[16] Fodor has opted for functionalism which is one of the counter stones in cognitive science, that is, the idea that mental states, events and processes can be identified and characterized in terms of their causal role in producing behavior. But functional explanations are empty, as Moliere's sleep inducing function of opium shows, unless a mechanism which can carry out the function can be specified. In one of Moliere's play a physician asks how it is that opium puts people to sleep, and receives the reply that opium has "dormative properties." This is, of course, only a redescription of the fact that opium puts people to sleep and not an explanation how opium works or why it causes people to sleep. A universal Turing machine provides a conceptual tool for specifying the mechanism of the human mind. Turing machines can simulate or perhaps even duplicate[17] any formally specifiable symbolic manipulations and are (and this is very important for Fodor) mechanically realizable. This means that they can actually be built to carry out the manipulations.[18] Hence, if the mind is instantiating rule-guided processes its function can be simulated by a Turing machine (which as a machine is a causal system), and mental processes can be seen as formal operations on symbolic content or representations, that is, as computations.[19]

The Language of Thought

How to characterize the system of representations the mind computes, what Fodor calls the language of thought? The language of thought is what Fodor himself considers his most fundamental contribution to contemporary psychology. But the idea, as he is well aware, is not new even if Fodor's argument in terms of machine computation is. Historically the idea of a language of thought different from the language we speak has been motivated by several considerations. For example, public languages vary a lot but thought seems to be universal, and public languages are conventional and do not resemble what they refer to or are about. By postulating a meaning-bearing, nonconventional and universal language of thought these problems and others can be resolved. Already the Greeks saw this and both Plato (e.g., in *Republic, Cratylus*) and Aristotle (e.g., in *De Interpretatione*) seem to have accepted the idea of a language of thought. Aristotle speaks of universal states of mind as underlying and giving meaning to language. In Augustine's distinction between *verbum mentis* and *verbum vocis*,[20] the former being intrinsically meaningful and made apparent by Christ (the Interior Teacher), the idea is explicit. Both Augustine and the much later Descartes are taken by Fodor as intellectual forerunners. Descartes in his *cogito*[21] argument and in his dualism of mind and body operated with the notion of a language of thought.[22]

What then is Fodor's argument for a universal innate language of thought distinct from the languages we speak in? Before presenting this argument, it is useful to see why Fodor calls this internal representational system a language of thought, that is, what similarities he sees between the public and internal languages, which warrants speaking of both as languages.

The representational system must share a number of features with natural languages, the most important being that indefinitely many distinct representations can belong to the system. In neither language nor thought is there in principle an upper limit to the complexity or length of a sentence or a thought, and in both it is possible to produce or understand novel sentences or thoughts on a basis which is finite. Furthermore both language and thought are concerned with truth.

> But productivity isn't the only important property common to natural languages and whatever system of representation is exploited in deciding what to do. It is evident, for example, that the notion that the agent can represent to himself salient aspects of the situations in which he finds himself presupposes that such familiar semantic properties as truth and reference are exhibited by formulae in the representational system.[23]

These crucial similarities between thought and natural languages entitle us to conclude that there is a language of thought, that is, that thought is essentially linguistic, Fodor argues.

One could also add that psychological phenomena such as thinking, reasoning, believing, and problem solving all seem to involve mental states directed at statements or propositions. One thinks, fears, desires *that* it is going to snow. And since propositions are what sentences express, it is not farfetched to claim that we think in words and sentences or something of the same kind.[24] This is reinforced by the fact that reports of thoughts, for example "X thought that snow is white" is similar to report of speech "X said that snow is white." Furthermore, in addition to the similarities mentioned above, both language and thought exhibit systematicity, that is, the ability to understand or produce some sentences is not isolated, but intrinsically connected to understanding or producing other sentences.

So it seems plausible to claim that when we think, learn, decide or perceive we stand in a certain psychological relation to what is essentially a linguistic item. In light of this it is not surprising that the idea of a language of thought, in this sense, is accepted by many contemporary philosophers and psychologists. In philosophy, linguistic Kantianism, that is, the view that conceptual schemes or a priori concepts of the mind are linguistic, is widely accepted.[25] Psychologists as well adhere to the same view. Developmental psychologists such as Vygotsky, Piaget, and Bruner, although denying that thought initially is linguistic, see fully developed thought as linguistic.[26]

Much controversy in contemporary philosophy and psychology is not about the linguistic nature of thought, but about the origin and nature of the language of thought. For example, is the inner language of thought universal or relative to particular cultures or societies; is it learned or innate; is it identical or different from the individual's natural language? These questions, of course, are central to learning.

Before turning to Fodor's view about the origin and nature of the language of thought, which is, beyond doubt, the most controversial aspect of his theory, let me present his views on the meaningfulness of the framework. Learning to speak a language involves not only being able to combine words in a grammatical way, but also to learn what the words and sentences mean, and thus being able to make sense of utterances never encountered before. According to Fodor's theory of the mind, one can do this because the mental framework, the language of thought, is itself a language with meaning. To account for this is, thus, an important part of Fodor's project.

The Semantics of the Language of Thought

Historically, an important part of the language of thought hypothesis has been the assumption that the language of thought is intrinsically meaningful. For example, Augustine's *verbum mentis* is intrinsically meaningful in that it is made apparent by God.[27]

Fodor seems to endorse this idea. In *The Language of Thought* he makes a distinction between "wave form" or the word or sentence which is the physical input/rendering and a "message" (p. 111, p. 151). Words or the wave form are not self-illuminating, but the message or "internal representation" are ambiguity free, implying that they need not be semantically interpreted. In communication the message is translated, by the speaker, into the public language and then translated by the listener into message form again. Communication or understanding occurs when the messages are the same for the speaker and for the listener. The message itself need not be translated or interpreted in its turn. Indeed, to avoid making the language of thought dependent on the meaningfulness of public language and to avoid an infinite regress of semantically interpreted languages of thought, Fodor has to adopt such a view. It should, though, be pointed out that Fodor, especially in some later writings, is very careful not to commit himself to any semantic theory. In the introduction to the book *Representations* he declares that the intentionality or meaningfulness of mental states can not be handled by the computational approach to the mind.[28] In "Methodological Solipsism Considered as a Research Strategy in Cognitive Psychology"[29] he considers a way out of this dilemma by arguing that the inner language is meaningful by virtue of its form only.

> the computational theory of the mind requires that two thoughts can be distinct in content only if they can be identified with relations to formally distinct representations.[30]

This solution though, leads to another problem, namely that if the inner language is just a formal system, is it not just a system of meaningless syntax? And since no linguistic system is self-interpreting the basic intuition of Fodor's model, namely that thought is a meaningful representational system is lost.[31]

Fodor's initial reaction to this dilemma was not to give up the idea that thought is computational, that is, that it has only formal properties, but to argue that cognitive theories in psychology can not deal with truth, reference and meaning, hence that they can not deal with the language of thought as a representation of reality or as referring to the world. If mental processes have access only to the formal or syntactic properties of mental representations, this leads to the consequence that there can be no psychology of perception or knowledge, because knowledge is involved with truth and perception with "what is there." Truth is a semantic notion, as is reference; but since this can not be specified in a purely formal system, they can not be handled by the computational theory of the mind. Fodor does not think that this discredits or "falsifies" his basic assumptions. It only shows, he argues, that the theory cannot be applied to certain problems which traditionally have been considered part of psychology.[32] Or put another way, since in an important way only formal properties of the representations make a difference, the world does not make a difference to one's mental states, and the task of psychology is not to trace the organism-environment interaction, but to study the mental processes qua formal operations, just as the way we study a machine or computer. A machine has no access to its interpretations, (this is the task of the programmer), but its computations are in no way affected by this. Hence the processes can be understood and explained without taking into account what they are about.

In a later book *Psychosemantics* (1987) Fodor seems to think that the only way out of this situation, while sticking to the ideal of trying to develop a scientific psychology, is to rescue or rehabilitate causal or denotational theories of meaning. He does not claim to provide a conclusive argument in favor of a causal theory of the semantics of the language of thought, but sketches what he takes to be the basics of such a theory; language of thought tokens of 'water' and 'brisket' stand in a certain causal relation to water and meat and semantical interpretations of mental symbols are determined by causal nomological relations. Thus the fact that the language of thought can represent is a result of its being causally connected with objects, events, and so on, in the environment. By this Fodor tries to naturalize the semantics of the language of thought and hence fit it into a scientific account.[33]

What consequences does this stance and his general theory of mind have for his conception of learning?

Fodor's Strong Preformist Thesis

According to Fodor the language of thought is innate and consists of a body of information in which items are deductively related to each other, or, in Fodor's terminology, they are related to each other by formal operations or computations. This is, of course, similar to the view expressed in the *Meno*, where the slave boy's learning and cognitive capacities are explained in terms of the intrinsic structure of the knowledge. Fodor, like Plato, proposes a strong preformist or innateness thesis as the only way to escape the paradox of the impossibility of acquiring new knowledge unless one already possesses the knowledge in question. But there is more to Fodor's argument than this, namely the connected claim that the language of thought is unlike a natural language in that it is not conventional.[34]

So what are Fodor's arguments for the claim that the language of thought is innate and that it is not conventional?

First, he says that it is obvious from the fact that organisms that do not talk can think, that the language of thought is not identical with any natural language. Animals clearly can act similarly to humans, for example, mastering disjunctive concepts,[35] in ways which imply that their mental processes are sufficiently complex to be thought of as computations in a representational system like ours. The presence of a language of thought which is not equivalent to any natural language becomes even more evident, when we turn to preverbal children learning their first language. The learning of a natural language, as English or French, necessarily presupposes a language which is equally complex, powerful, and rich in semantic content as the language one has to learn. It also has to be different, otherwise the language need not be learned. Fodor does not rely on empirical evidence from child psychology to make this point, but put forth a philosophical argument of what learning, that is, the acquisition of knowledge, entails.

To learn a language, or for that matter concepts is, according to Fodor, a process of hypothesis formation and confirmation, it is a process of induction where one confirms or disconfirms a general hypothesis about all Xs on the basis of experience of a few Xs. More specifically, learning a language involves among other things learning semantical hypotheses rules on the basis of experience. From having observed that a number of Xs are F, the individual forms and confirms that 'all Xs are Fs.'

But how is the alteration of knowledge to be accounted for? To benefit from the experience of Xs and Fs the organism has to represent Xs and Fs, it also has to entertain the hypothesis that all Xs are F, and finally the organism has to employ a rule of confirmation to fixate the belief that all Xs are F. All this implies, Fodor argues, that learning is a matter of forming and confirming hypotheses. And this, as we have seen, presupposes a representational system (representations of Xs and Fs), or, in Fodor's terminology, a language of thought. But this representational system (and here comes Fodor's central argument) has to be as semantically rich as the language or conceptual system one is learning, because one cannot learn a language in which terms express semantical properties not expressed by some language one already knows.

> If learning a language is literally a matter of making and confirming hypotheses about truth conditions associated with its predicates, then learning a language presupposes the ability to use expressions coextensive with each of the elementary predicates of the language being learned.[36]

So clearly the language of thought that enables a child to learn the language of its community must be equal in semantic richness.

Nevertheless, the language of thought has to be different from the learned natural language, if we at all want to argue that it is learned. And natural languages are clearly learned since no child comes to master it except by a long process of training and interaction with other speakers.

What is the origin of this intrinsic representational system of the language of thought? Clearly, Fodor argues, it cannot be learned because this would require another language of thought which in turn requires another language of thought, and so on, in an infinite regress. So it has to be innately known, or, as Fodor sometimes puts it, it is a biological necessity. This implies that the language of thought is not determined by public learned conventions, but by rule-governed processing of information somehow instantiated by the brain.

To sum up, Fodor's claim is that the language of thought, although like natural languages in some aspects, as mentioned above, is different in that it is innate and not governed by conventional or social rules.

Furthermore the language of thought is a biological necessity[37] in the sense that it is hard-wired into our brains by evolution. Since Fodor takes himself to be a neo-Darwinian, the explanation of the origin of the language of thought must be sought in the evolutionary past of the human species. Fodor, though, does not elaborate on this; and later I will argue that this view is problematic, that is, his conception of language of thought is incompatible with evolutionary theory.

FODOR'S THEORY OF LEARNING

As we have already seen perception, deciding to act, cognition and language mastery are all explained in terms of the language of thought hypothesis. As another example of going beyond information given, learning is also explained in terms of the language of thought, which, unlike natural or public languages, is universal and nonconventional. How then are public languages as English or French learned and what is the role of the language of thought? Since Fodor discusses learning primarily in the context of language acquisition I will follow him here, but it is quite clear that what he says applies to all areas of conceptual learning.

For Fodor learning a language or a new conceptual system is, among other things, coming to grasp what the term or predicate means, that is, its intension. This is to learn the extension of the term or predicate and following Davidson's theory of meaning[38] this is to learn their truth rules.

> one understands a predicate only if one knows the conditions under which the sentences that contain it would be true.[39]

> many philosophers now believe that learning a natural language involves (at least) learning a truth definition for that language.[40]

Furthermore:

> Learning a language (including, of course, a first language) involves learning what the predicates of the language mean. Learning what the predicates of a language mean involves

learning a determination of the extension of these predicates. Learning a determination of the extension of the predicates involves learning that they fall under certain rules (i.e., truth rules).[41]

Learning is based on experience of public and conventional languages that the child/learner encounters. But experience, language heard, is not only incomplete or sometimes irrelevant but also full of mistakes, false starts, and so on, so the learned truth rule is underdetermined by experience. But there is an even more fundamental sense in which learning the rules of a language is underdetermined by experience. The meaning of words are more general than the individual single experiences they refer to. Or, put another way, truth rules are universal statements, but experiences are not universal but particular.[42] Because of this, learning from experience is an inductive process, that is, a case of nondemonstrative inference. Learning is a process of hypothesis formation and confirmation, of testing hypotheses about the predicate one is learning. For example, a child has learned the concept of red, when his or her hypotheses about what kind of things count as red correspond to the rule which underlies the use of the word 'red.' But the hypothesis to be tested and confirmed must, as already explained, contain predicates co-extensive with elementary predicates in the language to be learned, because to learn that all Xs are Fs one has to have the concepts of X and F. Or to learn that P falls under rule R, one has to be able to represent both P and R. To repeat:

> But one cannot learn that P falls under R unless one has a language in which P and R can be represented. So one cannot learn a language unless one has a language. In particular, one cannot learn a first language unless one already has a system capable of representing the predicates in that language *and their extensions.* And, on pain of circularity, that system cannot be the language that is being learned. But first languages *are* learned. Hence, at least some cognitive operations are carried out in languages other than natural languages.[43]

So to learn a language or concept one has to have a language as complex, rich and semantically powerful as the language one is learning. Of course there does not have to be an one to one correspondence between the two languages, but their scope has to be the same. The language of thought's representational power is given or innate, but it may well be that complex concepts such as 'airplane' decompose into simpler components like 'flying machine.'[44] This underlying language which makes learning possible is the language of thought and it is unlearned. The last condition is important because if the language of thought has to be learned, its learning has to be explained presumably in another language of thought, and so on in an infinite regress. Fodor's view does not imply that the language of thought is present at birth, only that it is known or understood without being learned.

This line of argumentation clearly says that unless there is a language of thought learning is impossible. In Piatelli-Palmarini's *Language and Learning*, for example, Fodor, along with Chomsky, takes this argument to be self-evident. Like Socrates in Plato's *Meno*, they seem to suggest that if we do not already know what we are learning, we can not learn it.

> you can't carry out an induction, it is a logical impossibility to make a nondemonstrative inference without having an a priori ordering of the hypotheses. This general point about nativism is so self-evident that it is superfluous to discuss it;[45]

As we have seen, Fodor's explication of this is that in one sense we already know what we are learning (we already possess a representational system as rich as the one we are learning) and in another sense we do not (we do not know the specific natural language we are trying to acquire). Like the slave boy questioned by Socrates our minds have an intrinsic structure, and learning involves utilizing this structure, but it does not add to or go beyond what is given any more than working out the consequences of what is already known.[46]

What then are the more detailed consequences of this line of reasoning for a theory of learning? How does Fodor answer the four problems specified in chapter 1, namely the questions of the framework, the mechanism of learning, the role of experience and the limits of learning?

1. In characterizing the nature of the framework or unlearned givens from which learning has to start, that is, the language of thought, Fodor is following in the footsteps of Plato but without adopting Plato's metaphysics. Instead the framework is characterized in terms of modern linguistic and computational theory. The productivity of the language of thought, which is the centre of Fodor's argument, is characterized in terms of recursive, transformational rules. Both the productivity of language

learning and use are explained by making the underlying language of thought productive. The productivity of action, perception, and language are all explained in terms of a mental framework consisting of formal rules. As already mentioned the framework is innate, or in Fodor's terms, a biological necessity, that is, it has been hard-wired into our brains throughout human evolution.

It is clear that Fodor is committed to a strong innatism because if the language of thought is not innate or an inherent property of the mind there is a threat of infinite regress of languages of thought. Fodor argues, though, that his innatism is not so very different from the one the empiricists are committed to. It is more a question of degree and of the nature of the innate concepts than a qualitative difference.[47]

All classical theories of concept attainment, empiricist and rationalist alike, operate with a distinction between primitive and complex concepts. For example, an empiricist like Hume makes a distinction between images and ideas, where the latter are built from the former by some combinatorial mechanism such as association. The primitive images and indirectly the ideas have their origin in the environment, either directly via the senses or indirect as innate ideas. A rationalist such as Plato claims that all knowledge is innate, but in both approaches the primitive concepts are unlearned, or given to the mind. The empiricists take the sense organs' structure to be innate, and this structure determines not only sense impressions but also limits concepts. In this sense the primitive concepts or impressions we receive are innately fixed, and if we had other sense organs we would get other concepts. Hence, Fodor argues, the empiricists have to accept that primitive concepts are "triggered" or given by experience, not learned from experience. Since the combinatorial processes (like association) also are given, there is not much left over to be learned, or, in other words, what can be learned is limited by the structure of our minds. The difference between the rationalists and the empiricists is that the empiricists take only sensory input or images to be unlearned or given while the rationalists claim that nonsensory concepts are given as well. The rationalist assumes that not only are our sense organs innately structured, but also our thought. Both simple and complex concepts are given. In addition, both approaches have to presume that the combinational mechanism is inherent in the mind. Fodor's conclusion is that neither the rationalist nor the empiricist should speak of learning, because in both cases the basic concepts are given not learned.

Furthermore, Fodor argues that rationalism combined with neo-Darwinism does not deny that concepts ultimately come from experience, because they have been hard-wired into our brain in the phylogenetic development of the human species. He has, though, failed to give an account of how this is possible.

The rationalists, according to Fodor, have a more powerful theory, that is, one that can account for productivity, and is more supported by evidence.[48] Even if Fodor argues that his strong preformism is supported by empirical evidence, it is clear that his basic argument is a priori—it is "so self-evident that it is superfluous to discuss"[49] that one already has to know what one is learning. He begins his argumentation by noting the productivity of human psychological functioning, but in attempting to explain this fact he seems to lose track of human specific behaviors or functioning, and relies totally on his a priori argument. In spite of this he often stresses that his theory or basic hypothesis is empirical. To sum up, Fodor's answer to the first question, that is, the nature of the basic given framework, is to assume a rich and productive innate structure, in terms of which learning proceeds.

2. The second question any learning theory has to deal with is the nature of the relationship between what is known and what is learned, that is, the nature of the process or mechanism which makes this possible has to be specified.

For Fodor learning is a process of hypothesis formation and confirmation; it is clearly a rational endeavor. Both what is learned and what is utilized in learning is propositional knowledge.[50]

Learning is in a fundamental sense working out what is already there, as is shown by the fact that Fodor argues that we cannot learn a language or conceptual system unless we already possess one of the same semantic richness. In an important sense there is no learning, only a fixation of belief or a confirmation of hypotheses which corresponds to truth rules in the natural language learned. Hence a theory of learning is not called for, since there is no learning, only an account of how the given language of thought is actualized, made explicit, in the acquisition of a natural language.

Denying that anything fundamentally new is learned, Fodor sees learning as translation from the language of thought into public language. Here again he comes close to Augustine's view,[51] as well as Aristotle in *De Interpretatione*. The child is like a foreigner entering a country, where he or she does not speak the language. He or she already has a language, not only the language spoken in the foreign country.[52]

> But the argument I just sketched suggests, on the contrary, that Augustine was precisely and demonstrable right and that seeing that he was is prerequisite to any serious attempts to understand how first languages are learned.[53]

In the final analysis, though, this of course means that learning theories claiming that something genuinely new is learned are mistaken; and not surprisingly Fodor not only criticizes behavioristic theories, but also argues that Piaget, Bruner, and Vygotsky are equally mistaken. Their mistake consists in assuming that cognitive capabilities can be decomposed into stages, where the concepts expressed in the earlier stages are weaker and different from concepts in later stages. They furthermore assume that the transition from one stage to the next is a process of learning. Focusing on Piaget, Fodor argues that if the difference between two stages is understood as either a difference in the concepts' expressive power or the range of application of the concepts, the theory is untenable. Fodor's argument can be summarized this way:

> one cannot learn that P falls under R unless one has a language in which P and R can be represented. So one cannot learn a language unless one has a language. In particular, one cannot learn a first language unless one already has a system capable of representing the predicates in that language *and their extensions*.[54]

From this it follows that one already has to have a concept coextensive with the concept one is learning; hence the assumption of different stages is mistaken. Or, one has to say that the transition between stages is not a matter of learning. But if one insists on different developmental stages, as Piaget does, it is impossible to account for learning. Fodor also makes it clear that he thinks that Piaget lacks a theory of learning.[55] Piaget describes the transition from one stage to the next in terms of changing equilibrium, that is, the correspondence between conceptual schemata and the world increases, but this does not tell us anything about how the change is accomplished, or what learning is. It only characterizes the end result.

Fodor also criticizes Vygotsky (1962) along the same lines. However, the argument is not stated explicitly in terms of learning but in terms of communication. Fodor's target is Vygotsky's claims that children and adults have fundamentally different concepts. But if this is the case, Fodor asks, how can children and adults communicate, how can children understand adults and vice versa. To understand a concept in an adult expression, a child has to have a concept coextensive with the concept of the adult. Hence the apparent possibility of communication rules out the difference that Vygotsky postulates.[56]

Again we have an argument for the impossibility of learning something genuinely new.

3. Although Fodor claims that learning is not the acquisition of something new, the role of experience in ontogenetic development is not denied by him. Its role is not to provide new concepts or new content to the mind or language of thought, but to trigger or select the relevant parts of the language of thought. Concepts are triggered or selected by their instances, so ostensive definition seems to be a way to activate the language of thought. But this is too simplistic because the triggering is a process of hypothesis confirmation. The hypothesis is given by the mind, but experience confirms or disconfirms it, that is, experience has an epistemological and causal role at the same time. The details of these roles are not clear in Fodor.

The similarity between Fodor and Plato should be clear because just as in Plato's account experience, by providing instances, makes what is latent or potential in the mind actual. To this Fodor adds that what is latent is also a product of experience, only phylogenetic "experience."

Furthermore it is an individual mental process because it is the individual who, when confronted by experience, utilizes his or her own private language of thought. Other people play no essential role in teaching the child language. This is similar to Piaget, but dissimilar to views that claim that interaction with other speakers is crucial. Wittgenstein, Skinner, Bruner, and Vygotsky all see this as fundamental, but their account of the social differs.[57] The Domestication Model, likewise, sees the social interaction between the learner and other people as crucial.

4. The fourth question that any learning theory has to deal with is that since not everything acquired counts as an instance of learning, the standards or limits of learning have to be specified. By now it should be clear that the language of thought sets the limits of learning.

> In particular, one cannot learn a first language unless one already has a system capable of representing the predicates in that language *and their extensions*.[58]

So nothing really new is learned. The representational power of the language of thought is as powerful as any language one can learn, but of course Fodor allows for the emergence of new concepts both in the individual and in science. As already mentioned this can be understood, he suggests, as complex concepts being made up of simple concepts. If we can characterize the language of thought, we have characterized the limits of learning; and as mentioned in the foregoing section, this rules out radical shifts in conceptual or linguistic systems, as proposed by Piaget and Vygotsky, among others. His theory furthermore has little room for social conventions and interactions to shape what is learned.

What we learn is totally limited by the structure of our minds, or more specifically by the formal transformational rules that our brains instantiate. This emerges clearly in Fodor's discussion of semantics. Learning a language involves at least learning its semantics. To learn what English or French words and sentences mean involves translating them into the language of thought, to go from wave form to message, the latter being intrinsically meaningful or self-illuminating. This implies that the semantic relationship, the relation between the symbol and what it stands for or refers to, is built into the mind or is innate. Hence there is no need to learn this relationship. On this account whether or not we mean the same is a matter of having our minds structured in the same way, not a matter of communication or agreement.

This idea is further developed in *Psychosemantics* (1987) where Fodor, as mentioned, sketches a causal theory of the semantics of the language of thought:

> symbol tokenings denote their causes, and the symbols types express the property whose instantiations reliably cause their tokenings.[59]

CONCLUSION: THE MYTH OF LEARNING

Fodor's starting point for his theory of mind was the failure of behaviorism to account for productivity, that is, that cognition, learning, action, and perception all essentially involve going beyond information given.

Fodor's most fundamental building stone was the assumption that the mind is representational. He assumes that the very possibility of psychology rests on there being a representational system of thought—a language of thought.

It is clear, especially from his account of learning, that his theory has led him to conclusions which are strangely opposed to his basic intuitions. He seems to have ended with a psychology or theory of mind which rules out learning. All our concepts as well as the recursive rules we utilize are innately fixed. Strictly speaking, there is no theory of learning because there is no learning. Furthermore, productivity does not involve radical novelty, because nothing essentially new is possible in Fodor's system.

He has solved one of the critical problems of learning, productivity, or the ability to go beyond information given, by suggesting that the framework—the mental processes are productive. The tension between productivity and the framework mentioned in chapter 1, namely that they seem to pull in different directions, has been resolved by assuming that what one has to know in order to "learn" is itself productive. Or put another way, the productivity of learning and behavior is explained by postulating productivity on another level—in the mind. This solution seems to operate with, or can be described in terms of the pre-socratic principle of "like knows like," as, for example, Heracleitus's idea of *Logos*. He like Empedocles said that we know the world by parts of the mind that are similar to the world, for example, by earth we know earth, by love love, and so on. In Fodor's case, by language we know or rather learn language.

If the language of thought, its concepts and their meaning is innately fixed, we end up with a notion of a solipsistic and unchanging mind. This seems to be as problematic as behaviorism, and is at odds with Fodor's own stress on productivity and the representational nature of the mind. It furthermore does not take biological or social aspects of learning into account.

Before turning to a possible alternative to a limited behaviorism and Fodor's strong rationalism, namely to a Wittgensteinian conception of the mind and of learning, let me turn to and elaborate the main criticisms that have been levelled against Fodor's theory. This discussion will also point to the problems and issues the Domestication Model of learning has to solve.

CHAPTER 3

Problems with
Fodor's Account of Learning

Fodor's theory of mind has given rise to many issues and become one of the most debated theories in contemporary philosophy of mind,[1] and has led Fodor to develop his views further.[2] It would take me far beyond the scope of this book to summarize and evaluate the debate to which his work has given rise. I will consider only those criticisms which pertain directly to his theory of learning. My focus will be on the status of Fodor's explanatory theory (i.e., whether it is a priori or empirical), the basic assumptions accounting for productivity (i.e., the nature of the language of thought) and generally on the nature of the framework, and his claim that his account is the *only* remotely plausible theory. This, I hope, will show the reader that even if Fodor's theory of a language of thought seemingly is a very clever solution to the problem of the tension between the framework and productivity, he fails to solve the tension which is at the very center of the problem of explaining language learning.

IS THE THEORY EMPIRICAL OR A PRIORI?

Fodor Confuses the Description with What It Describes

My first criticism is methodological and is relevant to Fodor's theory of learning insofar as, if it is correct, the theory is not an explanatory theory. It can not be empirically tested, but is rather a conceptual analysis of what learning, thinking, and so on, entail. As such it has more the status of an a priori account, and Fodor has committed the very mistake which he accuses Ryle of,[3] namely that of confusing conceptual analysis with causal or explanatory analysis. Hence he does not provide a new empirical theory of learning.

When a person learns a language what is learned can be described in certain ways, for example, in terms of syntactical or semantical rules. The same holds for learning to play tennis or learning to ride a bicycle. The behavior can be described in terms of rules. What the cyclist does to keep his or her balance can be described in terms of specific rules, for example:

> When starting to fall to the right turn the handle bars to the right so that the course of the bicycle is deflected towards the right, then counteract the thrust to the left by turning the bars to the left.[4]

The cyclist is not following this rule or any other consciously, and there is no reason or evidence to suppose that it is followed unconsciously. Furthermore, the motion of the planets can be described in terms of differential equations but no one would like to suggest that the planets are computing these equations in order to move.[5]

The fact that we can describe the motion of the planets, cycling, or language in terms of a set of formalized rules does not in itself imply that the planets, the cyclist, the speaker, or that the language-learning child is actually guided by the rules which are used to describe the behavior in question. Perhaps they are only behaving in accordance with the rules. To claim that a specific set of rules actually are followed or used to "produce" the behavior, the theory has to specify things. First it has to specify what specific rules are actually followed. Since rules are always underdetermined by behavior in the sense that one and the same behavior can be described by different sets of rules, reasons must be given why a set of rules have preference over another set, which equally well describe the behavior, but which are not actually followed. For example, the behavior of a bicyclist trying to maintain his or her balance could be described in a rule different from the one given above. Another example is that a verbal utterance can be described using many different types of grammatical rules, for example, the school grammar's simplified rules, or the rules of a phrase structure grammar or those of a transformational grammar. Second, and more important, the structure of the causal mechanism involved in rule following must be specifiable independently of the description of the behavior in question, so as to avoid confusing the conceptual issue with the causal issue.

The first problem is of little interest here since we are not concerned with which specific rules the child is learning; but it illustrates the difficulty of ascribing or attributing rules to a specific behavior. It also gives rise to the general methodological question of the underdeterminacy of language, or of the problem that perhaps not all linguistic behavior can be captured in rules.[6]

Philosophers such as Dreyfus, Dennett, and Heil[7] have all, in somewhat different contexts, criticized Fodor for failing to meet the second requirement, and hence for confusing description with causal mechanisms.

Dennett claims that Fodor has confused the conceptual issue (the mechanism of description) with the causal issue (what actually is taking place) when he argues that the structure that could causally explain our beliefs, thoughts or language is the same as the structure of the syntax of the formulations we use to describe language, thoughts, or beliefs. Dreyfus makes the same point:

> Likewise, we need not conclude from the fact all continuous physicochemical processes involved in human "information processing" can in principle be formalized and calculated out discretely, that any discrete processes are actually taking place.[8]

Heil argues that even if Fodor can show that it is possible to construct a computer that computes according to the rules specified in the description:

> It scarcely licences the conclusion that any device which performs the task in question necessarily does so in anything as the way the comput ing machine does it.[9]

In *Psychological Explanation* a central part of Fodor's argument for the computational nature of the mind is that it is not an empty explanation like Moliere's famous example of the sleep inducing powers of opium, because we can actually build computational devices that perform the task according to the rules we have specified, and because we know the causal mechanisms involved in such a device. We can specify the causal mechanisms, for example, on and off switches, independently of any particular program we want to run on the device. Heil counters this by saying that it is a trivial fact about any computing device that in order to get it to perform a certain task we first have to describe the task in question in such a way that the computer can perform it. If we are successful the computer will perform the task, but this is a fact about how we have programmed the computer. It does not licence us to conclude that *any* device which performs the task necessarily does it in the same way. Fodor's answer to Heil would be, I think, to refer to Turing's article "Computing machinery and intelligence" (1950). Like Turing, he would argue that if a computing device or any other entity has the same predictive power as the one we try to explain, that is, produce the same behavior, we have good reasons to assume that the same kind of processes are at work. If we could construct a computer program that could predict what a human would say in different contexts, we have good reason to assume that we have hit on the very same information processes as are taking place in the human mind.

So Fodor can and sometimes does answer this type of criticism by claiming that the assumption that mental processes are computational is only an empirical hypothesis which will be confirmed or disconfirmed by empirical data. But especially in *The Language of Thought* the hypothesis—that the mind *actually* is a computing device, not only that it can be described as such—is treated more as an a priori truth than as an empirical assumption. It is derived from a specific analysis of what productive behavior, perception or learning entails, namely the recursive application of rules. Chomsky's analysis, which Fodor accepts, that language can be described in terms of a set of universal recursive rules does not entitle him to conclude that the child is actually following the rules (in the sense of using them), as already discussed. To do this he has to show some independent evidence; but since the rules do not seem to be followed consciously, introspection can provide no evidence. Independent behavioral evidence seems ruled out as well because it would have to be described or characterized in a specific way, that is, in terms of formalized rules, before it even could be considered as relevant behavior. Among others, Ericsson and Simon (1984) claim that this problem can be overcome. Verbal reports, like thinking-aloud protocols, can help us gain information about the internal structure and the details of the mental mechanisms. For example, they claim that verbal reports very often contain all the information necessary for the performance of a task. This method is, of course, useless in the case of children who do not possess a language. In addition, awareness and reporting of linguistic rules or other rules is very rare.[10] Hence Fodor's theory, unless he develops a way to deal with these problem, seems to be empirically irrefutable since there could be no falsifying evidence either from behavior or introspection. If we came across a behavior, a skill for example, that could not be specified in computational terms, Fodor's reply would be, I suspect, that the behavior is either not intelligent or that it is not productive, or he would say that we have *not yet* found relevant formalizations. If we find the correct formalization, that is, the correct description, explanation will follow.[11]

Somewhat similar to the way Ryle's[12] conceptual analysis of "clever clowning" does not necessarily tell us what goes on, or does not go on, in the clown's mind, Chomsky's universal grammar or Fodor's truth rules do not necessarily tell us what goes on in the speaker's mind. Fodor's theory is not only irrefutable but seems to have committed the very mistake which he himself accuses Ryle of,[13] namely confusing or reducing a causal problem to a conceptual problem. Fodor is well aware of the distinction, as is shown by the fact that he uses it against Ryle.[14] It is only unfortunate that he seems to forget it when he develops his own theory.

Underlying Fodor's confusion is, I think, the fundamental assumption that the structure of what is learned tells us how it was learned. Fodor echoes Socrates in *Meno*, where the question if and how it is possible to teach and learn virtue can be answered only if we know what virtue is. We do not need to know anything about the pupil's initial endowments or knowledge, or his interaction with the environment, but only the knowledge, behavior or thought that is to be learned, because from this the initial knowledge can be deduced. Both for Fodor and Plato nothing new is really learned because this would be paradoxical, hence learning is really recollection or re-presentation of what is already in the mind. The starting point in learning is the same as the end point, there is no process of constructing or creating knowledge. This is not strictly correct, because not everything has to be inherent in the mind. Fodor could argue that all he is claiming is that the mind is equipped with an axiomatic system, rules of transformation or inference and rules of construction (grammar). One has to grasp the axioms but not the consequences. This, again, seems to be similar to the view that Plato presented in *Meno*.[15] If the end product—language or knowledge—is all we need, the theory is solipsistic in the sense that we do not need to consider the relation between knowledge or language and the world, but it is enough to consider the internal structure of what the individual knows. Furthermore, we do not need to take into consideration the biological and psychological make up of human beings, because learning can be accounted for only in terms of formalized rules describing what one is learning. This of course fits very well with Fodor's basic assumption that the mind in essential aspects is a computer, that is, a rule-governed information processor.

Learning as Computation

Fodor's basic assumption is that all reasoning, perception and mastery of language can be reduced or described in terms of computation, specifically the forming and confirming of hypotheses. Again we see the similarity with Plato, who in the later part of *Meno* argues that all knowledge must be stated in explicit definitions or a set of rules that tells us what to do. If knowing how to act virtuously cannot be converted into knowing that or explicit definition, it is not knowledge but only true opinion. And if it is not knowledge, it cannot be taught or learned. Fodor seems to be arguing in a parallel way when he discusses learning, namely that unless the pupil possesses relevant knowledge explicitly stated or formulated in hypotheses, learning is impossible. Both Fodor and Plato here seem to reduce knowing how to do certain things like acting morally or speaking meaningfully, to knowing that such and such is the case, or knowing an explicit definition. In Fodor's case at least learning—forming and testing hypotheses—involves calculation or transformation of representations.

The idea that reasoning or mental processes are computations is not uncommon,[16] but both in Fodor and Plato it has the consequence that nothing can be taught, known or learned unless it is explicitly represented. Dennett brings out the last feature of Fodor's theory in his review of *The Language of Thought*.[17] He claims that Fodor is committed to the view that nothing can be believed, thought, or learned unless it is explicitly represented.

> Fodor seems to think that the only hypotheses which could *determine* the extension of a natural language predicate would have to be confirmed hypotheses explicitly about that predicate and having the explicit form of a truth rule.[18]

To learn the extension of "is a zebra" the child has to conjoin all confirmed hypotheses about zebras, that is, the child's concept of 'zebra' is the set of truth rules it has confirmed. But, Dennett argues, is it not the case that we have beliefs about zebras (e.g., that they do not wear green overcoats), without having entertained this hypothesis:

> We have all believed it for some time but were not born believing it, so we must have come to believe it between birth and, say, the age of fifteen, but it is not at all plausible that this is a hypothesis any of us has explicitly formed or confirmed in our childhood, even unconsciously. It is not even plausible that having formed and confirmed other hypotheses entailing this fact about zebras, we (in our spare time?) explicitly *computed* this implication.[19]

Just as Plato's slave boy does not know unless he has explicitly defined the knowledge, Fodor seems to be ascribing not only representation, but explicit and unlimited representation to the learning child. All this seems to follow from his assumption that mental processes are computations; and, given this assumption, his theory seems irrefutable. Let me explain.

He is committed to the view that believing or knowing something is computation. This requires explicit representation, and entails that anything that is produced at a particular time or occasion was already inherent in the mind. In many cases Fodor has no record or evidence of this explicit inherent representation, but infers these characteristics from his description or characterization, which gives him exactly the qualities he needs to get his theory to work. Again, we have to question the empirical status of his theory.

Here Fodor's reasoning is not very different from Skinner's[20] claim that however novel a response seems, for example the response to an armed robber for the first time, it can be explained in terms of an inferred reinforcement schedule (unless it is considered a totally random response). Skinner, referring to something like stimuli generalization,[21] would, I think, argue that the "threat stimulus" encountered when being robbed is similar to relevant stimuli in the past which were followed by reinforced responses similar to the one exhibited towards the robber. Both Skinner and Fodor infer from their description of the behavior (stimulus/response and formalized rules) what must have taken place before, and both conclude that the behavior or knowledge must have been explicitly performed or represented before. So both Fodor and Skinner give an account of something seemingly new in the individual, in terms of earlier behavior or mental structures that are the same as the new ones. Productivity seems to be a myth. Neither can their theories be refuted, because there is no independent evidence for their inferred givens. Again, Fodor's argument for the nature of the language of thought can be traced back to the idea that unless one knows what one is learning, learning is impossible.[22]

Another case of Fodor seemingly proposing an empirical hypothesis is found in his discussion of why the language of thought is different from natural languages. This argument is empirical and not conceptual, he claims, and says that since both preverbal children and nonverbal animals can think, the language of thought is different from any natural language. But this is not a straightforward empirical question. The question is not whether animals or infants can solve problems or process information or whether their behavior can be described in terms of formalized rules, but whether or not this is enough evidence to ascribe thought or propositional attitudes to them. For example, there is no agreement about what would count as evidence that a nonverbal creature possesses propositional attitudes, since the only uncontested evidence we have is what the organism says rather than what it does. Nonlinguistic behavior can be characterized by many different and distinct ascriptions of beliefs. So it is clear that Fodor has to provide more arguments.[23] Just referring to empirical evidence of similarity in behavior between verbal and nonverbal creatures will not convince the sceptic. One way Fodor could answer this is to refer to Turing (1950) and claim that if we can predict a child's or an animal's behavior on the basis of ascribing propositional attitudes to them, we are justified in ascribing such things to them. But again these considerations are not really central to Fodor's argument which is a priori. He claims that the language of thought has to be different from natural languages to avoid an infinite regress of languages.

Can the Language of Thought Hypothesis Really Explain Productivity?

Clearly, Fodor thinks that the productivity of language, learning, perception, and action can be explained in terms of the productivity of the language of thought; but is this really an explanation? Is this explanation not unsatisfactory in that the problem of productivity is "solved" by creating exactly an analogous one—the productivity of the language of thought: How is the productivity of the language of thought acquired? Does the idea of a language of thought make sense? Can its productivity explain the productivity of speaking, of action and perception?[24] To meet this challenge Fodor has to show that his language of thought hypothesis can explain the productivity and is not just a repetition of of the same characteristics on a different level or an empty reformulation of the question in explanatory terms. His account of the language of thought has thus to show that it makes sense, can explain what it sets out to explain, and how the productivity and meaningfulness inherent in it came about. Fodor's claim that since we know the causal mechanisms of computing devices we also know the causal mechanisms of the mind and its internal structure does not help, because it does not make sense to speak about the brain as a rule-guided device or the mind as instantiating rules (or a program), and neither does it make sense to attribute semantics to a system transforming purely formal and abstract rules. To evaluate this we have to turn to Fodor's basic assumptions and characterization of the language of thought.

ARE FODOR'S BASIC ASSUMPTIONS TENABLE?

Fodor's Strong Preformist Thesis

According to Fodor one's learned language can only provide mnemonic devices and shortcuts for thinking, but never change it in any other way.[25] This means that individual experience adds nothing essential to the language of thought, but only has the role of "triggering" or "selecting" and confirming the relevant hypotheses.[26] A consequence of Fodor's conception of the language of thought is that the public natural languages never in any essential respects influence or determine thought or the cognitive capacity, and Whorfian and Wittgensteinian claims that certain thoughts and concepts are only possible given a specific natural language are ruled out, because everything essential is already fixed in the mind.[27]

The innateness of an inner language of thought as rich, powerful, and complex as any language one can ever learn, has
another radical and very problematic consequence, namely that
it rules out the ontogenetic development of higher mental processes such as problem solving and language. Cognitive development, understood as the development or acquisition of increasingly powerful conceptual or linguistic systems, is ruled out, and
all that so-called development amounts to is a maturation of the
biological system (the brain). In addition, the improvement of
performance conditions such as attention span and memory are
important. Another way that learning takes place is through the
new combination of concepts or linguistic structures already
given by the intrinsic structure of the mind, or the working out
of the consequences of an axiomatic system. As already mentioned, theories of cognitive development, such as Bruner's,
Vygotsky's, and Piaget's are all misconceived according to
Fodor.[28] Fodor thinks it is self-evident that one can not learn a
language or conceptual system different from the one one
already has. In Bruner's, Vygotsky's, and Piaget's theories it is
assumed (in different ways) that the child's concepts and knowledge are very different from the adult's and the system of knowledge the child is trying to master. It is clear that if Fodor's view is
accepted all that is essential to the cognitive capacities of human
beings are a result, not of ontogenetic development, but of phylogenetic development. In the epilogue "Creation Myth" in his
book *Psychosemantics* he claims that not only is there an innate
language of thought, but in order for the child to benefit from
experience—especially social experience—there has to be innate
common-sense psychology as well. Here Fodor points to the
speed and ease by which children learn to interact, both linguistically and in other respects, with adults. The only way to understand this, he suggests, is to assume that children are innately
equipped with psychological knowledge of the kind we, as
adults, use every day.[29] The role of experience in shaping the
mind in ontogeny seems small indeed.

Since Fodor nowhere denies or contests the validity of the
theory of evolution, he is faced with the problem of explaining
how a rich, complex, and powerful language of thought was
acquired and retained by the mechanism of natural selection,
long before this system, either as a whole or in parts, could have

been utilized in action or communication. Since the innate language of thought is a biological "necessity" it must have been acquired at some point in the phylogenesis of humans. According to evolutionary theory new structures are the result of random mutations and selection pressure. But it is hard to entertain the idea that one big mutation endowed the human species with a complete conceptual system including concepts used in nuclear physics. What use would a massive mutation have been to an isolated individual with no one to talk to? And why has it taken so long for scientific concepts to appear in history if all of humanity has possessed them throughout its entire history? Several small mutations seem also to be an implausible explanation, given that concepts such as 'electron' or 'valence' are very specific yet related to other concepts, and therefore cannot be accounted for in terms of isolated mutations. A way out of this dilemma can perhaps be found if one takes into consideration the fact that many anatomical and behavioral systems are redundant, that is, having evolved for one function they can take on another function. Furthermore two or more different systems or organs can perform the same function alongside each other, allowing one to slowly change and take on another function. In this way language could have co-developed with another structure which in itself had survival value. Or, another possibility is that language is perhaps the result of the brain's enhanced capacity.[30] But as I hope to show later in discussing the Domestication Model of learning, if this fact is taken into consideration, we do not need the hypothesis of a fixed and explicit language of thought.

So Fodor's theory seems, if not incompatible with modern evolutionary theory, at least very implausible in light of this theory. Since that theory has a wider application and has more empirical support than Fodor's theory, his theory is more likely to be mistaken, and the burden of proof is without doubt on Fodor and not on evolutionary theory in this case.

It is also problematic to argue, as Fodor does, that new concepts are reducible to old and less complex concepts. Baker and Hacker (1984) argue that many concepts are not like this at all. For example, family resemblance terms which are not united under a unitary concept and terms like 'substance' can not be defined by enumeration or formal definitions. They also raise the question whether there are any absolute principles for counting how many meanings a word has.[31] Theoretical concepts in the sciences cannot be accounted for by reductions or eliminative definitions of observables, but are rather defined implicitly by the complex of propositions, or theory, in which they occur. P. Churchland in her review of Fodor's *The Language of Thought* argues that Fodor ignores this and also gets into problems because:

> either the (overtly) theoretical concepts of science are innate, or on the other hand, they are reducible to truth functional combinations of innate concepts. Taking the first alternative, it will have to be admitted that the ancient Greeks, the Huns, and perhaps even Cro-Magnon man, possessed a Mentalese graced with such concepts as 'electron' and 'valence', and the wonder is that the relevant theory was so long in articulation. On this alternative, we attribute to Mother Nature a thoroughly uncanny prescience in outfiting our representational systems, for it appears that science in our genes scoops, and scoops systematically, the science in our libraries.
>
> The second alternative fares no better, for there is not the slightest reason to believe that theoretical predicates are reducible to elementary predicates, should there be such. Quite the reverse; there is good reason to believe that theoretical predicates are not so reducible.[32]

Boden argues that the weak point in Fodor's theory is that new concepts can only be generated by explicit definitions in terms of existing concepts. He is ignoring the possibility that meaning can be partially defined. For example, theoretical concepts in the sciences, although rooted in observation statements, are not definable directly in observation-terms. Meaning-postulates and inferential networks linking them to other parts of the theory and to observation-statements can give us partial definitions of new terms. She rejects Fodor's extreme nativism, but maintains that a "fairly complex" representational system must be presupposed.[33]

Another way to refute Fodor's extreme nativism, as well as a more modest nativism, is suggested by T. Wasow. In a review of Fodor's *The Language of Thought*[34] he argues that Fodor, in assuming that thought is computational,

> need postulate only that our "language of thought" have at least two symbols and three operations.[35]

since any algorithm can, in principle, be carried out by a Turing machine which uses only two symbols and three operations. If this is all that needs to be attributed to the language of thought, Fodor's claim that it is as rich as any language we can learn, has been reduced to the claim that there has to be something, in order to learn.[36]

So it seems that Fodor's extreme nativism flies in the face of evolutionary theory, and is not necessary because the assumption that thought is computational does not warrant an extreme nativism.

Is the Language of Thought Intrinsically Meaningful?

In *The Language of Thought* Fodor argues that the language of thought is a system of representation that has semantic content (p. 30), and that one of the crucial aspects of learning a language or conceptual system is to learn a semantical rule. How can this semantical content be accounted for or explained? What is the relationship, if there is any, between the mental representation and the external world which it represents? How does the learning of a semantical rule involve learning about the world, or is this learning only, as it were, a change in the internal state of the organism?

More generally this is related to the issue of solipsism, that is, whether or not mental states, thoughts, beliefs, and the like, require the existence of something outside themselves.

According to the Cartesian conception of mind, thoughts, feelings, and so forth, are private to the person experiencing them, and in themselves say nothing about whether a specific content is related to a particular thing in the external reality (Meditation 3). Thus the relationship of the mental content to the world is an entirely different matter, which need not be resolved in order to account for mental representation. Fodor in "Methodological Solipsism Considered as a Research Strategy in Cognitive Psychology" adopts this position when he argues that cognitive psychology can not deal with meaning, truth, and reference. The only way to account for differences or similarities between two thoughts, according to the computational theory of the mind, is in terms of their (internal) formal properties. Two thoughts or beliefs are the same if they are formally isomorphic. By this Fodor does not imply that introspection (as was the case for Descartes) is the only way to identity or individuate beliefs. Instead, as a proponent of functionalism, he argues that two thoughts are the same if their functional role is the same, that is, if they share the same pattern of relations (causal) to stimuli, behavior, and other mental states. This implies that the meaning of the language of thought is intrinsic to itself, that one does not have to go outside the individual's mental framework or ultimately the brain.[37] The same, of course, holds for learning the semantical rules. They do not involve learning about how concepts represent the world but are a matter of activating the relevant internal relations, because the representing "function" is, as it were, built into the language of thought. But is the language of thought really something that can represent? Before we even start to ask how the symbols or representations in the language of thought are related to what they are about we have to ask whether or not it even makes sense to see the language of thought as capable of representing or symbolizing. To discuss this I will turn to an argument that is based in the work of the later Wittgenstein and this will also function as an introduction to the type of criticism presented in chapters 4 and 5. This criticism attacks Fodor's functionalism or more specifically his claim that mental states are analogous to the internal states of a digital computer, arguing that mental states no less than computational states are not the sort of thing that can be representational. Heil in his paper "Does Cognitive Psychology Rest on a Mistake?"[38] argues that it does not make sense to attribute semantical properties to the language of thought because it is not the sort of thing that can refer to or signify independent states of affairs. Heil thinks that one of the merits of Fodor's work is that he, unlike many other proponents of cognitive psychology, makes explicit and acknowledges basic assumptions, and even if Fodor is aware of difficulties with these assumptions they are

more serious than Fodor imagines.[39]

What, then, is Heil's argument to show this?

It is clear that Fodor in *The Language of Thought* takes the language of thought to

incorporate all the semantical features which makes representation possible.[40]

Since learning a natural language such as English is a matter of learning the semantical rules of English, and this is only possible by formulating hypotheses in the language of thought about relevant semantical rules, it is clear that this aspect of learning—how English is related to the world and signifies—is parasitic on the semantics of the language of thought. Fodor argues that the language of thought is intrinsically meaningful or "ambiguity free," meaning that it has not to be interpreted or translated into another language to be meaningful. Without this assumption his theory would lead to an infinite regress of languages of thought interpreting languages of thought. So learning on Fodor's account requires a language which is intrinsically meaningful. How does Fodor account for this?

Fodor here appeals to his analogy between the mind and a computer, claiming that both the language of thought and machine languages have their semantics built into them.

> The critical property of machine language is that its formulae can be paired directly with the computationally relevant physical states of the machine in such a fashion that the operations the machine performs respect the semantic constraints on formulae in the machine code.[41]

Analogously one can consider the nervous system as the physical state of the language of thought, that is, its formulae or truth rules can be paired with the nervous system in such a way that the concepts, and so on, respect the semantical constraints. For this analogy to work it is assumed that the internal states of a computer can represent or signify independent states of affairs in a way which does not rely on natural languages or something else with semantical properties.

If the semantical content of a computational state is understood only in terms of the role it plays in the inferential structure of mental states, stimuli, and so forth, then the problem does not arise because meaning is not a question of signifying independent states of affairs. As pointed out, in *The Language of Thought* Fodor seems to want the internal code to be meaningful in the sense of referring to the external world. This is very problematic according to Heil, since nothing can represent or refer by virtue of its formal structure alone.[42]

He points out that a state of a computer is symbolic by virtue of a link between the state and the world provided by the programmer, and this must be so (and here he relies explicitly on the later Wittgenstein) because structure alone cannot represent or signify anything other than itself.

Why, then, according to Heil can structure or formal properties not signify? Why is the meaning of a sign not something
intrinsic to the sign or the cognitive system? First, he says, a
structure or a picture, however detailed cannot include its own
principle of application, whether to an external object or to a
psychological internal state. He asks the reader to consider
Wittgenstein's simple example of a stick figure, which just as well
can represent a man walking up a hill, a man sliding down a hill,
a man standing still, a warning to use sticks, and so on.[43] Adding
more detail, as an arrow, does not help one to apply or understand the picture because the arrow has to be interpreted in its
turn, and so with all structural additions to the picture. No
amount of detail of a picture or the formal system will solve the
problem. Representation is not a matter of a further internal ele-
ment, but rather something external to the picture linking it to
what it represents. In the case of a computer the programmer
provides this link using his understanding of natural language,
and in natural languages the job is done by the conventions of
use for a sign.

But cannot a picture, or in the case of Fodor the formal
properties of the language of thought, represent by being isomorphic with what they represent? This is in essence the picture theory of Wittgenstein's *Tractatus*, which when translated into
Fodor's terminology would entail the view that brain states or
states of the language of thought have internal structures that
correspond to states of affairs. In Heil's words:

> Structures in the brain, then, would represent those states of
> affairs whose structure they happen to match.[44]

This view, according to Heil, involves two assumptions, namely
(1) every state of affairs is capable of being represented as having
a natural structure, and (2) representation is explicable in terms
of structural isomorphism.

But is there one natural way to divide up natural objects or
for that matter an internal state? Can reality be decomposed into
"simple" parts and can language be analyzed into primitive
undefined terms? In the *Tractatus* Wittgenstein seemed to hold a
view like this,[45] but later rejected it. In the *Philosophical Investigations* (PI 48) he does this by pointing out that it makes no
sense to speak of absolute simples of objects or linguistic expressions. What the parts of a chair are depend on the context in

which this question is asked. For a carpenter it could be the wood, but for a chemist the atoms. He also asks what are the parts of a sentence. Is it the letters, the words, or something else? If we do not know in what context the question is raised, there is no answer. If there is no way to give a natural structure to any object or state of affairs and to linguistic expressions, how can we determine if two structures are isomorphic? Anything can be isomorphic with anything else:

> Structural equivalences turn out to be ours for the asking; we may make them pretty much as we choose.[46]

Setting these serious difficulties aside and agreeing that two things have the same structure, can we then have a case of representation? Heil claims that we cannot because only when the structure is used in a certain way, that is, when it has been assigned an interpretation do we have representation. In other words, Fodor must postulate the presence of a homunculus or a programmer to make the language of thought meaningful. Fodor's attempt to stop the infinite regress by appealing to the internal structure seems unsuccessful. He has either to give up the view that the internal language is representational (which made his theory plausible in the first place) or accept a homunculus-like entity. In neither case can learning be explained in a satisfactory way. A similar argument is put forth by Searle[47] in his so-called Chinese Room argument. His point is that understanding a language involves more than manipulating or transforming symbols, that is, it involves interpretation or the ascription of meanings to the symbols. To make this point he explores the analogue between a computer program, which manipulates symbols according to a syntax but lacks semantics, with a person who does not know Chinese, manipulating Chinese symbols according to syntactical rules. He describes the case of someone locked up in a room with a rule book (in English) for manipulating Chinese symbols. When given a question in Chinese through a slot in the door the person in the room looks up the string of symbols in the rule book and gives an answer based on what the rules say for combining signs. The answer that is returned to the people waiting outside the room could be in perfect Chinese, but this does not show that the person manipulating the symbols according to the rule book really understands Chinese. He or she could very well answer a question about mathematics, literature, or anything else correctly (and thus give the impression that he or she has understood the question) on the basis of following rules given in the rule book, but without understanding a word of Chinese. Hence, Searle claims that the hypothesis or claim that the mind is a rule-following device like a computer program cannot work, because:

> syntax alone is not sufficient for semantics, and digital computers insofar as they are computers have, by definition, a syntax alone.[48]

Fodor has not yet given up the idea of semantics as a matter of syntax, but tries to account for this in a causal theory of meaning;[49] but the problem of how to apply rules in novel situations is still a problem. Before turning to this, a few remarks on Fodor's book *Psychosemantics* (1987) and its causal theory of meaning are in order, however.

In this book Fodor, as already mentioned, proposes a causal theory of meaning. By his own admission the proposed theory is only a sketch and needs to be further developed. Fodor himself states that he has not yet solved the the problem just posed, but it seems that his account only works by incorporating a certain amount of what he calls meaning holism, namely that the content of beliefs and their meaning is related to other parts of the belief system and language. To avoid wholesale holism, which is incompatible with his causal/nomological theory, he has to give a principled way of restraining interconnections; but he fails to do this. His combinational semantics is a first step, but the criteria for deciding when an expression is a combination and when it is not is missing. The consequence of holism is that we cannot really know what a belief is, or whether two persons or the same person at different times have the same belief content. It becomes impossible to identify belief content and decide if two contents are the same. A consequence of this is that one cannot state that two beliefs are the same and hence can not state any generalizations or laws covering beliefs. Whether or not Fodor will succeed in spelling out criteria by which meaning holism can be halted remains to be seen, but even if a causal account of semantics of the language of thought were to succeed, the problem of productivity would remain and so would the problem of how the language of thought can be the basis of learning, or translating into, a natural language such as English.

The Language of Thought and the Following of Rules

Let me finally turn to a challenge to the computational model of the mind, which like the one just discussed stems from Wittgenstein and more specifically from his analysis of following a rule.

The model that Fodor advocates implies that the mind essentially is a rule-following device. Computers and the human mind are alike in that they both transform information according to specific rules. This is especially evident in the case of language learning and mastery, which, not surprisingly, is Fodor's example par excellence in *The Language of Thought*. Clearly, to learn a language is to master syntactical and semantical rules as well as conventions or social rules governing linguistic discourse. According to Fodor, to master a semantical rule is to have implicit or explicit knowledge of a rule:

> no one has mastered 'is a chair' unless he has learned that it falls under the truth rule ' <Y is a chair> is true iff X is a portable seat for one.'[50]

Clearly Fodor here is concerned with knowing a rule as knowing that such and such is the case, that is, knowing a rule is to have propositional knowledge. It is clear from Fodor's discussion that knowledge of rules and an internal representational system is enough to explain human cognitive conduct.[51]

But to master a rule involves more than having this kind of knowledge, one also has to *know how* to apply the rule to actual instances of (in this example) chairs, including instances never encountered before. Fodor in both *The Language of Thought* and in *The Modularity of Mind* (1983) acknowledges this, but the issue is not pursued.

More specifically what is the problem of rule following which creates problems for Fodor's approach? Assuming that rule following in, for example, language or in mathematics involves both having implicit or explicit knowledge of the rule and being able to apply the rule, this approach leads to an infinite regress of rules for applying rules and is unable to account for the ability to apply a rule in novel situations. The last problem is especially interesting, since the central role of the language of thought hypothesis is to explain the productivity of natural languages.

First, let us turn to the problem of infinite regress. Any rule, mathematical, grammatical, or the rule for reading a map, can be correctly or incorrectly applied. A map of the Toronto Subway system cannot guide one's travel unless one knows how to use it; that is, knows what it represents in relation to the actual subway system. Detailed knowledge of the map itself is useless for a practical purpose such as getting from one place to another, unless one knows how to apply it. In the same way it is not enough to assume that a child is born with an innate representational system and linguistic rules. We also have to assume that the child knows how to use it. But how does the child know how to apply cognitive representations or rules? Does the child have another system of rules or another representation guiding the application of the "first" system of rules or representations, and yet another another system of rules to guide this system and so on in an infinite regress?[52] This will be further elaborated in chapter 5, in discussing Wittgenstein's rule-following argument, especially as it has been explicated by S. Kripke in *Wittgenstein. On Rules and Private Language* (1982).

LEARNING AS TRANSLATION

According to Fodor learning a first language is a matter of translating from the language of thought to the language in question. But what makes this possible? Translating from one natural language into another natural language is, according to Fodor, possible because of shared semantical representations—the language of thought—but this account cannot hold for translating between the language of thought and the first natural language because here there is no shared representational system. This would lead to an infinite regress of internal representations which Fodor rightly wants to avoid. But how are we then to understand this translation which is crucial to Fodor's conception of learning? Fodor does not provide us with anything which can solve this problem.

Even if one grants Fodor the claim that the language of thought is intrinsically meaningful this does not help because—to allude to Meno's paradox—how can we get from what we know (the language of thought) to what we do not know (a natural language), unless we already know the last or if what we know has something (everything?) in common with what we know already, that is, they are the same. Hence we do not need to postulate an inner language of thought which is different from natural languages. It does not aid in learning language. The language of thought hypothesis is no explanation, neither is it really needed.

IS FODOR'S THEORY THE ONLY "REMOTELY PLAUSIBLE THEORY"?

Early in *The Language of Thought* Fodor claims that his theory is the only remotely plausible theory of language learning. This is said with the failure of behaviorism in mind, but in light of the many problems with his theory other alternatives seem at least as plausible. Only if they have more serious problems than his theory, should they be rejected in favor of his.

There are several alternative theories which can claim to be at least as plausible as Fodor's theory. For example, Bruner and Vygotsky both reject the idea that learning, or at least initial learning, is a matter of forming and confirming hypotheses. Instead, they suggest that learning is best understood in terms of acquiring a skill, which is socially mediated and requires practice.[53] Furthermore, Bruner argues that non-linguistic representational systems (enactive or iconic) are involved in learning. Both Bruner and Vygotsky have ideas similar to the ones hinted at above, that is, in the discussion on following a rule.

Even for Piaget, who sometimes seems to see learning or conceptual acquisition in terms of hypothesis formation and confirmation, Fodor's account of learning is not the only alternative. Flanagan lists several different ways in which the basic elements of Piaget's theory can be preserved without having to accept Fodor's alternative. For example, just as in evolution, through the interaction between individuals and the environment which leads to new structures, and just as individual maturation of innate structures leads to new forms, an individual could have all necessary representational resources at the time it projects a hypothesis, with out always having possessed them.[54]

So Fodor's approach to learning is certainly not to be accepted by default. Even if all these theories turned out to be mistaken, or unable to account for the facts, it is not a good reason to accept Fodor's theory to say that it is the *only* theory.

> for that theory might be worse than none. Inability to explain a fact does not condemn me to accept an intrinsically repugnant and incomprehensive theory.[55]

As we will see in later chapters there is, though, a viable, and more than remotely plausible theory of learning, namely the Domestication Model. This approach acknowledges the problems just discussed and tries to combine insights and empirical data from Piaget, Vygotsky, Bruner, and even Skinner. But more about this later in chapter 7.

CONCLUSION

Although there clearly are problems with Fodor's claims and explanations of learning, he has attempted to answer a very difficult problem. In following up Chomsky's stressing of the problem of productivity as essential to understanding language and language learning, he has contributed to the literature on learning and helped clarify the issues that need to be resolved.[56] His work has, for example, shown that in order to explain learning we have to make the framework productive. But the preceding considerations show that Fodor has failed to solve the problem of productivity, of how new knowledge builds on old knowledge, yet can go beyond it. His theory of an inner language of thought has created more problems than it can solve and does not give us a tenable account of what we call learning. It is not an empirical hypothesis, cannot be falsified, it does not succeed in giving an explanation, and is incompatible with evolutionary theory.

To develop the above criticism more fully and to discuss what I take to be an important and interesting theoretical alternative to Fodor's conception of learning, I will next turn to the later views of Ludwig Wittgenstein. Wittgenstein is especially interesting because his criticism of his own early work can be applied to Fodor. The later Wittgenstein is the main opponent whom Fodor sets out to refute with his theory. So Fodor can be read as a critic of the later Wittgenstein while at the same time the later Wittgenstein can be read as a critic of Fodor. My reconstruction of a Wittgensteinian theory of learning will then be taken as basis for a theory of productivity or learning. This theory does not conceive of productivity in terms of rule-following. Furthermore, it does not see learning as an abstract or formal process of changing or transforming knowledge, and it does not divorce learning from concrete biological and social contexts. Instead it shows how biological and social factors make up learning and enhance each other.

CHAPTER 4

Wittgenstein 1:
Background and the Rejection of
a Language of Thought

As is seen from earlier chapters I have chosen the philosopher Ludwig Wittgenstein both as the basis for my criticism of Fodor's theories and as a basis for an alternative account of learning. Wittgenstein was one of the most influential philosophers during this century, whose first book *The Tractatus Logicus-Philsophicus* influenced new developments in logic as well as the so-called logical positivists, and with his later works, especially the *Philosophical Investigations,* common-sense or ordinary language philosophy. Not only was he very influential in in these areas, but his ideas have for a long time been dominating, at least in the Anglo-American philosophy, the philosophy of mind. In spite of this enormous influence his interest in learning has by and large been overlooked[1] and this and the next two chapters are attempts to remedy this and bring out Wittgenstein's interest in learning, and show how his views can be used both to criticize Fodor's views and for the development of an alternative and more viable account of learning.

My aim in this chapter is to show first that Wittgenstein is concerned with the same problems as Fodor, namely the problem of the framework and the problem of productivity. Next, I will sketch an argument to show that even if Wittgenstein did not explicitly present a theory of learning, a fruitful reconstruction of such a theory can be made. This reconstruction will become the chief focus of the next two chapters. The comments and remarks by Wittgenstein on which my reconstruction is based grew out of his criticism of his own earlier views, thus these will be dealt with first. I will argue that Wittgenstein's own earlier views are very similar to some of Fodor's in many important respects. Wittgenstein's criticisms can be read as if they were criticisms of Fodor-like accounts of learning. Wittgenstein functions, thus, as both a test of Fodor and as a source of a viable theory of learning. The viability of Wittgenstein's theory, or rather of a reconstruction of a theory on the basis of his critical remarks and a few positive hints on what learning entails, will then be discussed in the light of empirical evidence from biology, psychology, and sociology. The account of learning which emerges from all this will be what I call the Domestication or Transactional Model of learning.

My discussion of Wittgenstein consists of three parts. In this chapter I will show why Wittgenstein rejects the account of meaning as something mental, in the next chapter I will discuss the account of learning associated with this mentalistic approach of meaning and the following chapter is presenting my actual reconstruction of what I claim to be Wittgenstein's account of learning.

THE PROBLEM SITUATION

Introduction

As we saw in chapter 2, Fodor's theory of learning was primarily a response to the failure of behaviorism. Undoubtly it is more difficult to reconstruct or specify the problem situation for Wittgenstein than for Fodor. His writings cannot be seen as a response to a specific theory or school in the way Fodor responded to the failure of behaviorism in light of the newly developed theory of mental computation. Add to this the well-known obscurity of Wittgenstein's writings and the many, often contradictory, interpretations and the situation becomes complex indeed. Nevertheless, I think that Wittgenstein can be read as fruitfully dealing with problems very similar to the ones that occupy Fodor.

Throughout his writings Wittgenstein's central focus was language, in particular the problem of representation or meaning; and although he does not state his problem as explicitly one of learning, in his later writings he is very much concerned with tracing the conditions for learning and teaching language. This should come as no surprise both for biographical and philosophical reasons. Having left philosophy behind after completing *Trac-*

tatus and returning to his native Vienna at the end of the First World War he attended the Lehrerbildungsanstalt and taught for six years (1920–1926) in small village schools in Lower Austria. This is not as eccentric as it is sometimes made out to be; his great hero Tolstoy had founded a school for peasant children in the 1850s, and contemporaries such as Buhler, Adler, Popper, and one of his own sisters were also engaged in similar activities. It would be strange indeed if several years of teaching children did not influence a sensitive and intellectually active mind such as Wittgenstein's, especially since theories of learning and educational reforms were very much a part of the *Zeitgeist* in Vienna.[2] It should also not be forgotten that the only book Wittgenstein actually published during his life time besides the *Tractatus* was a word book or dictionary to be used in elementary schools. Wittgenstein initially became interested in philosophy through his engineering studies and perhaps this new and different practical experience of teaching contributed to his reconsideration of parts of his earlier view. The main reason for his reentering of philosophy was though his conversations with other philosophers like Sraffa and Ramsey in the late 1920s and possibly attending the lectures on the foundations of mathematics by Brouwer in 1928.[3] Whatever the validity of these biographical speculations his later writings show an increased interest in learning and teaching. In writings after the *Tractatus* he returns again and again to this. It is no coincidence that *Philosophical Investigations* starts with a criticism of St. Augustine's account of language learning in terms of ostensive definitions,[4] or that he in *Zettel* says:

> Am I doing child psychology?—I am making a connexion between the concept of teaching and the concept of meaning.[5]

His conception of language, especially in his later works, forces him to confront the problem of how it is possible to go beyond information given (i.e., the problem of productivity or induction) and the problem of the framework or Meno's paradox (i.e., that meaning is already presupposed in any process of learning), what I have argued in chapter 1 are the *two* problems of learning. His concern in the *Philosophical Investigations* was to clarify what was wrong with these questions and the assumptions about language they presuppose. Unlike Fodor, his aim is not to come up with an empirical theory. Nevertheless, Fodor and Wittgenstein, from quite different starting points, confront the same problem.

Wittgenstein's interest in these two problems has been brought into focus by two recent interpretations of Wittgenstein's later writings; by Saul Kripke on one hand and Merrill and Jakko Hintikka on the other. Wittgenstein's interest in productivity or the problem of induction in the realm of linguistic discourse has been made clear by Kripke in his discussion of rule following and the private language argument.[6] The Hintikkas' book shows, I think, that Wittgenstein's doctrine of showing and saying (i.e., that one cannot speak of language or rather of meaning) and the contextuality of meaning leads him to a very special solution to the problem of the framework.[7]

Two Problems of Learning

Fodor and Chomsky are, as we have seen, impressed by the fact that children learn to speak language meaningfully, but are critical of the behavioristic and other prevalent accounts, both everyday and philosophical. Wittgenstein, although not explicitly interested in language learning, was concerned to clarify the question of how we come to speak meaningfully. In this he comes to critically discuss different accounts of language and learning. In spite of differences in approach all three find themselves in a dilemma that is reminiscent of Kant.

Problem 1: The Problem of Productivity.   The kind of dilemma I am thinking of arises from two opposing factors: (a) the uncontested existence of a certain kind of knowledge (in Kant's case the synthetic a priori; in Fodor, syntactical and semantical rules and in the case of Wittgenstein knowing how to speak meaningfully), and (b) from a theory or set of presuppositions in terms of which this type of knowledge is impossible (Hume's epistemology for Kant; behaviorism for Fodor; and Augustinian or Tractatus-type theories for the later Wittgenstein).[8]

Chomsky argues, in Language and Mind (1968), for example, that: (a) language clearly is possible, yet (b) if the empiricist account of language (especially in the form put forward by Skinner) is correct, then language, especially linguistic creativity, seems to be impossible. This clearly presents a dilemma. Chomsky, like Kant, set out to escape the dilemma by rejecting empiricism. The same holds for Fodor, who in The Language of Thought argues that (a) language learning, linguistic creativity (i.e., that we can understand and produce utterances or expressions never encountered before) is an uncontested fact, and (b) this is impossible to account for in empiricistic terms, or more specifically in behavioristic terms. Following Chomsky he rejects empiricism and develops the rationalistic, innatist account of language and learning I have discussed in previous chapters.

Now, I think that a parallel dilemma can be found in Wittgenstein. He clearly takes for granted that (a) linguistic communication and creativity takes place. He stresses linguistic creativity less than Chomsky and Fodor but his discussion of both 'understanding' and even more his discussion of 'following a rule' is concerned with how a word or a concept can be applied to circumstances not encountered before (PI 179, 186, 189). He is here concerned to clarify the logical grammar of "Now I can go on" or showing how going beyond previously given information or experience, both linguistic and nonlinguistic, is possible. He thus claims that (b) conceptions of language, for example Augustine's as well as other's which explain language in terms of inner psychological or rational processes, if investigated carefully, seem to make language impossible.[9]

Wittgenstein's solution to this dilemma, or to use Kripke's words 'the sceptical paradox,' is parallel to Chomsky's and Fodor's. He rejects the theoretical approach in terms of which language is rendered impossible, and proposes instead an approach to language in terms of social conventions, or in his own terminology 'language games.' He does this by showing that the argument leading up to the sceptical paradox and a mentalistic account of meaning is absurd and that the the premises from which it follows are so as well.

If this crude comparison is correct, Fodor and Wittgenstein can be interpreted as dealing with the same Kantian questions: "How is language, communication and linguistic creativity possible?" "How is it possible to go beyond information given; or how is learning possible?" Their answers are, though, similar only insofar as both answers involve rejecting certain theoretical assumptions which they claim render language impossible. The important difference is that Wittgenstein criticizes theories of the kind Fodor takes to answer the "Kantian" dilemma, and vice versa, that is, Fodor argues that theories of the type that he ascribes to Wittgenstein[10] are incapable of accounting for language and conceptual formation. Each even argues that the type of solution presented by the other gives rise to the dilemma in the first place, and each rejects the other's solution to the problem of productivity.

In spite of these differences it should be clear that Wittgenstein and Fodor share an interest in the problem of productivity.[11]

Problem 2: The Problem of the Framework.   What about the dilemma or the paradox presented by Meno in Plato's dialogue and adopted by Fodor, that is, that either one already knows what one is learning or one does not, and in both cases learning is impossible? Is this a problem for Wittgenstein, and if so, how does he deal with it? Or, in other words is the problem of the framework a problem for Wittgenstein?

M. and J. Hintikka describe what they take to be a central theme throughout Wittgenstein's writings, namely what they call "language as the universal medium."[12] One can not say meaningfully in language what the relationship between language and the world is because any attempt to do so presupposes that this is understood. Hence the meaning relationship is already known or it is impossible to learn by going outside language; or in the words of the Hintikkas one is a prisoner in the language one already knows. In Wittgenstein's early book *Tractatus* this is implicit in his well-known picture theory of meaning. Here the logical form of a proposition, that is, the structure it has in common with the reality it depicts, cannot be said or made explicit in language but is shown. A proposition can display or make manifest its logical form; it is presupposed in what we say but can never itself be talked about. In the later *Philosophical Investigations* Wittgenstein rejects the picture theory of meaning but the idea of language as the universal medium (PI 120) remains. Here he is also concerned with how meaning can be taught and learned, and concludes that since meaning is use, the semantic relation can not be made explicit in linguistic rules or definitions. It can only be shown by examples of language in the context of the appropriate language game (PI 71, 75). But how can the child break into this system unless he or she already knows what the examples show or display, that is, unless he or she has already grasped what the meaning relation is? Are we not again stuck in Meno's dilemma that in order to learn we have to know what we are supposed to learn, or else learning is impossible?

I would like to argue that much of Wittgenstein's later writings can be understood as an attempt to answer this question. It was not idle talk when he said in Zettel:

> I am making a connexion between the concept of teaching and the concept of meaning.[13]

His remarks on learning are not only there, as sometimes presumed, to elucidate general problems of language and meaning but they are also there to solve the problem of what I have called the problem of the framework in chapter 1. These remarks are central for his account of meaning and language. The rejection of any kind of language of thought as underlying meaning and learning, his theory of language games, of forms of life and the account of learning as training are all interwoven in his attempt to deal with the problem of the framework. The specifics of this will be discussed in chapters 5 and 6.

Hence Wittgenstein, like Fodor, is concerned with the two central problems of learning, but while Fodor makes it absolutely clear that his aim is to present a new and more valid psychological account of what we call learning the same can not be said about Wittgenstein. On the contrary, he is explicitly denying that he is doing child psychology and also claims that philosophical doctrines are nonsense. Does this mean that Wittgenstein cannot and should not be read as presenting remarks or claims which can be developed into a theory or model of learning?

DOES WITTGENSTEIN HAVE
A THEORY OF LEARNING AT ALL?

It is unquestionable that the main thrust of Wittgenstein's later work is primarily critical, consisting mainly of the exposition of paradoxes inherent in different philosophical positions. He thought that his positive contribution consisted in showing the "nature of philosophy," not to contribute a psychological theory (e.g., PI 123, 124, 127). Hence one has first to ask whether he has any positive theory of learning and concept formation and use at all.

Description, not Explanation

Wittgenstein makes it clear again and again that he is interested in description, not explanation. In philosophy, he says,

> We must do away with all *explanation*, and describing alone
> must take its place.[14]

The only legitimate interest is to describe the use of terms such as
understanding, learning, thinking, and so forth, in everyday language, not to present theories or explanations of learning or
understanding. This attitude is expressed in his "idolatry of ordinary language" (PI 98, 124), as well as in his view that criticism
or change of linguistic habits on purely intellectual grounds is
not legitimate (PI 127). Philosophy's role is not to produce philosophical doctrines, which are metaphysical nonsense, but to clear
away misunderstandings (PI 119, 127; see also TLP 6.54).

Furthermore, he denies that he is engaged in a scientific
enterprise:

> our considerations could not be scientific ones.[15]

> we are not doing natural science.[16]

Wittgenstein, thus, made a sharp distinction between philosophy
and a science like psychology (PI part 2, p. 232).

Another possibility, supported by some textual evidence, is
that Wittgenstein only used references to learning to illustrate
some other point. He on several occasions referred to the pedagogical use of speculations on how we learn a word.

> One thing we always do when discussing a word is to ask how
> we were taught it. Doing this on one hand destroys a variety of
> misconceptions, on the other hand gives you a primitive lan-
> guage in which it would be used. Although this language is not
> what you talk when you are twenty, you get a rough approxi-
> mation of what kind of language game is going to be played.[17]

This quote and others (PI 77 and BB p.11) indicate that Wittgenstein was not interested in the topic of learning except as a didac-
tic help. For example, the quote above seems to be aimed at getting his students to start thinking about how aesthetic concepts
are used and differ from other concepts, for example, empirical.

From this it is clear that Wittgenstein is not presenting a psychological theory. Nevertheless he is interested in the conditions
for, among other things, learning. He is interested in conceptual,
or in his terminology, grammatical questions, and he does not
hesitate to discuss these even if it is mainly in a negative way, in
order to clear away misunderstandings (PI 90, part 2, p. 232). In

the process of discussing the logical grammar of psychological concepts he nevertheless makes some remarks of a more positive nature on, for example, learning language as a matter of training (PI 5, 6, 9).[18]

Conclusion: The Connection between Meaning and Learning

In spite of these considerations I think that Wittgenstein can be read as dealing with the problems of learning, if not by presenting a new psychological theory, then at least by raising the two most central problems of learning and by suggesting an account of learning as training and teaching as providing examples, as an alternative. The rest of this chapter and the next two are devoted to supporting this reading of Wittgenstein. But let me first give a general indication of why learning is central to Wittgenstein and why, I think, it is not only a pedagogical "trick" to become clear about particular language uses or misuses.

Given the account of meaning as use (i.e., something public) that Wittgenstein develops in the *Philosophical Investigations*, learning to speak meaningfully must be learned in close interaction with others and by participating in language games. The connection between learning and meaning, thus, becomes crucial (Z 412). An individual's understanding of meaning is a result of his or her participation in the language game, of how other individuals have shown or corrected the learner's use of words or linguistic expressions, hence how something is learned becomes a determining factor in what one means. Meaning is not a feature of the individual's mental structure or of the linguistic item itself but is a negotiated and constantly changing social construction. Meaning and learning are tied together, the possibility of learning language is the possibility of meaning and vice verse, because meaning is something acquired not given, as is supposed by theories postulating a language of thought of the kind Wittgenstein rejects. To speak meaningfully is not something given or unlearned but acquired by participation in language games, which is clearly a social process; and it is not surprising that Wittgenstein says as much about the teacher as about the pupil.[19]

Wittgenstein when discussing learning, as in discussing everything else, is not interested in empirical facts (e.g., at what age is a particular syntactic rule is grasped, etc.) but only in clarifying what is needed in order to prevent misunderstandings (BB 18,

125). Without removing the misunderstandings underlying individualistic assumptions of psychology and learning, people would be tempted to invent hidden and mysterious processes to account for meaning and learning. But he goes further than this and presents both an alternative account of meaning, and I argue, the beginning of an account or theory of meaning.[20]

WITTGENSTEIN AND THE LANGUAGE OF THOUGHT

Relationship between Early and Later Philosophy

One controversial aspect of Wittgenstein's philosophy is the relationship between his early philosophy in the *Tractatus* and the later *Philosophical Investigations*. A reason for this is surely that although Wittgenstein's views undoubtly changed radically, some themes from his early philosophy remained and were even developed. In trying to reconstruct his account of learning it emerged that the later work contains a severe criticism of certain aspects of the early work (language of thought), but that the later work also keeps and develops themes (e.g., language as the universal medium as one aspect of the the showing and saying distinction) from the earlier writings.

There is continuity, not only in interest and problems, but also in substantial claims. Since the ideas on learning partly grew out of the *Tractatus*, both as criticism and as developments, I will sketch relevant aspects of this work before turning to his later philosophy. I will consider the *Tractatus* only to the extent it can throw light on his later concern for learning, and hence pass over many of the ideas more frequently discussed by Wittgenstein scholars.

Tractatus *and the Language of Thought*

Tractatus does not deal with the problems of learning, but as already mentioned the foundation for Wittgenstein's later concerns is laid here. The later ideas are closely tied to his dissatisfaction with some of the views of *Tractatus*, but they are also developments or generalizations of early ideas. For example, his idea of language games seems related to, or has one of its its roots in, the belief that philosophical and ethical utterances show their meaning, not by depicting reality, but in the activity of which they are part; and in the idea that language is part of man's natural endowment (TLP 4.002).

In the following I will argue that Wittgenstein in the *Tractatus* asks questions very similar to the ones asked by contemporary theories of meaning and language, namely, the ones accepted by Fodor and Chomsky.[21] The *Tractatus* was designed to solve other problems than the ones that concern Fodor, yet Wittgenstein comes up with a similar approach to meaning and language.[22]

Russell said in his introduction to the *Tractatus* that Wittgenstein's main problem was

> what relation must one fact (such as a sentence) have to another in order to be *capable* of being a symbol for that other?[23]

or, in other words, what gives the lifeless symbol its meaning? Wittgenstein's answer is that the thought is what gives meaning to a sign (TLP 3.5, 4). It is thought, not the public or natural language, which is the locus of meaning, and Wittgenstein makes a clear distinction between the thought and the linguistic sign or proposition.

> In a proposition a thought finds an expression that can be perceived by the senses.[24]

and public language is a source of confusion:

> Language disguises thought.[25]

The thought itself (the logical picture of facts) is intrinsically meaningful due to the fact that it is isomorphic (TLP 2.2, 2.16) with what it depicts or refers to by sharing a form with reality. And the thought is the complete analysis of a proposition, because analysis or interpretation always comes to a halt at the thought (TLP 3.25), that is, there is no ambiguity at this level.

The last aspect, namely, that thoughts are self-illuminating or the meaning locus brings Wittgenstein, according to McDonough,[26] close to Russell in an article[27] where he develops very similar ideas. Russell relies on Brentano's concept of the mental, namely that the mental or the thought is intrinsically related to its object, that is, it is relational or intentional in its very nature. In Wittgenstein's words it includes its own pictorial relationship.[28] Wittgenstein says that without this one would have an infinite regress of thoughts interpreting thoughts (TLP 4.02).[29] Wittgenstein's doctrine of showing and saying is a natural accompaniment to this idea of a language of thought in the sense that if a thought is intrinsically meaningful and if the pictorial relationship is included in the picture this cannot itself be expressed in language or thought because it is has to be presupposed.

a proposition describes reality by its internal properties.[30]

but it shows its sense:

> What expresses *itself* in language, we cannot express by means of language.
>   Propositions *show* the logical form of reality. They display it.[31]

So we cannot say in language what the meaning relation is because to do so must already presuppose it, but it can be shown or displayed, that is, directly grasped.

The above sketch of Wittgenstein's ideas makes it clear that in the *Tractatus* he operates with a language of thought hypothesis which in important respects is like the hypothesis that Fodor takes as a starting point for his account of learning.

1. Thinking is a kind of language, and thought is isomorphic with language (compare to the claim that language of thought has to be as rich in its combinatorial possibilities as natural languages), but its structure is often concealed by the surface grammar. The language of thought is self-illuminating or is intrinsically meaningful, or in Wittgenstein's words contains its own method of projection (TLP 2.1513; BB p. 34). Thought is, in this sense, the meaning locus and if Russell's (1919) interpretation of Wittgenstein is correct the mental is the essence of meaning.

2. The thought is meaningful by virtue of its structure. Wittgenstein says that a proposition depicts reality by virtue of its internal properties (TLP 4.023) and Fodor, as we have seen, claims that meaning is "located" in the formal structure of the language of thought.

3. Both present a denotational account of meaning.

4. Both are sceptical of the possibility of elucidating the semantic relation (e.g., Wittgenstein's showing-saying distinction and Fodor's "methodological solipsism").

5. From different perspectives they both are led to solipsism and the claim that the individual is a "prisoner" of his own language of thought. (TLP 5.62, 5.63, and Fodor's idea of a fixed innate language of thought).

It is clear that both Wittgenstein and Fodor present a view which is descended from the philosopher Frege. For example, the capacity to understand new sentences or thoughts is explicable with reference to the meaning of words and their different forms of combination. The meaning of words is conceived in terms of a thought or proposition.[32] For Frege the thought is not something psychological or mental, but the objective content which is capable of being the common property of several thinkers. Fodor on the other hand makes the language of thought into something private, a property of the individual which cannot exist independently of the thinker. It is very difficult to determine whether Wittgenstein is closer to Frege than to Fodor in this respect. The idea of 'thought' is considered to be extremely obscure in the *Tractatus*. It seems that thought for him is the meaning locus and that it is intrinsically meaningful, but is it a mental entity like Fodor's language of thought? Pitcher[33] claims that Wittgenstein did not want to postulate any independent entities such as Frege's "ideal thoughts," and Black[34] says that thought is a proposition in use. More helpfully, he also refers to some passages in *Notebooks* which seem to place Wittgenstein closer to Fodor than to Frege's "Platonism."

> Thinking is a kind of language. For a thought too is, of course, a logical picture of the proposition, and therefore it just is a kind of proposition.[35]

> I don't know *what* the constituents of a thought are but I know *that* it must have some constituents which correspond to the words of Language. Again the kind of relations of the constituents of thought and of the pictured fact is irrelevant. It would be a matter of psychology to find out.[36]

In *Tractatus* (4.1121) Wittgenstein himself says that what he is doing is not empirical psychology but philosophy, but he does not deny that thoughts are psychological entities.

> Does not my study of sign-language correspond to the study of thought-processes, which philosophers used to consider so essential to the philosophy of logic? Only in most cases they

got entangled in unessential psychological investigations, and with my method too there is an analogous risk.[37]

Further support for reading Wittgenstein in this way is that the psychological conception of thoughts could very well come, indirectly, from Russell, who in the already mentioned article said that the possibility of having the mental accompaniment

makes the "essence" of 'meaning' of the words.[38]

Further support for this reading, that is, that meaning is something mental, is found in *Philosophical Investigations* where he criticizes not only Augustine but his own earlier views for making meaning into something mental (PI 693). So I will take it that Wittgenstein, at least in his later work, understood what he said earlier about meaning in this sense. If not, much of his criticism of *Tractatus* does not make sense.

The above applies to Wittgenstein's account of the meaningfulness of factual propositions but not to his account of ethical and philosophical discourse. From the point of view of the analysis of factual propositions, ethical and philosophical discourse is nonsense and their meaning is given in another way. In the *Tractatus* Wittgenstein does not give an explicit account of this but he hints that their meaning are not their logical form (they do not depict anything in the world) but is given by the activity of which they are part. This is very different from the language of thought idea. I will argue later that Wittgenstein's hints or undeveloped ideas, which appeared in his discussion of the nature of ethics and philosophy are developed and are applied to language and learning in the later work.

Rejection of the Language of Thought Thesis of Tractatus

As already mentioned, the later Wittgenstein rejects the idea of an intrinsically meaningful language of thought. His arguments about what is wrong with this view are an important part of the *Philosophical Investigations*. Here he deals with the problem of productivity, for example, in his discussion of rule following or "now I can go on," and he reinterprets the "showing-saying" doctrine in terms of the issue of the framework. Later we will see what consequences his reinterpretation of the two problems of learning has.

Philosophical Investigations opens with a quotation from Augustine on language learning,[39] but is at the same time an attack on Wittgenstein's own earlier views. The quotation has three main themes, (a) learning through ostensive definition, (b) language as essentially consisting of names, and (c) that language expresses private mental occurrences. These were all important aspects of the conception of language that Wittgenstein repudiated in his later work. Augustine said:

> I grasped that the thing was called by the sound they uttered when they meant to point it out...I gradually learnt to understand what objects they signified; and after I had trained my mouth to form these signs, I used them to express my own desires.[40]

The likenesses with Wittgenstein's own views in *Tractatus* become even more evident if one considers the text which surrounds the quotation in the *Confessions*.[41] Here Augustine makes distinctions between inner and outer language, and he treats the inner language of thought as self-illuminating or intrinsically meaningful and takes natural language to be necessary for communication but not for thought. Whether or not Wittgenstein took Augustine's view to be pre-theoretical, it is clear from other writings by Augustine that he was committed to the language of thought idea (see chapter 2 above). This idea, as mentioned above, has been very influential throughout the history of philosophy and, intentionally on Wittgenstein's part, his criticism extends far beyond Augustine. It is explicitly an attack on Wittgenstein's own earlier ideas, and furthermore Bloor argues that Wittgenstein can be read as an attack on the so-called act-and image-psychology prevalent in the beginning of this century.[42] Let me now turn to the later Wittgenstein's criticism of Augustine. I remind the reader that this is also a criticism of some of his own earlier views and that they can also be applied to Fodor.

The first thing Wittgenstein comments on is that Augustine assumes that

> individual words in language name objects—sentences are combinations of such names.[43]

This is a crude description of the theory of language presented in the *Tractatus* where he claimed that language is made up of combinations of names:

> The simple signs employed in propositions are called names.[44]

> A name means an object. The object is its meaning.[45]

In *Philosophical Investigations* he finds this too simple because although some words in language are names, not all words are names. Factual propositions are only one aspect of language; it is the old center of the linguistic town but just as a real city has many suburbs so language has many different functions beside the naming function. What was only implicit in the *Tractatus*, namely that there are two types of linguistic discourse, factual on one hand and philosophical and ethical on the other, now becomes the center of attention.

> As if there were only one thing called "talking about a thing." Whereas in fact we do most various things with our sentences. Think of exclamations alone, with their completely different functions.[46]

But even the case of naming is not to be analyzed as was done by Augustine or himself in the *Tractatus*. Consider his example of the builder teaching his helper the name of different materials that are needed for building a house. Here learning the names is not a matter of grasping the logical form or isomorphism between the thought and reality but a matter of conforming to commands. Hence the picture theory of meaning and the language of thought is no longer acceptable.

Wittgenstein goes further in his rejection of the Augustinian and *Tractatus* analysis of language. Central to the picture theory of meaning was the idea of logical form which in its turn presupposed that language and reality can be divided into absolute simples.

> Objects are simple.[47]

> The requirement that simple signs be possible is the requirement that sense be determinate.[48]

Later this is rejected in strong terms:

> But what are the simple constituent parts of which reality is composed? What are the simple constituent parts of a chair?— The bits of wood of which it is made? Or the molecules, or the atoms?—"Simple" means: not composite. And here the point is: in what sense 'composite'? It makes no sense at all to speak absolutely of the 'simple parts of a chair.'[49]

> Well, does the sentence consist of four letters or nine?—And which are *its* elements, the types of letters, or the letters? Does it matter which we say, so long as we avoid misunderstandings in any particular case?[50]

Reality and our sentences (propositions) cannot be divided into absolute 'simples', because the way we divide sentences, and so on, depends on the wider context in which the expressions are used. Given this all talk about isomorphism in form is idle, anything can be made out to be isomorphic with anything else, and this can no longer make the thought self-illuminating or intrinsically meaningful by sharing the same form as reality. Here the later Wittgenstein raises a criticism which applies to Fodor as well.[51]

Later in the *Philosophical Investigations* Wittgenstein goes further in his criticism by arguing that there can be no such thing as a private meaningful language of thought. The so-called private language argument strikes close to the heart of the language of thought hypothesis because if there is anything we should be able to name by connecting it with something mental it is our own sensations, but as Wittgenstein shows even this is impossible. Suppose one attempts to give the name "x" to a sensation one is experiencing; how does one know that the next time one is experiencing what one takes to be the same sensation that it too is the same as "x." One has to have a standard by which to measure its accuracy but the earlier sensation is no longer before the mind and a memory image of it could be mistaken. But what could this standard be? There is no way of telling the difference between seeming to be the same and actually being the same, hence there is no difference between only thinking one is having and naming the same sensation and actually doing this (PI 243ff).

> When one says "He gave a name to his sensation" one forgets that a great deal of stage setting in the language is presupposed if the mere act of naming is to make sense. And when we speak of someone's having given a name to pain, what is presupposed is the existence of the grammar of the word "pain"; it shews the post where the new word is stationed.[52]

Wittgenstein here warns against the temptation to explain what we see or hear in the public world, by referring to something mental. But this will not do, because meaning is not something mental but is public.[53]

Kripke (1982) argues that Wittgenstein in his discussion of following a rule comes to the same conclusion when speaking, not of naming inner sensations, but of grasping meaning rules, namely that any attempt to account for this in terms of a private language, dispositions, and so forth, leads to scepticism.[54]

A fifth aspect of the Augustinian picture is that natural language is necessary for communication but not for thought. Yet again this idea is rejected, because some thoughts presuppose language. Animals can think in a rudimentary way (PI 650) but thoughts of more abstract or complex concepts are impossible without language (PI 342). Also, thinking about sensations seems to be necessarily dependent on language, as the private language argument has shown. The same point is made in his famous "following a rule argument." The last two points are developed further in chapter 5.

And he concludes in the last section of Part 1 of the *Philosophical Investigations*

> And nothing is more wrong-headed than calling meaning a mental activity! Unless, that is, one is setting out to create confusion.[55]

Criticism of Image- and Act-Psychology.   Wittgenstein's attack on meaning as mental activity is an attack on Augustine, himself and the views of Russell referred to above, and on deep-seated views in the Western intellectual tradition. For example, psychology in the beginning of this century in the German speaking world (e.g., Wundt and the so-called act-psychology), accepted the view that meaning and mental activity belong together. The two sides in the "imageless thought controversy," which emerged as a reaction to the failure of the Wundt-school to get uniform introspection results, that is, images, did not disagree that meaning is mental. The defendants (like Wundt) argued that words have meaning according to the accompanying picture or image while the other side (Kulpe and Buhler) argued that words are given meaning by the mental act directed at the object named or talked about. They spoke about tendencies, attitudes, expectations or even more often about awareness of meaning, rules, or determination. It was the act of thought, rather than the content of thought which gave it its meaning.[56] Toulmin (1973) and Bartley (1973) both claim that Wittgenstein was influenced by Buhler in this matter but Bloor's (1983) interpretation that Wittgenstein rejected both accounts seems more correct. As already mentioned, the *Philosophical Investigations* ends with a clear rejection of meaning as mental; and there are more specific arguments. Even if Wittgenstein did not intend this, the 'private language' argument can be seen as directed at the so-called image psychology (Wundt, etc., see below), and the following rule argument as directed at act-psychology in Buhler's version.

In the *Philosophical Investigations* Wittgenstein argues that calling up an image to match the word is just as problematic as calling up a word (PI 73). Furthermore, if the picture theory is rejected nothing in a mental image itself can tell us what it is isomorphic with, and refers to (PI 140). Hence, in rejecting his own earlier and Russell's views he also is showing that Wundt and his followers present an untenable account of meaning.

The mental act school is also rejected in a parallel way. Wittgenstein uses introspection[57]—the school's own method—to show that there is no such thing as an act of referring or meaning. Rejecting the idea that a special experience of understanding is present when we understand a word, he argues that meaningful language does not depend on an underlying thought (BB. pp. 155–56, and in a different context PI 329, 330). Furthermore, the process or intentional act seems to be very mysterious, and never the same from one occasion to the next (i.e., the same criticism that the act-psychologist brought against the image-school). In discussing ostensive definition he says:

> And if I ask how that is done, you will say you concentrated your attention on the colour, the shape, etc. But I ask again; How is *that* done?...But do you always do the *same* thing when you direct your attention to the colour?[58]

> For neither the expression "to intend the definition in such-and-such a way" nor the expression "to interpret the definition in such-and-such a way" stands for a process which accompanies the giving and hearing of the definition.[59]

The same points come up again when Wittgenstein discusses understanding (PI 138, 140, 151–55). To talk and understand something meaningfully is not to be guided by a queer process or performing some mental act. Yet further arguments, or a version of the same, is given in sections 186–88 where he discusses the puzzle of productivity, that is, that in grasping the meaning of a word or a mathematical rule we are able to apply the word or the mathematical rule to a potentially infinite number of cases. He rules out the suggestion that a new act of meaning is needed at every use of the word or rule and also that the initial act, so to speak, traversed all the infinite steps in one act of grasping the meaning or the rule. Meaning is not something mental.

What I hope this shows is that the later Wittgenstein clearly rejected the idea of a language of thought. Philosophical analysis, introspection (the scientific method of psychology at his time), and the study of behavior show that there is no such thing as a mental picture or mental act giving meaning to what we say, or underlying our ability to learn. There is no mysterious and hidden picture or process, only what is in plain view, the behavior, language, and its context. Hence learning, or the problems of productivity and the framework cannot be understood in terms of a language of thought. This criticism applies, as we have seen, to Fodor and his account of learning. If this theory is unsatisfactory, the question becomes: Is there an account of learning which escapes these problems and which can be developed into an empirical theory? Before answering this question we have to look more closely at Wittgenstein's rejection of the account of learning which have been associated with the mentalistic account of meaning which he so forcefully critiziced.

CHAPTER 5

Wittgenstein 2:
Learning is Not Based on
the Language of Thought

REJECTION OF THE
"AUGUSTINIAN-TYPE ACCOUNT OF LEARNING"

As mentioned in chapter 4, the opening section of *Philosophical Investigations* starts with a quotation from Augustine, which explicitly deals with learning. If we are to follow Wittgenstein's methodology—to look at what is right before us, "what is in plain view," and not beyond it—the issue of learning repeatedly comes up in his discussion of meaning, and although learning was not a central topic for Wittgenstein what he says about meaning throws light on the two fundamental problems of learning. He explicitly criticizes Augustine, but before doing this he briefly gives his own account or picture of learning as a process of ostensive teaching whose central part is not the mental association or connection of sounds with objects, but training (PI 5–9). He thus, early on, gives an indication that he thinks there is an alternative account to the traditional mentalistic theories of learning.

Let me first return to his criticism of Augustine, which, as we already have seen, seems to be both a criticism of his own earlier views, related philosophical positions as well as a criticism of psychological theories of his time. In exploring this criticism of the idea of a language of thought, the problems with Fodor's account of learning will become even more clear. Thus, in this chapter I move away from dealing exclusively with the language of thought, and focus on the accompanying account of learning. This chapter will help to make the shortcomings of Fodor-like theories clear and show which considerations underlie Wittgenstein's own approach to learning. Although what Wittgenstein gives us on Augustine in the *Philosophical Investigations* does not amount to a theory of learning, I will call the approach that Wittgenstein attacks "Augustine-type accounts of learning." The reader has to keep in mind that the views discussed below not necessarily are Augustine's, but are used by Wittgenstein to draw out what he takes to be an important misunderstanding in Augustine as well as a whole tradition of philosophy of mind and language.

The Problem of the Framework

This section will deal with Wittgenstein's criticism of the Augustine-type solutions to the question of the framework and the discussion is focused on what the structure of the mind has to be for learning to be possible. Many of the central themes in *Philosophical Investigations* deal with this problem, showing that the Augustine-type approach as well as the solutions are misconceived. I will thus discuss what he has to say on the topics of ostensive definition, understanding, reading, private language, and thinking. These are all themes in the quote from Augustine that opens the book and are developed throughout the first part of the *Philosophical Investigations*.

Ostensive Definition.   What is wrong, then, with the Augustinian picture of learning a language as a matter of ostensive definition and the accompanying idea of learning as a process of translation from inner language to outer language (PI 32)?

Wittgenstein turns first to ostensive definition, namely the idea that we learn what words mean by having the objects they refer to pointed out to us. He argues that an ostensive definition can never by itself fix the meaning of a word. Only if the learner knows what the teacher intends when he or she points to something, that is, the shape, form or color, can the definition function as a learning tool.

> the ostensive definition explains the use—the meaning—of the word when the overall role of the word in language is clear.[1]

because

> an ostensive definition can be variously interpreted in *every* case.[2]
>   The person one gives the definition to doesn't know what one wants to call "two"; he will suppose that "two" is the

name given to *this* group of nuts!—He *may* suppose this; but perhaps he does not. He might make the opposite mistake; when I want to assign a name to this group of nuts, he might understand it as a numeral.[3]

and

we shall only say that it tells him the use, if the place is already prepared.[4]

All this makes it clear that in order to be able to learn from an ostensive definition one already has to know something. But what does one have to know? In section 32, Wittgenstein compares the Augustinian account of learning a first language with learning a foreign or second language. Thus, given this approach one already has to have a language in order to learn a language, hence implying that learning by ostensive definition is like translation from an inner known language to the outer conventional language one is trying to learn. This would seem to suggest that learning and understanding are possible only if one has a language of thought just as Fodor argued.

In the following sections (PI 33–36) Wittgenstein goes on to show that the mental act which is supposed to accompany the grasping of an ostensive definition is an illusion in the sense that it has nothing to do with ostension. Later he also argues that a private language of thought is impossible (see section on "The private language argument" below), hence it seems to follow that Augustine's account makes learning impossible.

Wittgenstein clearly does not accept this conclusion and gives some hints on what he takes learning to be, namely training based on man's natural endowments (PI 5, 25). Although Wittgenstein in these and related sections is primarily interested in attacking the referential theory of meaning he indicates in what direction one should look to better understand the acquisition of language. This indicates, I think, that Wittgenstein rejects the idea that postulating a private inner language of thought is the only possible solution to the problem of the framework, that is, the problem of what one has to know in order to learn. If confronted with Fodor's theory, one can assume that Wittgenstein would have rejected it on similar grounds.

Let me now turn to his arguments against a language of thought as a framework for understanding and learning.

Understanding or Grasping. Wittgenstein can also be read in terms of providing a rejection of the Augustinian view that learning is understanding or grasping (PI 1), that is, he rejects the idea that learning is to be explained in terms of underlying mental processes. Reflection and introspection of what is happening when we understand or learn a word give the impression of insight, understanding, or conscious grasping of a connection or rule of meaning. In section 138 Wittgenstein is investigating 'understanding' and here his prime interest is the experience we have of understanding something "in a flash," as when we suddenly understand a term which meaning has be unclear to us. Although we sometimes seem to grasp a word in a flash, to understand a word is to be able to apply it over time, to use it again and again in the appropriate circumstances and to be able to apply it to new circumstances. How is this to be accounted for?

He is here concerned with how to understand the understanding or grasping that is mentioned in the Augustinian picture, namely as something mental like a mental picture or feeling:

> I grasped that the thing was called by the sound they uttered...I gradually learned to understand what objects they signified; and after I had trained my mouth to form these signs, I used them to express my own desires.[5]

As mentioned in chapter 4, Wittgenstein rejects the idea of *Tractatus* or Augustine (or image-psychology) that understanding means having a picture before one's mind, even a picture including its own application. He then turns to an example of a pupil learning a series of numbers pointing out that although we certainly speak as if there is such thing as a flash or definite point in time when the pupil understands the mathematical rule he or she is supposed to apply, this is not understanding. Neither is there an mental act or sensation of grasping or understanding a rule. The last point is further supported by pointing out that there is no unique experience or mental act that one can call understanding. Furthermore, we need not consider introspective evidence in order to know that we understand or are able to go on, that is, apply a rule or a word to a new situation.

Again Wittgenstein wants to say, I think, that all theories that postulate a language of thought misread the picture or "snapshot" of understanding—they look for something mysterious, hidden, and mental behind the picture, when they should be looking more closely at the picture itself, at what is in plain view. If they look at what is actually going on when someone understands something or when we use the word understanding they would see that understanding is not a state (PI 149), process (PI 152, 154) or experience (PI 153), but something public a person does in specific situations. They would then also discover that what counts as understanding varies with the context and is given by the circumstances, and that there is no definite point at which one can say that understanding or grasping takes place. Understanding is not the name of a mysterious mental process but a skill or a public activity or behavior (PI 150).[6] And learning is not a matter of understanding, at least not if understanding is conceived as a conscious or at least in principle conscious mental process involving a rational insight. He also rejects the idea that learning and understanding is a more or less mechanical (and unconscious) mental process. This, I argue, is the message he wants to convey by his extended discussion of reading.

Translation as Reading. As already remarked Wittgenstein understands Augustine to imply that language learning is a matter of translation from an inner language of thought to whatever language is spoken around the child. Again we have the same picture as in Fodor, of learning as a matter of establishing a link between what is in the mind (the language of thought) and an outer public language. Wittgenstein has already argued, for example, in discussing understanding, that there is no mental act of understanding or grasping connecting something like a language of thought with the language learned. This is continued in his discussion of reading but here he focuses not so much on the language of thought as on the process or mental act that is supposed to link the private language to the public that one is learning to understand. He is interested in how one gets from one language, the language of thought, to another, the public language one is learning. Reading is chosen because it as well involves going from one language (the written) to another (the spoken). Reading for Wittgenstein is linking one symbol—the written or printed sign with another symbol—the spoken word. He is explicitly not concerned with reading as a process of understanding, but rather reading as a "translation" from one sign to another, that is, rather as a case of a mechanical reading machine (PI 156). He is again interested to show that something which we uncritically take to be a matter of a psychological process is not something of the kind. Furthermore, reading is not letting one set of rules guide how another is understood, it is not a matter of rule-following. In the same way, I would like to argue, he claims that getting from a language of thought to another language is not a matter of being guided by rules.

In choosing to analyze reading in order to criticize Augustine's picture of language and its related account of learning, Wittgenstein makes use of a technique found throughout *Philosophical Investigations*. This technique is to replace internal mental constructions with external nonmental counter-parts, to place in plain view what one is investigating. With this Wittgenstein means that whenever someone tries to explain something by referring to something hidden or mysterious, such as a private language of thought, mental picture, or act, this should be replaced by something which is analogous but not hidden, such as a physical picture, model or drawing.

> In fact, as soon as you think of replacing a mental image by, say, a painted one, and as soon as the picture image thereby looses its occult character, it ceases to seem to impart any life to the sentence at all.[7]

If this is done, thought, language, or learning is no longer surrounded by a "halo" (PI 97), and the picture can be rearranged so as to show us what is actually taking place, which can help us to correct our mistakes.

Wittgenstein here considers reading as:

> the activity of rendering out loud what is written or printed;[8]

He is separating it from understanding what is read, that is, in effect studying human beings as "reading-machines," and goes on to show that what makes something into reading has nothing to do with a hidden process connecting the written and spoken symbol. It cannot be accounted for in causal terms, in terms of a brain process, in terms of specific sensations, mental occurrences (PI 159, 165, 168), or in terms of guiding or derivation. First, if it were a process or derivation or being guided by the written sign, the sign itself would have to contain its own rules of application or translation. This Wittgenstein has already rejected, but he repeats his argument again. Neither is it a sensation that links the two signs, because there is no characteristic sensation of reading, and even if there were it would not make uttering words into reading. And it is not a brain process because we do not need to know what brain processes are taking place before we are justified in saying that someone is reading. Undoubtedly brain processes take place, but they can play no part in what counts as reading.

What then is reading? Wittgenstein's answer is that reading is a change in behavior, it is something which is not hidden but can be observed in plain view. Furthermore, there is no one process or behavior that counts as reading in all contexts.

So if the translation from a private language of thought is like the mechanical process of rendering a written sound out loud, there is nothing hidden or mental about it, hence the Augustinian picture, as well as Fodor's, is wrong once again.

The Private Language Argument.   This argument, which is one of the most well-known and controversial aspects of Wittgenstein's later views, can be read as an answer to a serious challenge to Wittgenstein's view that learning a language does not require a language of thought. Augustine or someone like him (e.g., Fodor) could perhaps accept that understanding a mathematical rule or speaking meaningfully about public objects is the result of training, but how could training or interaction with a teacher, however rigorous the training, teach the child to speak about sensations, like pain? We speak about them and children clearly learn sensation words in spite of the fact that the sensations are private and cannot be shared or pointed to by the trainer-teacher. How can a teacher train, show, or explain to the child a particular use when the referent is not only unperceived by the teacher but can not ever be known? According to the Augustinian picture this is possible because the child is directly acquainted with his feelings and can name them before translating them into the public language spoken around him or her.

> after I had trained my mouth to form these signs, I used them to express my own desires.[9]

Wittgenstein thinks this picture is confused and unintelligible.[10] It presupposes inner private ostension which is impossible. Furthermore, if we look closely at what is taking place when we speak about sensations, we see that in talking about sensations we are not engaged in "naming talk." Sensations are real but do not enter the language game in which sensation words are used and learned except indirectly, via their natural expressions.

What then is wrong with the idea of private ostension? The first problem concerns how the child knows what to look for in the inner stream of consciousness, how does he or she know that this feeling and not that feeling is pain? Furthermore, even if the child somehow could identify the referent of the word "pain" he or she would be in the same position as someone who is shown an object and told that it is called "tove." In the latter case the person does not know if "tove" refers to the color, the shape, the texture; and similarly the child does not know if "pain" refers to the unpleasantness, the sharpness, or the dullness of the pain, because pain is not only painful, it can be all these other things as well (BB p. 2).

> When one says "He gave a name to his sensation" one forgets that a great deal of stage-setting in the language is presupposed if the mere act of naming is to make sense. And when we speak of someone's having given a name to pain, what is presupposed is the existence of a grammar of the word "pain"; it shews the post where the new word is stationed.[11]

But let us assume that an imaginary child somehow has managed this feat. Perhaps his or her language of thought provides the necessary "sign posts," but even if he or she has succeeded in naming sensations one can still ask: Does this mean that the child fully understands the word when he or she has impressed on her- or himself the connection between the private sign and the sensation?

> But "I impress on myself" can only mean: this process brings it about that I remember the connexion *right* in the future. But in the present case I have no criterion of correctness. One would like to say: whatever is going to seem right to me is right. And that only means that we here can't talk about 'right.'[12]

Wittgenstein's point is that even if one has named a sensation at one time, at a later date when one wants to identify something as "the same sensation" the previous sensation is no longer before one's mind and the memory image of it could be mistaken, and hence there is no way of telling if it is the same or only seem to be the same sensation.

If all these objections somehow could be overcome, and each child somehow knows from his or her own case what "pain" means, he or she would still not know what someone else means by "pain," so communication about sensations is an illusion. Furthermore, the referent of the word pain becomes irrelevant in speaking about pain, because the word pain could refer to different things, even nothing, in different people (PI 293, 315, 271). Hence what was the starting point for the argument in favor of a private language of thought, namely communication and learning where inner private sensations are talked about, is ruled out by this very argument.

With this Wittgenstein does not want to deny that sensations are real (PI 304, 307, 308), but their role in learning sensation language is only indirect. Sensation words are only learned via the public nonverbal expressions or displays which are naturally and normally connected with the sensations. Sensation words are not names for this behavior or display, and do not name the sensations but rather replace the natural expressions (PI 244, cp. 582, PI 2, p. 189). The cry is replaced by verbal expressions of pain. Because of this they can be learned and used in talking about something that is not directly accessible to others besides the subject him- or herself. This will be further discussed in the next chapter when Wittgenstein's suggestions are compared to behavioristic accounts of learning (see section on "Learning as Operant Conditioning," chap. 6).

Thinking.   The private language argument is further utilized in his discussion of thinking.

In sections 316ff. in *Philosophical Investigations,* Wittgenstein deals with the concept of thinking, and again he seems, among other targets,[13] to argue against his own earlier views as well as Augustinian-style language of thought theories. According to the latter views we think and our thinking makes our language meaningful and helps us learn language, so surely there must be something like a language of thought. That is, there has to be a process or act of thinking independent of language. Wittgenstein, as in his discussion of sensations, does not want to deny that we think, only that thinking is not a mental process which determines or establishes meaning. He points out that when we speak meaningfully there are not two separate processes taking place alongside one another, one (thought) lending meaning to the other (language).

> When I think in language, there aren't 'meanings' going through my mind in addition to the verbal expressions: the language itself is the vehicle of thought.[14]

> Is thinking a kind of speaking?...But what constitutes thought here is not some process which has to accompany the words if they are not to be spoken without thought.[15]

Furthermore, neither mental images nor pictures can establish meaning.

> These words may lead me to have all sorts of images; but their usefulness goes no further.[16]

The idea of a language of thought, of thought as underlying language, comes from a misleading idea which Wittgenstein himself accepted in the *Tractatus*.

> In a proposition a thought finds an expression that can be perceived by the senses.[17]

Speaking meaningfully is not to express a thought in the sense of informing someone of what goes on in one's head as a cry informs someone what one feels (PI 317). It is not a translation of a mental process (PI 316, 335). He does not want to deny that thinking is taking place or that it exists.

> Speech with or without thought is to be compared with the playing of a piece of music with and without thought.[18]

> This, of course, doesn't mean that we have shown that peculiar acts of consciousness do not accompany the expressions of our thoughts; only we no longer say that they *must* accompany them.[19]

In all this the point seems to be that the language of thought is mistaken if it is taken as that which renders language meaningful.

Why is this picture mistaken? To answer this Wittgenstein refers back to the private language argument and his discussion of understanding.

> The question what the expression means is not answered by such a description (the description of sudden understanding: author's remark, cp. PI 321); and this misleads us into concluding that understanding is a specific indefinable experience. But we forget that what should interest us is the question: how do we *compare* these experiences; what criterion of identity *do we fix* for their occurrence?[20]

If speaking meaningfully depended on an inner experience or train of thought one could never know what someone else meant with his or hers words and communication, and learning would be impossible. And this would not only be true when speaking about inner sensations, but about anything.

> If I know it only from my own case, then I know only what *I* call that, not what anyone else does.[21]

And of course one does not know even in one's own case what one means because one lacks independent criteria which could identify something as the 'same' (cp. private language argument).

To further stress the point that language and the learning of it is not based in thought he discusses the example of William James's case of a deaf-mute who reported that he, long before he encountered written language, thought about the world and god in a linguistic fashion is unintelligible (PI 342). The deaf-mute or the child is not like a stranger coming to a country with an unknown language; he or she is not like someone that already has a language only a different language (PI 32). Thinking or speaking to oneself is parasitic on public language and is something one has learned while learning language, not the ground of learning as the examples of the deaf-mute and Augustine suppose (PI 361).

> Our criterion for someone's saying something to himself is what he tells us and the rest of his behavior; and we only say that someone speaks to himself if, in the ordinary sense of the words, he *can speak*. And we do not say it of a parrot; nor of a gramophone.[22]

The criterion of thinking or saying something to oneself is not something unobservable which could be present in anything (a machine or a chair) by taking place in a hidden mind, but given by the linguistic and nonlinguistic context.

Where does the mistake of assuming a language of thought, which seems so persuasive to us, come from? Again Wittgenstein repeats the point already made early in *Philosophical Investigations* that we tend to generalize one account, namely that speaking is sometimes accompanied by thoughts, to be true of all cases. This is why we fall into the trap or fly-bottle of seeing the mental as determining meaning. But we cannot assume that words have meaning regardless of circumstances in which they are used. Language gets its meaning from the language game and form of life in which it is imbedded (PI 261, cp. 96). Meaning is something public, so what the child learns is something public and does not connect something private with what is public. Similar misconceptions lead us to postulate a language of thought as the basis of learning. But as is argued above it cannot solve the problem of the framework.

Wittgenstein's discussion of ostensive definition, understanding, reading, sensations, and thinking amounts to a very forceful rejection of the mentalistic conception of the framework of learning he ascribes to Augustine, but also takes to be prevalent in philosophical theories. Thus a very common and persuasive account, as Fodor has shown, of the framework is rejected. He also rejects, as we will see presently, an equally common and persuasive solution to the other problem of learning, namely the problem of productivity.

The Problem of Productivity

The problem of productivity was central to Fodor and made him develop his language of thought hypothesis; but as already mentioned this concerned Wittgenstein as well. He, though, as we will see, clearly rejects Fodor's solution.

Rule Following.   In discussing understanding Wittgenstein points out that understanding is something that stretches out in time and is something which enables one to deal with new situations. In this context he says very little on this topic, but returns to it in his discussion of rule following.

A very clear and explicit discussion of what is involved is presented by S. Kripke in his book *Wittgenstein: On Rules and Private Language* (1982) where he explicates the problem of applying rules to situations or instances never encountered before. This way of posing the problem is, of course, very relevant to Fodor, since he like Chomsky sees the creativity of language and thought as central, and its explanation as a crucial task for any linguistic or psychological theory.

Kripke sees what he calls Wittgenstein's sceptical problem as a paradox

> no course of action could be determined by a rule, because every course of action can be made out to accord with the rule.[23]

To illustrate the problem Kripke asks us to consider a pupil who has learned addition, but not yet added numbers higher than fifty-six. In grasping the rule of addition the pupil is guided by the rule in each new case of addition, that is, even if the pupil only has computed a limited set of sums in the past, the rule determines answers to an indefinite number of new sums, which haven't previously been calculated. But, and this is the sceptical challenge, if the pupil is asked to compute 57 + 68 the answer that the sum is '125' is compatible with and indefinitely many rules, for example, 'x + y = x + y, for all x and y'; or 'x + y = x + y if x and y <57, and 5 otherwise.'[24] Everything that the pupil has done in the way of addition, experiences, intentions, or behaviors up to this new instance of addition is consistent with both rules and with indefinitely many others, hence there is no way of determining what rule the pupil followed. This means that to explain the pupil's behavior, the answer 125, by saying that he was guided by the rule of addition is as unjustified as saying that he was not guided by this rule. Consequently the appeal to internal computational rules is useless in explaining how someone will act in a new situation.[25]

To illustrate this future, let us imagine a person who has seen a lot of tables, but not a table on the top floor of the CN Tower in Toronto. Let us further assume that we observe this person in many situations when he or she says "table" in the presence of what we normally call table. This person's behavior could be described by many different rules. One is the rule: "Everything with legs which one can put things on, but not sleep or sit on is a table," and another rule describing exactly the same behavior could be "Everything with legs which one can put things on, but not sleep or sit on, and is not at the top of the CN Tower in Toronto, is a table." Again, everything the person says is compatible with both rules, and there is no way of choosing one and not the other as the rule which the person is actually following. The appeal to rules is useless in explaining the behavior.

So to sum up, the Wittgensteinian criticism finds the conception of the mind as a rule-following device highly unsatisfactory because a given behavior or sequence of behaviors can be described by indefinitely many rules. Furthermore, as mentioned in chapter 3 in the critique of Fodor, rules lead to an infinite regress of rules interpreting rules. If we have a rule for table we need to know when to apply it, which means we need a rule for this, and a rule for knowing when to apply this rule, and so forth.

Wittgenstein's solution to the dilemma is to argue that rule following is grounded in shared practices, customs, and so on

(i.e., in the actual public habits of language use), not in characteristics of the minds of individual persons. In the case of language it
is linguistic practices, that is, authoritative interpretations of rules
of the participants in the language game/community, that justify
saying that someone means such and such, and that the present
usage accords with what one meant in the past. In Kripke's
words:

> Others will then have justification conditions for attributing
> correct or incorrect rule following to the subject,[26]

What mental states, calculations or experience cannot do, namely to fix a meaning, can be done by the community. For example,
a pupil learning to add must fulfil certain conditions, set by the
teacher, to be considered to have mastered addition. The pupil
must answer, not what he or she feels like, or thinks is correct,
and so on, but what other members of the community would
answer in the same circumstances.[27] If this argument is correct it
shows that language acquisition or any cognitive behavior cannot be explained solely by appealing to an internal language or a
language of thought. For a child to to learn he or she needs a
teacher and a community using the language or concepts in question. The appeal to individual mental representations or processes, computational or not, cannot explain what it is to speak a
language or solve a cognitive problem.

So, Wittgenstein's discussion of ostensive definition, of understanding, of reading and of following a rule, the private language
argument and the discussion of thought can all be read as attacking the view of language and the related approach to learning
which he himself was inclined towards in his earlier writings and
which he also ascribes to Augustine.

CONCLUSION:
A WITTGENSTEINIAN CRITICISM OF FODOR

By now it should be clear that Wittgenstein's later criticism of his
own earlier ideas (and those of Augustine) on learning can be
taken as criticisms of Fodor. This is of course to apply Wittgenstein's ideas to something for which it was not, and could not
have been, intended for. Nevertheless, reading Fodor in the light
of Wittgenstein is illuminating and brings the problems with

Fodor's account of learning into focus. So, before turning to my reconstruction of a Wittgensteinian account of learning let me summarize chapters 4 and 5 with respect to Fodor's theory.

In chapter 4, I showed that Wittgenstein's own early conception of language of thought is similar to Fodor's, that is, both seem to agree that language of thought underlies natural language and gives it meaning. The language of thought contains its own method of projection and is meaningful in virtue of its structure. Furthermore, the early Wittgenstein and Fodor agree that semantics can not be explicated and that the language of thought is solipsistic. The later Wittgenstein's criticism of this conception, that is, that denotational theories focus too much on names, that there are no absolute simples, that language is not grounded in thought, that there is no private language and that accounting for mental processes in terms of rule following does not make sense, is also a criticism of Fodor's conception. On the basis of Wittgenstein's criticism, Fodor's solution to the problem of the framework is clearly unsatisfactory.

In chapter 5, I focus on learning and explicate Wittgenstein's claim that learning cannot be based on a language of thought. Attempts to explain learning in terms of understanding, grasping, thinking, or other mental and rational processes such as hypothesis formation and testing do not make sense. The idea of a private language of thought is shown to be mistaken and so is the idea that learning is a matter of translation from one (private) language to another (public). Furthermore, Wittgenstein's following a rule argument, as understood by Kripke, strikes at the heart of Fodor's account of productivity, namely that thinking is computational or the recursive use of rules. Thus, Fodor's solution to the problem of the framework (his hypothesis of a language of thought) and his solution to the problem of productivity (rule following) is unsatisfactory.

What, then, is Wittgenstein's attempt to solve the two problems of learning? Can he provide a better understanding of learning?

CHAPTER 6

Wittgenstein 3:
Reconstructing a
Wittgensteinian Account of Learning

If I want the door to turn, the hinges must stay put.
—Ludwig Wittgenstein: *On Certainty*

INTRODUCTION

In this chapter I will first show the differences between Fodor's and Wittgenstein's approach to learning. It is clear that on basis of differences on the nature of language they conceptualize the the fundamental problem of learning very different. For Fodor the acquisition of language is a matter of acquiring productivity, but for Wittgenstein the central problem of learning is to account for the acquisition of limits to productivity.

After discussing the consequences of this I will tie it to what Wittgenstein takes to be the framework of learning, that is, the social process of training and the innate natural behaviors of of the child. I will also compare his approach to contemporary theories of language acquisition, for example, behaviorism and to some extent Piaget's and Vygotsky's theories. It will become clear from all this that Wittgenstein is not providing a new theory of language acquisition, but rather reorients our way of seeing the problem and provides pointers to the direction of such a theory. Only in this sense is there a Wittgensteinian account of learning.

While Fodor says that children generate language according to innate mental structures until they reach agreement with the language spoken around them by forming and confirming hypotheses, a Wittgenstein-inspired approach would say that children generate language by moderating innate behaviors until they reach agreement with the language spoken around them. This is accomplished by training.

So just as with Fodor, such an approach takes something innate as the starting point for learning, but unlike Fodor it is not an innate language of thought or linguistic competence, but specific behaviors and natural expressions (shared "biological" forms of life). These are not translated into their public linguistic counterparts but are replaced, extended, and refined by the encounter with public language. Something genuinely new is acquired, not only the externalization of something already present, either explic it or implicit, in the mind.

The process by which this takes place is not hypothesis formation and confirmation but a nonintellectual process of training. Training, or learning how to behave, involves persuasion (the nonrational acceptance of authority), exemplification, and goal-directedness. Differences in training lead to differences in what is learned. The acquisition of new behaviors and language is not explanation or hypothesis testing, at least not in the initial stages. These presuppose that one already knows what one is learning, that is, to understand an explanation or formulate and test an hypothesis one already has to have a conceptual or linguistic system as rich as the one explained and tested.[1] Instead it involves the unquestioned or blind acceptance of what an authority presents both in the form of examples and corrections, that is, it is like "following orders." Here reward and punishment seem to be important because without these the authority cannot get the pupil to react in the appropriate way. This persuasion or training is a social process because one could not learn to speak or mean objectively (i.e., speak in a consistent way) on the basis of one's own private experiences (PI 199, 202, 257), as was shown in the previous chapter.

The content of what one is learning is not inherent in the mind and only waiting to be awakened by experience, but is given by experience in the form of examples of correct language use. These combine with and also shape the child's innate or natural behaviors until they resembles what is expected of the surrounding linguistic community. Thus, in acquiring meaning and language the child is not acquiring propositional knowledge, statements, or linguistic rules, but new ways of behaving, for example, new ways of expressing pain. The child learns how to do certain things it was not able to do before, not a way of expressing in public language what it already knew before.

Learning or getting to know how to use language, or in other words training, is goal-directed. The goal is to speak in ways similar to other people. Without this, communication and discourse about the world is impossible. In this sense learning is a process of adaptation, one of assimilating new ways of behaving (e.g., imitation of speech sounds) and accommodating old ones (e.g., 'pain' instead of crying) in order to conform to "the way things are done."[2] But the adaptation is not static because meaning is open-ended (i.e., family resemblance) and it is always possible to transcend particular examples or habits of use. Learning is to adopt certain open-ended frameworks, stabilities, or norms. Having done this the child can change or extend what is learned—go beyond information given—to create new linguistic frameworks. Creativity and challenge (e.g, testing of ideas, etc.) is only possible given a stable but not determined or totally closed background.[3] According to my reading or reconstruction of Wittgenstein, learning does not involve going beyond information given but what is learned is the limit of language. Creative use of the indeterministic language is not a matter of learning, but possible first when one have acquired the limits of language use. On the basis of a finite set of innate behaviors and reactions, a finite set of examples and finite social encounters the child has come to master the limits of language as a "tool" which can be used to describe and communicate about the world in potentially infinite ways. The nature of language makes productivity possible, but learning or being trained in a specific language-game introduces limits to what otherwise would be arbitrary (PI 198).

All of what has been said above only applies to the first stage of learning. However, once a language has been mastered, either one's mother tongue or the basic concepts of a science, one can use this for learning in a way which involves explanations or hypothesis testing, but undoubtedly learning from examples plays a role here as well.

In spite of the fact that Wittgenstein's account of learning is mainly negative and that he provides few details, it allows for a viable alternative to Fodor's as well as other theories. Later I will try to show that what I call the Domestication Model of learning is based on ideas very similar to Wittgenstein's suggestions.

THE PROBLEM

In exploring the picture of learning he got from Augustine, Wittgenstein has shown us what is wrong with that picture, namely its reference to a language of thought. But Augustine's picture is not totally wrong, because if we focus on other aspects, look at it in a different way, or so to speak "rearrange" it, we discover what is "in plain view." So, let us, once again return to the quotation from Augustine which opens *Philosophical Investigations*:

> Their intention was shewn by their bodily movements, as it were the natural language of all peoples:...I heard words repeatedly used in their proper places in various sentences.[4]

The two points he makes here are that (1) there is something like a natural language of all people in their bodily movements and (2) words must be seen in their context. Thus, bodily movements like instincts and natural expressions of sensations, and the idea of meaning as use in a language game later become important in his positive remarks on learning.

Closely connected with this, or rather the basis for the "restructuring," is Wittgenstein's account of meaning in terms of family resemblance, which implies that meaning is not something fixed or context independent. In rejecting the idea of fixed "simples" of meaning[5] which constitute the building blocks of a language of thought, a fundamental rearrangement of the Augustinian picture of learning is accomplished. Wittgenstein argues that this view, namely, that what a statement of the meaning of a word entails is referring to certain characteristics which the object must have, is confused. He rejects all belief in shared essences or universals arguing that if we investigate all instances that fall under a particular concept or linguistic expression, we find that they have no property in common by virtue of which we group them together, and apply the same word to them. Instead:

> we see a complicated network of similarities overlapping and criss-crossing;"[6]

> I can think of no better expression to characterize these similarities than "family resemblances;"[7]

So for Wittgenstein there is no unitary meaning of a concept in the sense of the essentialist or the proponent of the picture theory, and consequently the teaching and learning of concepts and linguistic expressions has to reflect this.

Furthermore, Wittgenstein says that there is no fixed meaning which covers all possible cases of future use of an expression (PI 18, 79). Bloor refers to this aspect of Wittgenstein's claims as his finitism:

> the established meaning of a word does not determine its future applications.[8]

Beyond the limited set of current applications of a specific concept or word, the meaning and applications are not yet determined (PI 68, 70, 99). Nothing in the linguistic expression or the concept and their meaning determine future use. The future meaning depends on the new contexts and interests of the speaker or thinker, not on something inherent in the current use or meaning of a concept. For example, the concepts 'simple' and 'complex' have neither a fixed nor an absolute meaning, but their meaning and reference depend on the particular contexts in which they are used. A table can be referred to as a simple thing if we are counting the pieces of furniture in a room, but in another context, when discussing the design of a table it can be referred to as a complex of different structures.

The same point is made in the discussion of following a rule. A grammatical or algebraic rule does not determine its future application; but this is determined by its use in particular contexts of language games. The future use of a language rule is not determined by its past use and in this sense speaking meaningfully is always a potentially creative act. There are no absolute or unchanging determinants of meaning, and rules and general statements are thus unable to capture it.

This implies that meaning is context dependent, open ended and can always be changed. Hence it always goes beyond what is given by past uses, explanations and definitions. Thus, for Wittgenstein, productivity (or going beyond information given) seem to be the "ideal of natural order" of language[9] and conformity is what needs to be explained. The fact that we can communicate and mean the same thing or use our language in a consistent way becomes problematic. If language is always underdetermined one can go on in any direction and one can "deduce" anything; hence learning to speak must be learning to conform and to limit this "productivity." He is in a sense turning Fodor upside down. If a universal, fixed language of thought is rejected in favor of an open-ended one, conformity, not productivity, becomes the central issue. It is also clear that Wittgenstein in his discussion of rule following rejects any account of productivity in terms of rules or computation, for example, Fodor's.

The same problem surfaces in the discussion of private language. If our sensations, feelings, and thoughts are private how can we ever speak about them and mean the same thing as others, if what they mean is in turn private and does not conform to any independent standards? How can we communicate if our words can mean anything, if there are no extra-subjective criteria of what is right, wrong, appropriate, and so on? Wittgenstein argues that if a private language is understood as a language which is (logically) independent of other circumstances than the private mental states of the person then several problems arise. First, one would not know that another person means the same as I do (PI 347), which makes the possibility of communication and understanding other people problematic. But even worse, and this is the center of Wittgenstein's argument, we cannot know if we mean the same thing from one occasion to the next since the private mental state or act of meaning along with memory could constantly be changing (PI 258). What is needed is some criterion or "stage setting" which links the mental state to something outside itself (PI 257). Stage-setting does not mean that the meaning is determinate or that different persons mean the same thing, only that limitations are set for what they share.

If this is taken to be the background, the problem of learning changes from how to go beyond information given to how the child learns to mean the same thing in order to communicate. It is always possible to go beyond information given—even the simplest ostensive definition lends itself to innumerable interpretations. How, then, do we learn to limit productivity, so that we can conform to the "correct" interpretation? This is Wittgenstein's form of the problem of learning, which emerges out of his rejection of Augustine-type theories and his remarks on learning.

His answer, in the case of ostension, is that while ostensive definitions lead to unchecked productivity, ostensive training (PI 6) leads to "checked" productivity making shared discourse about ourselves and the world possible. The "trick" we use to teach children, mathematicians or professionals such as builders, doctors, and soldiers is to train them to act on paradigmatic examples utilizing their natural abilities so they can gradually build up complex actions which conform to the "rules of the game."

Wittgenstein's ideas on philosophical method also provide another insight into his ideas on teaching and learning, namely that the function of teaching is to reduce misunderstanding, which arises in particular situations, and to limit productivity (PI 119, 127, 145). This suggests that much of teaching and learning is not aimed at creating identical meaning, but reducing discrepancies which have practical consequences.[10] Wittgenstein's frequent references to philosophy as therapy and the treatment of an illness also fit with this conception of learning, that is, it suggests that learning or progress is a matter of imposing order or objectivity on something which is un-functional, disordered, or irrational (see PI 118, 119, 133, 254, 255, 309; Z 382, 452).

Put another way, in rejecting Fodor-like accounts of productivity, that is, in terms of rules and determining or "guiding" by mental processes, and opting for indeterminacy Wittgenstein has to put forward an alternative account of the framework as the basis of learning. In the following we will discover that he sees the framework as twofold. It consists of the individual's natural behavior, and of the examples and accompanying corrections from the surrounding linguistic community. The framework for learning necessarily encompasses more than the abilities, characteristics (mental of behavioral) of the individual learning something, that is, the surrounding linguistic community mediated by the child's care-givers.

LEARNING AS OSTENSIVE TEACHING

As mentioned, Wittgenstein does not deny that ostension plays an important role in language learning and that it has a role in our actual practices. He only opposes the function it is given in Augustine's picture, namely to connect a verbal sign (as a label) to the object. To understand the central, but different, role of ostension in Wittgenstein's account of learning it is necessary to say something about his thesis of showing and saying.

A central idea in *Tractatus*, part of which Wittgenstein never gave up, but rather developed in later writings,[11] is the distinction between what can be said and what cannot be said, but only shown or displayed.

What *can* be shown, *cannot* be said.[12]

Wittgenstein claims that what is presupposed in what we say, that which makes saying possible, can only be shown. By this he means that how words connect with the world or ideas cannot be explained in language, because this presuppose that the child already has a language.

But Wittgenstein also applies the showing-saying distinction in discussing ethical discourse (TLP 6.41, 6.421, 6.43). Ethical statements or judgments, although they look like propositions, do not convey information about the world, but show our basic presuppositions about what is right, good, bad, or wrong. Ethical judgments show this, but only in the context of the total situation or life in which they occur (TLP 6.43).

Following Toulmin and Janik[13] I would like to argue that Wittgenstein's views on ethics were very much influenced by Tolstoy. Tolstoy claimed that ethical judgments and ethical behavior can only be learned and given their standard use in the context of real-life situations, in the shared framework of a form of life, that is, in the total life situation in which they occur. In teaching ethics one has therefore to provide examples, not explanations or explicitly given general doctrines.[14] According to Tolstoy art, especially literature, is the best medium for this. For example, Tolstoy teaches religion, not through doctrines and explanations, but by showing in different stories what a religious man is like. This is done by showing how he behaves in particular situations.[15]

I think Wittgenstein held a similar view also in his approach to the teaching and learning of language. The basic presuppositions for language and communication cannot be said, only shown in their actual application. What signs fail to express, their application shows.

What signs slur over, their application says clearly.[16]

The explanation of this is possible only through exemplification.

> The meanings of primitive signs can be explained by means of elucidations. Elucidations are propositions that contain the primitive signs. So they can only be understood if the meanings of those signs are already known.[17]

Here Wittgenstein seems to be suggesting that only by examples can we hope to get people to recognize what is implicit or presupposed in their linguistic practice.[18] What Tolstoy did for ethics Wittgenstein transferred to language.[19]

Wittgenstein not only held on to this view in his later writings but brought them to the center of his philosophy. In these later works he rejected the picture-theory and the view that pictorial form or internal structure can convey meaning and hence application. Instead he argued that what can only be shown, the presuppositions of language and communication, is found in the language-game (i.e., the language and actions into which it is woven), and ultimately in forms of life. Here what can be shown is found outside language in the surrounding world; it is in plain view and not a hidden structure. Hence it comes as no surprise that the basis of the teaching of any language or rather language-game has to be the giving of examples, which include not only linguistic expressions but their use in actual situations. The teacher does not convey knowledge by giving the pupil an explicit rule, definition or explanation but more indirectly shows the pupil by presenting relevant examples or paradigm cases. Learning something new is not a translation of what is already known but a concrete showing of a limited set of examples.

> I just teach him the word *under particular circumstances*.[20]

It is important for Wittgenstein that the teacher does not know more than the examples him- or herself (PI 68, 208, 209). Consequently the use of examples or samples is not an indirect way of teaching "underlying rules."

> Here giving examples is not an *indirect* means of explaining— in default of a better.[21]

Further evidence for the importance of examples is found in Wittgenstein's view of philosophical method.

> Instead, we now demonstrate a method, by examples; and the series of examples can be broken off.[22]

Philosophical Investigations itself is, I think, a very good example of this philosophical method or way of teaching, consisting as it does of a collection of examples, not of explicit doctrines or theories.

But how can a child learn from examples unless he or she knows what they are examples of?[23] The idea that learning involves examples does not by itself solve the problem of the framework, because to learn from examples one has already to know what they are about. Having rejecting the language of thought of the *Tractatus* Wittgenstein's answer is that training complements the examples and enables the child to learn.

> A child uses such primitive forms of language when it learns to talk. Here the teaching of language is not explanation, but training.[24]

The early learning cannot consist of explanation, translation, and so forth, since the pupil doesn't yet grasp the presuppositions of language (PI 30). The pupil does not, for example, yet know that 'red' is a color word and cannot benefit from the ostensive definition 'this is red' when the teacher points to a newly painted house. The child is learning language by being induced into a language-game, through exemplification *and* training since what is being learned can only be *shown* not *said*. If the child does not already have a language the semantic relationship, that is, how words connect with the world, cannot be explained to him or her but only shown by examples of how the word is used.[25] Training, though, is crucial, because examples however paradigmatic can "show" many different things, hence further restrictions, such as being corrected by others, are needed. It is not enough for the child to hear language (like passively watching television), but he or she has to actively interact with with a speaker, who both provides examples of language uses and also corrects the child.

LEARNING AS APPRENTICESHIP

Wittgenstein's own examples of learning very often involve a pupil learning from a teacher. This is clearly seen in his examples of the builder and his apprentice which are found both in *Philosophical Investigations* (PI 2, 8–10, 15, 17, 19–21) and *The Blue and Brown Books* (pp. 77, 79, 81). Here his account closely conforms to that of an apprentice learning from a master. The apprentice is learning a trade (building) not by being given theoretical explanations, but by observing the master and taking a limited but increasing part in the trade or game. Learning is a matter of getting to "know how to do certain things" not "knowing that such and such is the the case" and it is done on basis of the masters' examples, corrections, and the pupil's initial natural behavior. Ostension, the pointing out of paradigmatic examples, is combined with shaping of the apprentice's behavior thorough corrections and encouragements.

This model of learning is very old—it goes back at least as far as Plato and his recommendations for primary education of the future soldies in the *Republic*, but unlike Plato who meant the training of his auxiliaries or soldiers to conform to the fixed, eternal model of the ideal soldier or the Form of Courage, Wittgenstein denies any fixed standards or rules of meaning in accordance with which the pupil is trained. Hence it is more fruitful to compare his analysis to something like Kuhn's (1963) who in speaking of scientific knowledge does not speak of one set of fixed rules for science but instead of different paradigms, that is, for both Kuhn and Wittgenstein there are no fixed rules or standards.

For Kuhn scientific training is dogmatic and authoritarian and relies on examples, together with rewards and corrections, rather than outright explanations. The student is treated as an apprentice and the examples of both subject matter and techniques are *displayed* in textbooks.

> these books exhibit, from the very start, concrete problem-solutions that the professional has come to accept as paradigms, and they then ask the student, either with pencil or paper or in the laboratory, to solve for himself problems closely modelled in method and substance upon those through which the text has led him.[26]

The textbook does not discuss different methods and the student is not invited to doubt or criticize what he or she is learning. Kuhn compares scientific training to the teaching of the playing of an instrument—both are relatively dogmatic initiations into techniques with inter-subjective standards or a problem-solving tradition, which the student is not equipped and not invited to evaluate.[27]

In a later article Kuhn[28] illustrates what he takes scientific training to be by comparing it to a child who learns some new names of birds. A young boy who already knows some bird names takes a walk with his father who points to some paradigmatic examples of birds and calls out their names. The child, after having observed his father, practices names on his own while his father either confirms or rejects the child's namings.

Because there are innumerable perceptual differences or similarities between, for example, two swans, the child can only learn by submitting to the authority of the father. The child's perceptual ability is a necessary starting point for the learning but the father's corrections serves as a guide to how perception is to be organized. Nature (child's perceptual ability) and culture (the father as a mediator of the "collective" rules of language) are both essential to the acquisition of the skill of naming birds.

For Kuhn as for Wittgenstein learning clearly is ostensive training; it relies on paradigmatic examples which can not be questioned by the pupil, and on rewards and punishments. Its staring point is the pupil's natural instincts or abilities which are organized or shaped by the training. The importance of particular paradigmatic examples are crucial in both accounts of learning, and the examples are always given in the context of a scientific tradition or a language game, that is, the example gets its meaning from the wider context of which it is part. This means that the pupil in learning examples also is learning in Kuhn's case a paradigm, and in Wittgenstein's case the language game.

Both take the underdeterminacy of perceptual or meaning judgments as the starting point and see learning as a process of imposing structure or limitations. Learning is not a matter of productivity but a matter of conforming to cultural norms. This makes communication and in Kuhn's case scientific creativity possible. For both, learning is an authoritarian learning of a skill, and for both it has a necessary social component.

Comparing Kuhn and Wittgenstein helps us to focus on certain central aspects of Wittgenstein's account of learning but it leaves important questions unanswered. What is the role of the initial abilities or instinctive reactions,[29] how do corrections and rewards work to induce learning? Neither Wittgenstein nor Kuhn has an answer to the last question, but one of the most influential theories of learning, operant conditioning, provides an answer. So, is Wittgenstein's account of learning an undeveloped version of Skinner's behaviorism?

LEARNING AS OPERANT CONDITIONING

Why did Wittgenstein choose to account for learning a language, which is something uniquely human in terms of training, where training is understood to be similar to the training of an animal—breaking in a horse or training a circus animal (cp. BB p. 77)? Training is not the only or even the most plausible way of teaching people to behave in certain ways. Professionals, scientists included, are as much trained by studying and having the rules explained as by imitating a teacher or a paradigmatic example. Part of the answer is found in the thesis of showing and saying, that is, the idea that semantical relations can only be shown, not said or explained in language.[30] Hence, the teacher cannot use language to explain to the child what is correct or incorrect use. He has to show examples of correct use, and correct and reward the child depending on how the child behaves in particular situations. This training, just as in the case of animals (BB p. 90), has to have its starting point in the child's natural or instinctive reactions (bodily movements) which then are shaped or replaced by behavior conforming to conventional language. (BB pp. 89–90, PI 244). Learning is a shaping of instincts through rewards and punishments, hence Wittgenstein's rearrangement of Augustine's picture, showing us what is in plain view, seems to leave us with a picture similar to behavioristic accounts of learning and operant conditioning.

> I do it, he does it after me; and I influence him by expressions of agreement, rejection, expectation, encouragement.[31]

In *Verbal Behavior*[32] Skinner like Wittgenstein rejects the assumption that in explaining verbal behavior one must refer to something taking place inside persons; such as their ideas, images or thought processes. He sees language, or in his terminology, verbal behavior as

> reinforced only through the mediation of other persons.[33]

His detailed account of how this takes place reads very much as something one would have expected to find in Wittgenstein if he had explained more in detail how learning takes place.

Skinner speaks of operants (behavior emitted without an obvious stimulus) and respondents (reflexive responses emitted in the presence of particular stimuli) which frequently are changed and come under the control of stimuli in accordance with the specific reinforcement schedule imposed on them. Starting from the organism's natural behavior (its unconditioned behavior)—it is trained to emit only those behaviors which are reinforced either by the physical environment, or in the case of language acquisition, by other human beings interacting with the child.

> A child acquires verbal behavior when relatively unpatterned vocalization, selectively reinforced, gradually assumes forms which produce appropriate consequences in a given verbal community.[34]

It is not necessary that all complex forms of language, vocabulary, and the like, are present in the child's unconditioned responses, only the building blocks.

> In teaching the young child to talk, the formal specifications upon which reinforcement is contingent are at first greatly relaxed. Any response which vaguely resembles the standard behavior of the community is reinforced. When these begin to appear frequently, a closer approximation is insisted upon.[35]

In this way the child's verbal responses, which in the beginning are just babbling, are gradually coming to resemble those of his or her peers and adults. The child will say "This is candy" and "The door is open" in presence of candy and an open door because these responses have been reinforced by adults who consider them appropriate in the circumstances. In the same way a child will learn the names of building tools and how to complete a series of numbers.[36]

The similarities between Skinner and Wittgenstein become even more striking if we consider their account of how a word like "pain" is learned. This is also an interesting case to consider since Wittgenstein's account of how "pain" is learned is his most detailed case study. And of course this is a crucial test case for learning given the problems exposed in the private language argument.

According to Wittgenstein sensation words such as pain are learned in language games where the word comes to replace natural expressions of pain.

> the verbal expression of pain replaces crying[37]

Nonverbal public displays of pain such as crying or holding the injured part of the body are naturally connected with sensations of pain, and by linking the behaviors to words such as pain, discomfort, and the like, the words are used as part of the natural expression and even instead of it. This is done through the encouragement and rejection of other speakers. To say "I am in pain" functions as an natural expression of pain. "Pain" does not refer to the pain behavior but expresses or is about the inner pain sensation. Wittgenstein claims that it is only in this way, by hooking up our public sensation words with public natural expressions of private sensations that we can come to talk about them. It should be noted that sensation does not play any direct role in the learning of pain but our language is about it because it replaces or extends our natural expressions of sensations (PI 244). In behavioristic terminology the verbal response pain has finally come under the control of a private stimulus, namely the sensation, by being exchanged (through reinforcement) for a natural expression of the sensation.

Skinner,[38] treats sensations such as headaches or stomach pains as private occurrences (which cannot be observed and hence the connection between sensation and sensation word can not be reinforced directly by the verbal community); but he believes in a way similar to Wittgenstein that these private stimuli can come under the control of public reinforcement. He proposes four possible ways or mechanisms by which this can take place.

Firstly, a child's utterance "I am in pain" is reinforced by smiles, comforts, and so on, only if uttered in the presence of anything which regularly accompanies the sensation, for example, damage to tissue, bleeding, swelling, and so forth. The connection between the public stimuli (the tissue damage) and the private stimuli need not occur in every case. It can be conditioned on the basis of an intermittent connection but the word will eventually come under the control of the private stimulus.

Skinner's second way of describing how sensation words are learned is very much like Wittgenstein's in that through reinforcing a verbal response in the presence of natural expressions (e.g., crying) of toothache we would attach the word "ache" to the private stimulus, the toothache.

Skinner's third way—that verbal responses or words begin as descriptions of overt behavior but eventually become attached to private stimulus was denied by Wittgenstein.

> the verbal expression of pain replaces crying and does not describe it.[39]

The reason Wittgenstein rejects accounts like this one by Skinner is that if the word pain is understood as a description, then the child in learning it already has to have criteria of when to apply it. This means that it has to have something like a language of thought.

Skinner's fourth way is "stimulus induction" meaning that a response which has been rewarded for one kind of stimuli naturally generalizes to stimuli which are subjectively similar. This way of seeing things would be unacceptable to Wittgenstein because it does not make sense to say of something that is private in the mind that it is subjectively similar. He would here use the private language argument against Skinner.

Even if Wittgenstein would reject two of the four ways Skinner suggests it is evident that the two remaining ways are very close to what Wittgenstein himself suggests. And these accounts are plausible because they explain not only how we can talk about sensations and report on them to others, but also why they are uncertain. We can talk about what they are because they were initially tied to public behavior; but we are crude in describing and uncertain in comparing them because our reinforcement schedules are all different. The account also explains why statements about sensations are incorrigible—just as it is absurd to question whether a bleeding and crying person is in pain, it is absurd to question someone saying honestly "I have a headache." The subject cannot be mistaken, but another person can, since it is possible to say one has a pain, without one actually having pain.

Was Wittgenstein a Behaviorist?   Given these similarities can it justifiably be concluded that Wittgenstein in accounting for how pain is learned proposed a rather underdeveloped behavioristic account of learning? Do we have to turn to Skinner to find a fuller picture—a picture which Wittgenstein should have exchanged for Augustine's picture?[40] I think the answer is *no*, not only because Wittgenstein explicitly said so (PI 307) but because much of what he says supports a non-behavioristic interpretation. The main reason is what Bloor (1983) has called Wittgenstein's finitism, that is, the idea that the established use or meaning never determines future application. Skinner thought it was possible to identify variables that control and determine verbal behavior, and to establish laws connecting verbal behavior and stimuli.[41] Wittgenstein would strongly disagree, arguing that meaning is *not* determined by use, either by the individual or by the society, but that use only delimits what an expression means in particular contexts or in particular circumstances. Baker and Hacker (1980) argue that Wittgenstein did not subscribe to behaviorism after introducing the concept of "family resemblance." There are no behaviors common to all instances of, for example, expecting someone or reading (just as there are no experiences common to all instances of understanding). Furthermore, family resemblance concepts, like mental concepts, are explained in terms of examples and to go beyond the examples is speculative. This is why there are no absolute criteria of "how to go on" or any rules for behavior. A behaviorist like Skinner would not accept this because it rules out the possibility of generalizations and laws. In this sense Wittgenstein's quasi-behaviorism does not allow for what the behaviorists wanted, namely scientific laws. It is interesting to note that Fodor in *Psychosemantics* rejects what he takes to be Wittgenstein-type meaning theories (i.e., what Fodor calls meaning holism) on the same ground, that is, that they do not make generalizations possible. Another consequence of Wittgenstein's finitism is that he is not proposing to reduce reference to the mind to references to behavior patterns or behavior dispositions. Reductionism would require that the mind is known independently of behavior and that there are some law-like connections between behavior and the mind. This is, as we have seen, rejected by Wittgenstein because mental ascriptions are not identical with behavioral descriptions. In spite of these crucial differences Skinner and Wittgenstein agree on the impossibility of a private language and on the limits of introspection. Skinner rejects reference to a private language and the use of introspection on the grounds that they are not objective and scientific. Wittgenstein argues that a private language is conceptually incoherent and that introspection can not give us knowledge of what most people take to be psychological occurrences, for example, understanding and thinking, because these are not something mental. Wittgenstein, like Skinner, places importance on encouragements, and so forth, in the process of teaching, but does not seem to give reinforcement the systematic role that Skinner gives it. One reason for this is surely Wittgenstein's disregard for psychological detail, but reinforcement schedules seem to be ruled out if behavior never can be captured in generalizations.

So even if Skinner and Wittgenstein show some similarities, there are also crucial differences.[42]

Before turning again to Wittgenstein's positive account of learning let me first in passing mention that neither is he an ontological nor a methodological behaviorist.[43] Although Wittgenstein sometimes seems to have been on the brink of proposing ontological behaviorism, for example, in *Philosophical Investigations* when he says:

> The thing in the box has no place in the language game at all;[44]

and in discussing chess (PI 337), he seems to deny the mental. But he clearly assumes that sensations and mental states are real:

> And now it looks as if we had denied mental processes. And naturally we don't want to deny them.[45]

Furthermore, *Philosophical Investigations* is full of references to introspective reports; but they are used to refute philosophical theories. He did not think introspection could reveal the essence of what we call mental events, because they are not primarily or only a matter of experience, even if experiences sometimes accompany them. Wittgenstein did not, though, want to deny that there are experiences of different kinds. This and the prevalence of introspective reports, and the fact that *Philosophical Investigations* reads like a stream-of-consciousness confession, should make it clear that Wittgenstein is not a methodological behaviorist either. It is legitimate to speak about and use introspection as basis for philosophical arguments, that is, to show that understanding, meaning, and the like, are not mental entities. Neither does Wittgenstein opt for Skinner's view in *About Behaviorism*[46] that introspection is observing inner physiological states. This is clear from his discussion of reading in *Philosophical Investigations*.[47]

Wittgenstein didn't endorse or express the views of logical behaviorism claiming that mental words are "descriptions" of behaviors and that learning such words is learning meaning rules connecting mental words with behavior.[48]

LEARNING AS ADAPTATION

Before turning to my final reconstruction of Wittgenstein's theory of learning and his account of the individual aspects of contribution to the framework, let me first recapitulate what is central in the above reconstructions.

1. Fundamental to the later Wittgenstein's conception of meaning is what I above have called finitism,[49] that is, that the established meaning of a word does not determine further uses. Given this, learning to think or speak meaningfully about the world and to communicate with others is not to go beyond information given, but it is rather to acquire restrictions or limits to something which in a fundamental sense could go anywhere, namely, meaning. Learning is thus a process of ordering, structuring or determining something which is potentially infinite in such a way that meaningful discourse becomes possible. To learn a language is to learn the limits of language, it is the acquisition of a framework.

2. The content of the framework is provided by concrete examples of correct language use and encompasses both linguistic and nonlinguistic aspects, that is, language-games. This is why ostension, that is, the giving of particular examples, plays such an important role in learning. This is crucial because the framework cannot be explained in terms of language or rules for language use because this leads to an infinite set of rules interpreting rules, or assumes that what is being learned is already known.

3. But examples themselves are as impotent as rules to convey what they are examples of so something more is needed which, without presupposing that language or thought is already there, can enable the child to acquire constancy of meaning both over time and in relation to other people. Wittgenstein takes social pressure in the form of reward and punishment from an authority to provide the necessary limitations. This is why his model of learning is one of apprenticeship, where the pupil/child learns from the master/adult not by getting explanations or by questioning the master/adult but by being shown what to do and submitting to the authority (OC 160, 204; PI 219). The model of apprenticeship also brings out that learning to speak and to think is a question of learning how to do things and not learning to understand or grasp general rules. It is learning to do something by submitting to authority.

4. This process has a lot in common with operant conditioning in that both start from the child's natural behavior or

instincts and in that both operate with rewards and punishments as the way to steer the child in the correct direction which is in conformity with the surrounding speech community. The crucial difference is that operant conditioning is deterministic while Wittgenstein denies this.

Given this I would like to say that for Wittgenstein learning is a process of adaptation, of adapting one's natural ways of doing things to the way things are done by the surrounding community. A young infant starts by babbling which includes sounds from all human languages but ends up uttering and recognizing only the sounds which are part of his or her mother language. Deaf children, just as normal children, have an instinctive understanding of pointing (unlike, for example, cats) but this gesture comes under the control of conventional use as is shown by the fact that sign languages vary from country to country. So, through social interaction the child adapts to the open-ended standards that are encountered.

The process of learning is a nonrational process but the result is rationality, which then is the ground for future learning. It is important to notice that I am only concerned with Wittgenstein's account of primary learning, which he must claim to be different from more advanced learning which takes place when language and rationality have been acquired.

The child's initial language learning is possible without an innate language of thought because linguistic facts, that is, examples of correct use and extra-linguistic facts, and shared natural behaviors and social pressure provide both content and limits to potentially infinite ways of using language. What then are the natural behaviors, instincts etc, which form the other necessary part of the framework?

Natural Forms of Life: The Starting Point for Learning

The starting point for learning or adaptation is not reason or thought but instinct and natural reactions, shared by all human beings:

> I want to conceive it as something that lies beyond being justified or unjustified; as it were, as something animal.[50]

It is a shared form of life (OC 358) which underlies all learning.

Wittgenstein never clearly defined or explained what he meant by form of life. But it is clear that form or, as he sometimes says, forms of life are the ultimate basis for language games and for meaning.

> What has to be accepted, the given, is—so one could say—
> *forms of life.*[51]

Wittgenstein in this quote and in other places speaks of forms of life and in *Zettel* he says that different forms of life and different educations (Z 387, 388) lead to different concepts. These remarks have led many to assume cultural and even individual relativism. But it is clear that teaching and communication presuppose something common (Z 389, 390). What is common in elementary language learning and concept acquisition is our shared human nature which makes certain behaviors or reactions natural. It rests on ways of responding which are common but peculiar to the human species (BB p. 90), hence learning has a biological basis (PI 415). He points out that we often forget this because it is right before our eyes and easily goes unnoticed as something self-evident. Wittgenstein is not interested in the details of human biology or natural history (this is undoubtedly a task for psychology or biology) but stresses that this is the necessary basis for language (PI p. 230).[52]

This contention, that is, that language is dependent on one shared form of human life given by our natural history is supported by several remarks by Wittgenstein. Language is part of our natural history (PI 25) and so are some forms of thought in that they are dependent on language (PI 344). The use of language leads to other species specific behaviors such as grief (PI p. 174). Other natural reactions are our reactions to colors (Z 345, 351) and "reacting to a cause."[53] But the important evidence of a shared form of life is found in the natural reactions or expressions underlying the learning (and meaning) of pain.

> words are connected with the primitive, the natural, expressions of the sensation and are used in their place.[54]

> The concept of pain is characterized by its particular function in our life.[55]

> It is a help here to remember that it is a primitive reaction to tend, to treat, the part that hurts when someone else is in pain;[56]

But what is the word "primitive" meant to say here? Presumably that this sort of behavior is *pre-linguistic*: that a language-game is based *on it*, that it is the prototype of a way of thinking and not the result of thought.[57]

Our language-game is an extension of primitive behavior.[58]

Similar remarks are made in connection with 'grief' (PI p. 174). Furthermore, common interest (Z 383, 384, 388) as well as agreement in judgement (PI 242) are mentioned as aspects of a shared form of life. This is why

If a lion could talk, we could not understand him.[59]

Although other human beings, their language or practices can appear mysterious to us it is possible to learn Chinese or to understand magic because there is a common ground of shared reactions and interests.[60] In the case of the lion this is missing and we cannot understand him even if the sounds he is uttering sound like English.

All this implies that language is the product of human physical and biological nature, but our natural way of behaving is only the starting point for language and does not determine language. It underlies children's learning of their first language and also the initial steps of learning a totally foreign language. But it is only on this level and to a certain extent in ordinary language that meaning is fixed or rather limited by our nature. This presumably underlies Wittgenstein's remark that our ordinary language can be taught to any human lacking it.[61]

In terms of Wittgenstein's metaphor of the city (PI 18), the old city with its different parts all rest on different natural ways of behaving (i.e., biological forms of life). The suburbs incorporate elements of this but also create new forms of life and new languages. But the city center does not determine further expansion or even rebuilding in the old city center, just as our natural history' does not determine language (See Z 352, 358, 364). Language is a product of our shared limited nature and of our collective creativity. There is an enormous freedom in language to create new things (the open-endedness of language-games) but it is not unlimited. It always builds on our natural history, and it is further restrained by cultural customs, practices and techniques. In addition, different interests imposed on specific languages (as English, Chinese, Finnish, etc.) and by different language games (as geography, physics, etc.) set limits.

In postulating a shared biological form of life, an innate and common orientation toward the world which makes for a continuity between innate reactions and socially shared ways of behaving, Wittgenstein avoids Meno's problem of having to know what one is learning.

Resemblance between Wittgenstein and Piaget. One of the most influential developmental psychologists during this century has been Jean Piaget.[62] This is not the place to discuss his theory, but it is useful at least to mention some similarities between him and Wittgenstein. One reason for this is of course to place Wittgenstein in the contemporary psychological tradition; but it is also useful background to the next chapter. In that chapter I will use some ideas from Piaget to illustrate my development of Wittgenstein's ideas in the Domestication Model.

Wittgenstein's approach to learning is, as I have reconstructed it, partly biological and resembles Piaget's in some respects. Like Piaget, Wittgenstein sees learning as a process of adaptation, of accommodating what is innate and assimilating new structures from the environment by a process of selection. For both cognition and learning are based on innate action patterns (Z 545, OC 204; Piaget's sensori-motor pattern).

But there are crucial differences. Wittgenstein speaks not of changing, mental structures, but of actual changing behaviors and reactions. These are not adapted to the natural environment but to the social environment of language games, and the selection is correspondingly social and not physical. Furthermore, different training leads to different concepts. There is no specific order of stages in learning and there is no specific end-state like Piaget's formal operations. Language is not acquired on the basis of thought structures as Piaget claims but thought becomes possible only with language. The child in Wittgenstein's account of learning is more passive than in Piaget's account, that is, he or she is not learning on his or her own by interacting with the world, but is trained by adults. Despite these differences some of Piaget's ideas, or rather his empirical studies, can be used to expand on Wittgenstein (see below in chapter 7).

Wittgenstein is preformist in a way similar to Piaget, that is, natural behaviors and instincts are the starting points for learning and the acquisition of knowledge, but to this he adds a social "preformism." Language requires certain natural behaviors but also models of correct use, and this is provided by the surrounding language community. These are the starting points, but the individual can transcend this. This is of course quite different from Fodor's preformism in terms of a language of thought.

Learning How to Speak

Although the starting point for learning in Wittgenstein and Piaget is quite similar the end point is, as mentioned, quite different. For Piaget it is mental structures or schemata but for Wittgenstein it is particular patterns of behaving or reacting. Furthermore, if Kripke is correct[63] Wittgenstein does not assume that what is acquired are dispositions or competence, hence his theory is different from behaviorism (e.g., Quine, Skinner) and from Fodor's theory as well. To learn to speak meaningfully is not to acquire a specific mental state (PI 692, 693), which enables one to act in a certain way but to acquire a technique or a skill—a way of behaving (PI 150, 199). It is the acquisition of knowing how to do certain things.

> Children do not learn that books exist, that armchairs exist, etc. etc.,—they learn to fetch books, sit in armchairs, etc. etc.[64]

Learning involves both linguistic and nonlinguistic skills as the quote indicates. Wittgenstein denies that acquiring ways of behaving, of knowing how, can be reduced to knowing *that* or to rules. One can be able to recite all grammatical rules without being able to speak because one must still know how to apply the rules. If this could be reduced to rules one would need rules to apply these rules and so on (see Wittgenstein's following a rule argument in chapters 5 and 6).

So acquiring a skill, or know how, is a prerequisite for all other knowledge and learning. Knowing is never only a matter of having propositional knowledge, or, in the case of language, having rules. Learning here can best be understood as analogous to moral learning in that it is clear that one would not say that a child had learned "It is wrong to steal" if the child could recite the rule but the next moment stole some candy.[65]

Skills or techniques imply standards, but the standards are open-ended, that is, one can train someone how to play chess but not how to become a great chess player. Furthermore, skills, according to Wittgenstein, cannot be reduced to each other. All language games are complete and independent but they can overlap and be combined (cp. PI 18).

The Necessity of Examples, Imitation, and Playing

Since innate behavior patterns could not and do not contain all that is learned in language, language being to a great extent social, the behavior has to be supplemented by examples of correct language use, that is, language-games. The child encounters a limited set of examples or language-games (PI 113) which are given by the adult/teacher, who does not know more than examples him- or herself (PI 68, 208, 209). As one sees from the importance of examples in Wittgenstein's account of learning, imitation has to play a central role in learning. It is clear that humans have a natural ability to imitate, but imitation on its own would lead to the acquisition of idiosyncrasies so it has to be supplemented by reward for correct imitation and punishment for incorrect imitation. Although Wittgenstein never explicitly spoke of imitation as part of learning it can easily be added to his account. I even think some of the examples in *Philosophical Investigations* and in *The Blue and Brown Books* implicitly involve imitation. This, though, makes the training of humans different from the training of animals; that is, we do not train a cat by having her imitate us but rather shape her behavior according to our goal. Since Wittgenstein stresses the similarity between animal and human training it is possible that he would not give imitation a central role, but I can not see how he can avoid it.

If Wittgenstein does not even mention imitation he at least mentions another aspect which I think has to be part of his account of learning, namely practice or play.

> Children are taught their native language by means of such games, and here they even have the entertaining character of games.[66]

Playing, for example, peekaboo and later games with dolls, cars, and so forth, enables the child to practice or exercise patterns of behavior, to recombine and refine them in situations when the consequences are not as serious as in "real" life. Play is the imitation of real situations and also enables the adult to correct and guide the child. Practice in this sense only is relevant to the acquisition of a skill because we do not acquire understanding (e.g., a factual proposition) by understanding over and over again. The importance and role of both playing and imitation will become clearer in the discussion of the Domestication Model of learning.

Training and Therapy

I have already mentioned above that innate structures, examples, imitation, and playing are not enough for learning. Something which picks out the "important aspects," what the examples are examples of, and so on, is needed. This cannot be based on subjective association or induction because individual consciousness cannot provide the objectivity necessary.[67] To solve this problem Wittgenstein suggests that agreements, encouragements, and rejection are central to learning (PI 208), that is, he must assume something like a pleasure principle as underlying learning. This stress of the corrective role of the adult/teacher means that he or she is not only a role model, that is, provider of examples, but also a corrector. The role of the teacher as a corrector comes much more to the foreground in Wittgenstein's idea of philosophy as therapy or the treatment of an illness. Like a sophist or a physician the teacher weeds out everything that isn't functional or useful for communication, that is, individual idiosyncrasies, inconsistencies, and whatever violate the limits of a specific language game. If we are to take *Philosophical Investigations* as a model this is done not by arguments and explanations in the traditional sense, but in terms of showing and appealing to examples. Hence higher learning seems to follow a similar pattern as elementary learning where the teacher provides a limited set of examples and tries to correct the pupil when he or she transcends the limits of language.

Wittgenstein's account of training (described in detail above in the discussion of operant conditioning) makes learning into a nonrational process, in the sense that initial learning does not require the use of rational faculties in, for example, the forming and testing of hypotheses. It is also a process of social adaptation in which behaviors, not mental structures, are made to conform to what is socially acceptable. Learning is also an intersubjective process. Other people are not only one aspect of the environment, like the physical environment, but are necessary. They "select" what is acceptable or not.

Here it is clear that Wittgenstein is quite close to the theories of Vygotsky.[68] The latter, like Wittgenstein, saw the roots of the child's learning in its instinctive reactions. Thought emerged out of the biologically based pre-linguistic problem-solving ability and the root of language is instinctual emotional reactions. He also saw language as a tool in human activity. Vygotsky's account, though, goes beyond Wittgenstein's both in detail and in that he includes more in learning than just training. Vygotsky, though, seems more of a determinist in the sense that public language determines the private use. A further difference between the two is that Vygotsky attempts to give an account of how language is internalized and comes to serve thought. This is crucial for any theory of learning and it is unclear whether Wittgenstein thinks of internalized language in the same way as Vygotsky, that is, that it loses some of its public aspects; and whether he thinks that thought and other internal states should be understood as mental skills.

The Limits of Learning

Learning how to to use language, or training, is goal directed. The goal is to come to speak and think in the same way as other people. Without this goal communication and discourse about the world is impossible. In this sense learning is a process of adaptation, one of assimilating new ways of behaving and accommodating old ones (e.g., utter the word pain instead of crying) in order to conform to "the way things are done."

But the adaptation is not static because meaning is always open-ended and it is always possible to transcend particular examples or rules. Learning is adopting a certain framework, certain stabilities or norms. Having done this the child can change or extend what is learned—go beyond information given—not in an arbitrary sense but in a way which is structured (family resemblance), but not determined by what went on before. Creativity and challenge (e.g, testing of ideas, etc.) is only possible given a stable but not determined or totally closed background.

Standardization is necessary for communication but also explains the success of language. Random, unsystematic, and diffuse expressions are weeded out and failures only stand out given a stable background. Furthermore, creativity grows out of conformity because creativity is appropriate to a context/problem (i.e., nonrandom) but is nevertheless not determined by the context. This view is expressed by Kuhn and although Wittgenstein has hardly anything explicit to say about creativity I think it is safe to extrapolate his views in the direction of Kuhn's. For Wittgenstein as for Kuhn[69] the limits or constraint on creativity are local (specific paradigms or language-games) while for Fodor or Chomsky they are global, the same for everyone at all times and places. If I have understood Wittgenstein correctly learning does not involve going beyond information given but what is learned are the limits of language, that is, what cannot be said but only be shown in training, and not what one *can* say. On the basis of a finite set of innate behaviors and reactions, a finite set of examples and finite social encounters, the child comes to master the limits of language as a tool which can describe and communicate about the world in potentially infinitely many ways. The nature of language makes productivity possible but learning a specific language-game introduces limits to what otherwise would be arbitrary (PI 198).

CONCLUSION

Wittgenstein's account of learning is mainly negative, that is, he is more concerned to correct what is wrong than give a positive account. He provides us with very few details of the specific factors involved in language learning and his account is far from complete. This should not surprise us: his writing is an example of what he teaches us—the only way to increase knowledge through teaching is by providing examples and corrections. The first stage of learning is always to learn the limits and the rest, the details of learning, he leaves to the scientists to work out. In spite of all this he shows that Fodor's theory is not "the only game in town." His aim was not to come up with a new psychological theory of learning but to show that productivity—going beyond information given—is possible without postulating an innate language of thought; that Meno's paradox can be overcome and that objectivity and communication is possible. He has done this not through a conceptual analysis of "learning" but by exploring the limits of language. Like Fodor he gets his conception of learning from his idea of the "nature" of what is learned. It should not surprise us that when he gave up his early account of meaning he also gave up the accompanying account of learning and replaced it with a new account. And he does this not by explanations but by engaging in a dialogue between his early mistaken self and his later reformed self—in the form of a confession.

Before turning to the task of developing Wittgenstein's approach to learning into an empirical theory, we have to look at possible difficulties. A good way to do this is to to turn to Fodor, who in all his work has attempted to show that Wittgenstein's theory is problematic and cannot be the base of an empirical theory of language and language learning.

Fodor's Criticism of Wittgenstein

In my presentation of Fodor I mentioned that one of the philosophers Fodor sets out to criticize and wants to provide an alternative to is Wittgenstein. He rejects what he takes to be Wittgenstein's behaviorism and reductionism, but as I have tried to show above Wittgenstein is not a behaviorist and in his view language or cognition cannot be reduced to behavior. Wittgenstein's argument that meaning is underdetermined rules out both these possibilities, as well as answers Fodor's (and Chomsky's) fundamental criticism of behaviorism and other empiricist theories, namely that they cannot account for productivity. But Fodor, especially in later works (*Psychosemantics*, 1987), seems to criticize Wittgenstein's account of productivity. He rejects, or rather gives a limited role to what he calls meaning holism, that is, the view that the meaning of a word or an expression is related to the totality of language or the conceptual system, and which he thinks is inherent in Wittgenstein's account of language and psychological phenomena (e.g., Wittgenstein's idea of family resemblance which Fodor relates to meaning holism). The problem with Fodor's criticism is firstly that he himself has to accept a limited meaning holism to get his own causal theory of meaning to work (see chapter 3 above), and secondly that his main and methodological argument is weak. This argument says that meaning holism has to be rejected because it rules out the possibility of a scientific account of mental processes and learning, because if meaning holism is correct there is no way to generalize over mental content of two different people or even one person at different times. Generalizations are impossible because the meaning of a concept is related to the total system of concepts and beliefs and as a small part of this changes so does all other concepts. But as the reconstruction of Wittgenstein's account of learning hints at, his account of productivity does not seem to rule out a scientific psychology or account of learning, as will be further developed in the next chapter. Meaning holism thus only rules out generalizations over mental content and is hence devastating for a theory which explains learning in terms of a language of thought but not necessarily for any other account.

Another of Fodor's criticisms of Wittgenstein and other so-called common-sense philosophers is that they only provide necessary grammatical truths, that is, they can say something about how we use language but nothing about psychological phenomena themselves, or in other words they confuse descriptions with what they describe. As I have argued in chapter 3 a case can be made that Fodor himself has confused description with what it describes and even if Wittgenstein clearly takes ordinary language as a starting point for his analysis he goes beyond it. He is not only explicating or describing common usage but primarily criticizes it, for example, the idea of a language of thought as underlying learning is closer to common sense than the account Wittgenstein sees as an alternative. Furthermore, if his account of learning in terms of training is correct and the adult's ascriptions of mental states to the child is part of the child's acquisition of for example sensation words or the concept of self, then the child's own concept of pain or self (and therefore its psychological organization) is a result of the folk psychology which is embedded, but perhaps not evident, in everyday language. This means that an analysis and criticism of language provide genuine insights, not only into language use, but also into actual psychological phenomena.[70]

Yet another criticism is that it is a tautology that we cannot learn anything which we do not already know. Wittgenstein's answer here is that we do not have a language of thought but that we have skills or know how, which in combination with examples and corrections of actual language use provide the necessary framework for learning. It is not necessary to possess a language to learn one, but one needs specific skills and an external language which can hook on to these.

I also hope that my reconstruction of Wittgenstein's account of learning shows that Fodor's theory is not the only game in town, that is, that it is a viable and better alternative to his language of thought hypothesis.

Although the criticisms that Fodor presents against Wittgenstein are not valid, Wittgenstein's own approach to and account of learning is by no means unproblematic.

Problems with Wittgenstein's Account

One of my criticisms against Fodor's theory was that it is not empirical and can not be falsified. The same can be said about Wittgenstein. Unlike Fodor he was clearly not trying to develop a psychological theory of learning (see chapter 4 "Does Wittgenstein Have a Theory of Learning at All?" above) but to provide conceptual clarification.

> For in psychology there are experimental methods and *conceptual confusion*.[71]

His main aim is negative and the thing he focuses on is exposing problems in language of thought-like theories, prevalent in the Western intellectual tradition and which he himself had held. But in spite of the fact that his stated aim is to clear up conceptual confusion, "help the fly out of the fly bottle," he provides some positive hints about learning in his remarks about training, forms of life, the role of examples, and so forth. It is on the basis of these remarks and hints that I have reconstructed an account of learning. The problem with Wittgenstein's text is that what he actually says is unclear, for example, about the role of reinforcement and what "forms of life" really means. If forms of life is interpreted as "shared biological structures," as I have done, the role of other people and society in shaping the language games is limited and so are the creative possibilities of language. On the other hand, if forms of life are seen as different social and cultural activities it is by no means clear how two people from different forms of life can understand each other, or how a child can learn from an adult, who obviously must have a different form of life than the learning child. Fodor's criticism of Vygotsky, Piaget, and the like (see chapter 2) seems to be a good criticism of Wittgenstein, if this is his claim. In the case of reinforcement and the role of the teacher we don't know from Wittgenstein's text if he had something similar to Skinner in mind and thereby would introduce something that would be incompatible with his finitism, or if he had something less deterministic in mind.

A consequence of this basic unclarity in Wittgenstein is that few commentators agree about how to understand him, and like Heracleitus's remarks, Wittgenstein's text lends itself to many, and sometimes contradictory, interpretations.[72] On its own Wittgenstein's text is not very helpful either from a philosophical or from an empirical perspective. His remarks cannot be conceptually criticized or empirically tested. Although he hated empty philosophical talk he seems to have occasionally engaged in it himself.

One reason for this is, I think, that unlike Fodor and Piaget, he made a sharp distinction between philosophy and science. The role of philosophy is to purge mistakes, perhaps describe or redescribe but not go any further. Yet, Wittgenstein's interest in the conceptual problems of learning lead him beyond mere criticism to describing an alternative, even if the description is sometimes unclear and incomplete. For example, he says nothing about the role of play or imitation in learning a language, and he tells us nothing about the innate behaviors and reactions language hook on to or how these change under the influence of language; nothing about what semantical skills look like and how they relate to other behaviors and skills; and as already mentioned, he speaks very lightly on the interaction between the teacher and the pupil. Thus, it seems, as I have said above, to be necessary to go beyond Wittgenstein and reconstruct a theory of learning which can be philosophically criticized and empirically tested. This, as also mentioned, goes against his stated intentions, but must be done if one wants to make empirical sense of his remarks on learning. In this case he himself failed to be a good teacher—he gave us examples but did not provide the necessary delimitations or training to interpret them. In this sense Fodor would be right in saying that Wittgenstein did not present a remotely plausible theory. Both my own reconstruction in the previous chapters and the Domestication Model presented in the next should be seen in this context—as an attempt to make his remarks clear so they can be discussed and also to put them in an empirical context so they can be tested and improved.

CHAPTER 7

The Domestication Model of Language Acquisition

INTRODUCTION

In chapter 1, I argued that there are two main problems inherent in any developmental theory of language acquisition, namely the problem of explaining linguistic creativity and the problem that meaning is already presupposed in any process of learning (the problem of the framework). These problems create a puzzle or dilemma in that the first implies that learning involves moving beyond what was previously known, while the second implies that this is impossible. In this chapter I will present what I have chosen to call the Domestication Model of language acquisition, showing that a reconstructed Wittgensteinian account of learning and meaning combined with what we already know about the biology, psychology and social interaction of young children results in a solution to the dilemma. The Domestication Model can handle productivity and the framework with equal facility and thus is an improvement over other explanatory models.

As we have seen, Chomsky and Fodor were very much impressed with the productivity of language, that is, that in learning the child is going beyond information given, whether it is faulty experience or generalizing to novel utterances, to say and understand sentences never encountered before. Fodor's solution that we must have a language of thought in order to learn a natural language is an account of this and an answer to the related failure of behaviorism. His language of thought hypothesis, though, does not explain what it sets out to do, it merely, as argued in chapter 3, reproduces the problems of learning on another level—in our evolutionary past. Fodor was right to reject behaviorism because it failed to deal with productivity, but throws out the baby with the bath water, that is, rejects social interaction altogether by focusing on innate linguistic mental structures. A reconstruction of Wittgenstein's solution to the problem of learning is based on his finitism (i.e., that past uses of a word or an utterance does not determine future meaning) as an account of productivity. He also takes into account the behavioristic insight that social interaction is integral to learning, as are shared biological forms of life. Wittgenstein, though, does not give us a detailed account of learning. His account of the framework is sketchy and he says very little about its characteristics. To see how a developed theory based on Wittgenstein's general approach would look and to measure it against empirical research I will link my reconstruction with theoretical and empirical research in psychology, neurophysiology, and biology. This will result in what I call the Domestication Model. This is an attempt to "flesh out" the Wittgensteinian approach by supplementing it with empirical findings.

In doing this I go beyond Wittgenstein's own preferences, and try to do more than "To shew the fly the way out of the fly-bottle,"[1] that is, I go beyond his philosophical analysis. In this I follow Bloor (1983):

> I will be going against certain of Wittgenstein's stated preferences, his chosen method, and perhaps his deepest prejudices. Nevertheless, I shall argue that this is entirely legitimate. Some purposes may be served by thought experiments, others are not. I shall replace a fictitious natural history by a real natural history, and an imaginary ethnography by real ethnography. Only in this way can we make a secure estimate of Wittgenstein's capacity to illuminate life, not as it might be, but as it is; and to describe people, not as they might be, but as we find them. There could be no more disciplined way to see just what his work amounts to.[2]

The usefulness of the Domestication Model lies in providing a promising alternative account of learning and thus showing that a language of thought theory is not the only "remotely plausible" theory. It is also an attempt to do what Wittgenstein urges us—to look and see what is before us and to rearrange our unreflected picture of language learning. Instead of Wittgenstein's thought experiment or imagined natural history it supplies empirical experiment and natural history. In the last sense the Domestication Model can also be seen as a test of Wittgenstein.

THE DOMESTICATION MODEL

This Model is an attempt to provide a solution to the two problems of language acquisition by showing that there is a framework which is language like and productive, yet not a language of thought. This rich framework, or, as we will see interacting frameworks, enables us to explain the acquisition without resorting to postulating a mental structure as rich as the one that is acquired. It enables us to account for acquisition in nonmental and nonrationalistic terms. It could also be called a Transactional Model or a Tri-Polar Model since it assumes that the framework necessary for language acquisition actually consists of three interacting frameworks, which are all in themselves productive, namely the innate biological skills of the individual, the social context, and language itself. There is already enough known about all these systems to enable us to account for language learning without postulating an innate language of thought or a rational process of learning, and without reducing language leaning to either biological, sociological, or linguistic facts. In this chapter I will first give a general presentation of the Model and then deal with the specific aspects of the different frameworks to paint a picture of language learning as a web of interacting activities emanating from different, yet overlapping, and in some aspects isomorphic frameworks.

Language is both man-made and a biological fact. It is possible because of species-specific biological characteristics, a unique ontogenetic developmental process, and the public language encountered by the child in interacting with other speakers. Language is learned, or rather trained, on the basis of some specific physiological and morphological characteristics and behavioral skills, by incorporating and substituting biological or innate behaviors with a public and socially shared language. Learning a language, or for that matter any conceptual system or cognitive skill which presupposes language, is like a process of domestication,[3] where a purely natural being, the infant, is socialized and its innate skills and behaviors are changed and added to by objective and socially shared practices, both linguistic and non-linguistic practices. Human biology is necessary but not sufficient for the acquisition of language, because although there are some speech specific traits, as Broca's area in the brain and the morphology of the human voice box, there are no innate language organs or a language of thought. Contrary to Fodor I will argue that language is not based in mental structures and processes, but is a result of a unique combination of different biological preconditioned behaviors and social training.

The theory of learning I would like to propose takes as evident that (1) language-like skills are required as a starting point for learning language and acquiring conceptual thought. It assumes, with Fodor and Plato, that the starting point for learning has to have some aspects in common with what is learned, but denies that it has to be identical; (2) actual language or conceptual experience is limited in the sense that what children overhear or their experiences are always a limited (and often faulty) set of examples of linguistic usages; and (3) language and concepts are learned and used in a communicative context. Both the starting point of learning (a set of skills and behaviors) and the social context in which learning takes place function to limit what can be learned, that is, impose limits and structure on language and thought which are inherently productive or unrestricted.

The starting point necessary to learn language or conceptual systems does not have to be the same as that which is learned. It does not have to be an innate language of thought as semantically rich as any language that can ever be learned. Instead it can be assembled from three different sources, namely innate and acquired nonlinguistic behaviors or skills; exposure to examples of language; and the social pressure of other competent speakers. Here the connection with Wittgenstein is clear.

One of the fundamental functions of the brain and accompanying behavior is to solve sensorimotor problems, that is, to interact successfully with the environment. In humans sensorimotor skills develop into more and more complex systems and eventually we get "cognitive-linguistic" problem solving. The same brain processes and behavioral mechanisms are responsible for both sensorimotor and so-called cognitive problem solving. Learning new motor and cognitive skills involves the assemblage and modification of preexisting or innately determined motor routines and a mechanism for error feedback. In purely motor skills this feed back comes from the physical environment. In the case of communication and language the error mechanism is the behavior and reactions of other people. Cognitive and linguistic skills thus share some fundamental elements with paradigmatic motor skills, and there is no sharp break between knowing how or the acquisition of motor skills, and knowing that or the acquisition of cognitive information.[4] I thus claim that all types of learning are based on the training of specific and innately based skills and that there is no fundamental difference between so-called lower and higher learning. Once language is learned though, it comes to play a special role in further learning, since it adds another skill to the already existing ones.

From this perspective it is fruitful to look at language acquisition as assembling and modifying two different sets of skills which become interrelated, with one overruling and shaping the other. Both types of skills have their origin in motor routines. Thus, learning a language involves a purely linguistic aspect; the perception and production of speech sounds in accordance with syntactical rules; and a communicative-semantic aspect; the communication of concepts in varying circumstances with different people. Although the production and understanding of sound clearly limit what we can mean or communicate, that is, limit sentence length, phonemic combinations, and so on, it is the semantic and communicative aspect which shapes and controls the purely linguistic aspects of language. A being producing at will a wide range of consonants and vowels in varying order or sequence will still fail to communicate or mean something. Both aspects of language are the result of the combination of different sets of behavioral or motor skills which all have an innate basis but which nevertheless are greatly changed as a result of interaction between the developing infant and its socio-linguistic environment. A precondition for this interaction is the plasticity and redundancy of the developing brain which only slowly reaches its growth potential.

The behaviors/skills involved in the linguistic "side" of language are present from an early age, some even from birth (discrimination of speech sounds) and others when the relevant anatomical structures have developed (the voice box for the production of sounds), but cannot be successfully used in anything resembling language until the communicative and semantic skills have developed enough complexity around the infant's first birthday. Both the linguistic and communicative-semantic skills undergo change and development during the infant's first year and will continue to do so, but it is first around this time they come together. At this point the linguistic skills have already been greatly shaped by the environment and have both in the realm of perception and production been narrowed to mastery of the sounds of the child's native language. The communicative-semantic side of language, which is based in object manipulation, imitation, play, and social skills, also is a result of the interaction between the infant and its sociolinguistic environment.

The development of both types of language skills, and their subsequent interaction, is best seen as a process of training or domestication. The developing skills of various kinds are shaped and changed by the sociolinguistic environment, that is, by adults who function as models to imitate but who also direct, encourage, and discourage the child's actual behaviors so they more and more closely resemble those of the speaking community, as the child is learning conventional skills. Although training the child to become a speaker is different from the deliberate training of, for example, a horse, the one resembles the other in that in both cases innate behaviors, not yet fully developed, are shaped and assembled together according to external standards. The training of the child is not a matter of simple conditioning but of a slow and painstaking process of incorporating the child into human community. This is done by what I later will describe as symbiotic interaction, that is, the adult not only encourages or discourages the child on the basis of its behaviors but on the basis of the attributed semantic and communicative meaning which the adult reads into them. Thus, by treating the child as meaning things, intending to communicate, and so forth, its purely natural behaviors are brought in line with and take on meaning and communicative intent, and we can begin to speak about language. This occurs, as I have already mentioned, around the child's first birthday but both the linguistic and communicative-semantic behaviors or skills are very underdeveloped at this time and it takes a few more years till we have fully developed language.

Although language is only found in humans, rudiments of related skills and behaviors can be found in nonhuman primates such as chimpanzees. They can be taught to use ASL (American Sign Language) for simple descriptions and requests resembling those of a two to three year old human child but do not develop language any further. This shows that, although language is species-specific, the skills involved in it are not species-specific but are present to some degree in some phylogenetically close species as well. What is unique to humans is not a specific language capacity but certain skills, for example, production of voluntary speech sounds, a slowly developing but complex brain which enables greater shaping by the sociolinguistic environment and enables humans to develop their manipulative, cognitive, and social skills far beyond that of our closest relatives among the primates. Once language has developed it also enhances these skills leading to further discrepancies with species lacking language.

What I have said above suggests that even if many of the skills and behaviors involved in language are genetically based, language itself is the result of a nongenetic mechanism, namely the interaction between developing and plastic skills and the sociolinguistic environment. I have also presupposed that language is a set of behaviors used in specific ways or skills to accomplish specific tasks. Language is not seen as an underlying heterogeneous capacity which unfolds in contact with the sociolinguistic environment but as a set of specific skills. The distinction Chomsky borrowed from Saussure between language (langue) and speech (parole) and expressed in his competence-performance distinction, is rejected. Language acquisition is not the acquisition of competence but the acquisition of specific behaviors, that is, performance. There is no need to assume any underlying mental capacities or competence to account for learning. Again, the similarity with Wittgenstein should be clear.

We need not specify the essence or universals that the child is required to learn. According to Wittgenstein there is no essence of language; there are only interconnected, crisscrossing, and overlapping language games. Languages are a result of historical, both social and biological, contingencies, and can change in an unpredictable way. Language games are human products but not private or individual but public and shared, that is, the result of human interaction and the genes or brain structure which makes this possible. The last limits but does not determine language. The child's "problem" is to apply or utilize general skills, or integrate a diverse set of specific skills to construct language skills sufficient to communicate and use for other purposes such as the gathering and processing of information. The skills need not be the same for everyone but it is only required that they allow effective interaction. It does not matter if my meaning of certain words, or my grammar differs from yours as long as they converge at some point and to some degree, or that language is sufficiently stable to enable us to gather and process information.

Above I have painted the picture of language as a result of the training of two different set of skills: the linguistic and communicative-semantic, developing in parallel but converging between the child's first and second birthday. This is reminiscent of Buhler's, Kohler's, and Vygotsky's claim that language and thought have separate roots. My claim differs in that although language is the result of two different types of skills, we have neither language nor thought until these two sets of skills converge and interact. Before this we have intelligent behaviors and utterances of speech sounds, but not thought and language. My reason for saying this is that I think that thought, that is, the internal and private but explicit contemplation of states of affairs, goals, and so on, presupposes language.

Below I will first briefly look at the reasons for supposing that language is species-specific. This is useful because it helps us to pinpoint specific skills and behaviors which in themselves or in combination are unique to humans. Next I will present a picture of the brain and nervous system, that is, the general neural substrata of language which is presupposed in my discussion of the development and acquisition of language relevant skills. This is an investigation of, in a Wittgensteinian terminology, the biological forms of life, or the biological framework. After this I will discuss linguistic skills, that is, speech perception, production, and syntactical skills, which also have a biological basis. Then I will turn to the communicative-semantic skills and specify some skills, namely, imitation and play, which are relevant to both sets of skills. Finally, I will describe the mode of sociolinguistic influence on these purely natural skills in terms of symbiosis between the child and its care-givers, mostly adults or sometimes an older child. This is an attempt to illustrate the social forms of life or framework and the language games involved in the acquisition of language. My description will necessarily be incomplete and at points speculative. The first is a matter of limited space but also because our knowledge is limited, in spite of a greatly increased study of infants during the last thirty years. It is also speculative when inferences are drawn from tentative or incomplete data. Nevertheless, I hope to show that the Domestication Model of language acquisition as the training of specific skills is compatible with what is widely accepted about children's behaviors and their development. It does not need the language of thought hypothesis and can avoid its problems; and in providing empirical content to Wittgenstein's speculations it is a development of his solution to the problem of linguistic creativity and the problem of the logical requirement that meaning is already presupposed in any process of learning (the problem of the framework).

In describing some of the biological and behavioral conditions for language acquisition I am not attempting to specify biological concepts by which the acquisition can be analyzed, that is, my approach is not reductionistic—human biology and behavior are necessary but not sufficient for language. I will rather show how our understanding of these and how they interact with social factors provide us with an account of the framework for learning which solves both the problem of productivity and prior structure.

IS LANGUAGE SPECIES-SPECIFIC?

In an obvious sense this is true—no other biological creature than humans speak or show linguistic capability. What counts as linguistic is controversial; for example, does a child speaking in one-word sentences show linguistic capability; or does a chimpanzee using signs from sign language really have a language? In spite of this difficulty most would, though, agree that no nonhuman primate or other animal has shown signs of mastering the complex syntax and semantics of natural languages. Chimpanzees trained in ASL can, according to some (Lieberman 1984), reach the same linguistic or proto-linguistic ability as a human child between two and three years of age, but all attempts to teach nonhuman primates complex grammar have so far failed. Primates can master manual gestures or artificial symbols (keys on a computer board and plastic chips) and employ these for simple requests and description but do not acquire rules of a complex grammar (Lieberman 1984). Although some of the primates have grown up and been treated more or less as human children they show much less spontaneity and productivity in their signing activities. So even the most optimistic interpretation of primates' linguistic capabilities shows that they fall short of any normal child's (Lieberman 1984, Lenneberg 1967).[5]

There is clearly social communication (as territorial and sexual signs) in all animals including primates, but their communication systems do not seem to be radically, if at all, more sophisticated than those of non-primate animals, and they do not seem to be precursors to language. For example, primates' vocalizations like cries and grunts seem closer to their human equivalent than to language, that is, they seem to have an automatic and emotional origin much as the cry of an newborn infant (Ploog 1979). Cries also lack the modifiability available in the ape's visual-motor behaviors, for example, hand gestures.

There seems to be no evidence suggesting that the auditory structures or neurological pathways in humans and primates are different; many mammals including newborn infants are able to make similar discriminations when exposed to human speech sounds (Lenneberg 1967; Lieberman 1984, 1988; S. Walker 1987). In contrast the human voice box or the supralaryngal airways and the larynx (the part of the throat where the vocal cords are located), differs from the voice box of primates (except during the first three months of the infant's life) and explains the failure to teach chimpanzees and other higher apes to speak. Lieberman (1984) has, though, shown in computer modeling of chimpanzees' sound producing organs that they can produce a wide variety of speech sounds. The fact that these sounds do not occur naturally and can not be elicited by human training indicates that something more is needed for vocalization; probably the voluntary control of speech sounds which seems, on the basis of aphasia studies, to be located in Broca's area in the brain. Although primates have homologues to Broca's area, this part of the brain seems uniquely human. The same uniqueness holds for cerebral lateralization (the selective localization of different functions in the two halves of the brain), which especially Lenneberg (1967) sees as central to the uniqueness of human language.

The human brain also develops more slowly and is more plastic than other primate brains; for example, infants are born with a brain weighing 24% of its final weight but the corresponding weight for a chimpanzee is 60%.[6] In the latter, development is completed in eight years which is six years shorter than the human's fourteen years. From this it seems reasonable to hypothesize that the language learning ability of humans is related to species-specific characteristics of primarily the brain and the vocal apparatus. Since children with articulatory deficiencies need not have impaired ability to learn language the brain seems to be of greater importance as opposed to the more peripheral aspects of language (Lenneberg, 1967). It is also clear that primates, for example, chimpanzees, do not develop or only develop to a much lesser degree some cognitive and manipulative skills utilized in language. For example, primates do not seem to develop the last stages in the acquisition of object permanence [7] and there is interesting evidence suggesting that they do not acquire important manipulative and play skills.[8]

Thus, the study of linguistic and other relevant skills in nonhuman primates indicates that we should start by looking at the brain, speech skills and manipulative skills in order to establish the linguistic-like content of the human biological framework for learning. We are thus looking for features isomorphic with language in one part of the total framework needed for the learning of language. I will first turn to the brain, arguing that it does not contain a productive language of thought, but that its plasticity in the young child allows for both productivity and molding by experience.

THE BRAIN

The brain is probably the organ of the human body that is least understood and there is widespread disagreement about both its general functioning (for example, whether specific functions as language are localized or depend on the interplay of many different parts of the brain (Lieberman 1984), and specific morphological and neurochemical details. Nevertheless, certain aspects of the brain's structure, function and developmental pattern, which are relevant to understanding the social training that constitutes the acquisition of language, are relatively uncontested.

Cephalization, the development of a large brain, is unique for humans but it seems that neither the relative weight of the brain to the body or its absolute weight,[9] which both are larger in humans than in nonhuman primates, in itself can explain the ability to acquire language. Lenneberg (1967) reports that nanocephalic dwarfs[10] in spite of an absolute brain weight similar to newborns and a brain weight relative to the body similar to a young teenager, attain the verbal skills of a five year old child. This is more than any chimpanzee has been able to achieve. Even more amazing is the reported case of a mathematical student from Sheffield University in England, who not only attained a first class honors degree, but appeared normal socially in spite of an estimated brain weight of fifty to one hundred fifty grams, or about one-tenth of normal brain weight (Lober 1980).

More important than brain weight in understanding learning and language acquisition seems to be the redundancy and plasticity of the human brain especially during childhood. The plasticity is shown by the ease with which the brain and especially the cerebral cortex can relocate and recreate functions following a trauma to the brain. The brain does not seem to be restricted to certain locations in order to perform certain functions. Both the plasticity and redundancy of the brain, especially when it comes to language and learning, are shown by comparative studies of aphasia in children and adults. Such studies are difficult to interpret due to different classificatory systems and the lack of circumstantial information about the patients. The relatively negative outlook of recovery in adult patients recently has been challenged with new and more persistent methods of rehabilitation (Konner 1989), but in spite of all this, it is clear that the recovery success and pattern of children with aphasia is markedly different from adults. For the latter the recovery of acquired aphasia is difficult and much less likely. Adults suffering from aphasia seem to lose the capacity of organizing and controlling specific aspects of language and are not able, or with great difficulty, to regain language. In contrast, children between twenty to thirty-six months, that is, right at the onset of language, start to relearn language in the same stages as they would have, had the trauma not occurred. Older children, four to ten years, seem not to relearn language in this way but nevertheless achieve full recovery. The young brain seems to have an extraordinary capacity for reorienting the neural substrata necessary for language, for example, from one hemisphere to another (Lenneberg 1967).

As already mentioned, the human brain is less developed at birth than any other primate brain. Children have less than 30 percent of the total brain weight at birth and although the growth is relatively fast in the beginning—from 24% to 60%[11] in a year, the pace of human development is much slower than in nonhuman primates. For humans the full development of the brain takes fourteen years compared to eight years in the chimpanzee and is much slower than in mammals in general. In contrast 40% to 60% of the the total brain weight is present in a newborn chimpanzee. The slow and ultimately higher level of development of the human brain is reflected in the fact that primates and mammals develop faster at earlier stages but also stop developing earlier than humans. Studies of the development of object permanence in monkeys, cats, and so forth, utilizing Piaget's techniques and concepts, show that cats, for example, achieve object permanence comparable to stage four at the age of eighteen weeks and chimpanzees at the age of twenty-four weeks. Children by contrast develop more slowly and achieve stage four at thirty-eight weeks, but after the onset of language they surpass all the animals (Fishbein 1984, Gruber et al. 1971).

All this seems to indicate that the slower development and greater plasticity of the human brain makes language possible or perhaps rather is open to be influenced and changed by the public language the child encounters and starts to use.

In a debate in France 1975 between Chomsky and Piaget, the French neurobiologist, J-P. Changeux (1980; see also Changeux 1985), proposed a view of the nervous system which is a compromise between innate theories such as Chomsky's and Piaget's theory of environmental influence. He is here implicitly addressing the question of the productivity of the biological part of the framework for language learning. He claims the genetic determination of the nervous system is very plastic and is limited only by a "genetic envelope." Many synapses[12] are not stable in the infant and become rigid first in adulthood, and the development according to Changeaux is regressive in that, for example, an axon[13] which in a newborn has twenty to twenty-five collated branches, at the age of two months has only four to five. Here development seems to be a loss of possibility, where the environment functions to stabilize certain neuron connections and "lets" others die. Hence, experience is necessary and shapes the nervous system. Changeux calls this process "selective stabilization" and to learn is to eliminate. Changeux, though, leaves the possibility open that it is not a simple triggering of predetermined functions (which would be Chomsky's view) but that the environment via stimuli could shape the system.

According to Changeux the plasticity of the nervous system is a necessity: it could not contain all information necessary for the complex function of our brain. The genes cannot possible contain all information necessary to specify all neuronal contacts. It seems that the injection of information from the environment is a necessity, because if it was a simple matter of triggering predetermined information the brain would have to be much larger than it actually is or could be. Hence it is reasonable to assume that the environment does more than trigger or select—it injects change inside the generally given parameters, that is, the genetic envelope.

Studies (Walker 1981) of certain areas of the brain, which seem to be associated with language such as Broca's and Werniche's areas, show that these areas are rich in so-called interneurons (a group of combinations of motor and sensory nerves) which develop or are continuously formed during early ontogenesis. Unlike the visual neurons which although sensitive to the environment are constrained rigidly by the genes, the neurons closely associated with language are plastic. It should be noted, though, that the anatomical features and even location of aspects of language capacity in the brain is highly contested. In itself this is not surprising if one accepts the plasticity and redundancy of the brain, which implies a great variation in the anatomical substrata of language. Traumas or any number of unknown factors can lead to unique functional organization of the individual brain.

There is a marked difference between innately determined motor patterns as swallowing which rapidly unfold and the painful emergence of language after years of practice. This is another indication that, although the neural substrata in Broca's area are genetically based, the specific neural mechanisms for language have to be built up and are not inherent in the brain.

Language, furthermore, seems to be closely bound to general maturation and is synchronized with other both cognitive and motor developments (Lenneberg 1967), making it seem less likely to be tied to specific language organs in the brain but rather is part of the general development of intelligent behavior, or as I will try to show, the interaction of many different skills. The brain does not contain language but is open to be shaped by linguistic as well as relevant nonlinguistic experience and practice.

Implicit in all of the above is evidence for a critical or sensitive period of language learning, that is, the facility with which one learns language weakens after puberty when the brain is fully developed. Someone not exposed to or having acquired language at this age seems unable to do so; trauma to the brain is more likely to result in permanent loss and it is very difficult to acquire the phonetic fluency of a native speaker (Lieberman 1984).[14]

My conclusion is that the development of neural substrata for language is possible partly because of the complex but plastic and redundant organization of the brain and partly because of the prolonged postnatal period of development. The malleability of the brain suggests that language is not hard-wired in the brain, but that it is a result of exposure to a linguistic environment given certain preconditions of the brain and anatomy of the voice box and auditory organs. Children not exposed to language, such as so-called wolf children and children not using language in a communicative context fail to acquire language in spite of normal brain and anatomy.

Harré and de Waele (1976) describe the human infants as a combination of a *nidicole*, that is, born after a relatively short period of gestation and totally dependent on its parents for survival and a *nidifuge* characterized by open eyes and other functioning sensory receptors as well as a relative independence of parents.[15] But the child does not become a real *nidifuge* until a year after birth. It is then that sensorimotor coordination allows for walking and talking, making the child relatively independent of adults. If the infant was a fully-fledged *nidifuge* at birth gestation would have been more than twenty months long, but the pelvic canal is too narrow to allow an infant with a head this size to pass through. Harré and de Waele speculate that man is a phylogenetic *nidifuge*

who has become a secondary nidicole because of his premature birth.[16]

As a consequence the helpless child grows up with a not ready formed and plastic brain in an environment which is social and linguistic from the very beginning and which it is able to perceive through its relatively well-developed perceptual apparatus, shown by especially its sensitivity to speech sounds (Eimer 1985). There are channels open between the environment and the brain, and language is learned on the basis of and utilizing the species-specific character of the human brain and its unique developmental pattern.[17] This allows for the environmental shaping of language representation in the brain given certain limitations and preconditions. The human infant is not like a zombie or ghost that can take on any form or ability, as was claimed by behaviorists like Watson, but is a creature restricted by its biological nature to perform a wide, but limited, range of tasks. Further support for the nongenetic, nonrigid, hard-wiring of language in the brain is that language seems to have evolved rather late in the evolutionary history of *Homo sapiens*.[18] What we know about the brain shows thus, that it is redundet, flexible, and open to the environmental influences to allow the nonindividual aspects of the framework for learning to shape what is genetically given.

In addition to a unique brain the infant is equipped with special anatomical and neural mechanisms for the perception and production of speech, to which I now will turn. These are features of the biological framework which are isomorphic with language and thus can provide parts of the basis for the learning of language. Again we are looking for specific behaviors as suggested by Wittgenstein, and not for Fodor's innate language of thought.

SPEECH PERCEPTION

Human infants have an innate perceptual mechanism which is well adapted to human speech and which prepares and enables them to utilize the language they encounter. Speech sounds consist of very complex acoustic units and structures which may vary from speaker to speaker and from one acoustic context to the next, so children's ability to discriminate speech sounds cannot be attributed to the simplicity of the speech signal. Among other things this is shown by the great difficulty encountered in constructing reading machines (Lieberman 1984, 1988).

The fetus seems to be able to sense sound in utero (Rathaus 1988), and newborns can sense sounds which have the loudness and pitch of speech sounds just as well as adults (Sinnott, 1983). Young children, even as young as a few days old to one month can discriminate speech in a way similar to adults, that is, they can ignore acoustic variation and detect discrete phonemes (Eimes

1985; Lieberman and Blumstein 1988). This was tested in experiments where infants were trained to suck on a rubber nipple when they heard a new sound, and by measuring the increased sucking rate (or in other studies, the heart rate) when an unfamiliar sound was introduced. These experiments have shown that infants can discriminate nearly all sounds of English and of many other languages as well (Lieberman 1984). Thus a few weeks old infant can discriminate two-syllable words. Since this ability is present from birth or very soon after, it is unlikely that this ability is learned, because there would not be time to practice these complex discriminations. So human infants seem to be equipped with innate neural detection mechanisms.

As was already mentioned, other primates and many mammals (e.g., rodents such as chinchillas), have no difficulty in making discriminations of human speech sounds, so this ability does not seem to be species-specific (S. Walker 1987), but becomes adjusted to human speech later in development.

Later, around six months, the child can recognize two vowels or nasal consonants as equivalent in spite of their being produced by different speakers and with different frequencies (Lieberman and Blumstein 1988), that is, they can treat as perceptually equivalent different tokens of a vowel. Childrens' ability to perceive speech sounds seems even more sensitive and richer than adults.' For example, certain sounds in Hindi[19] can be detected by a seven months old infant from an English speaking environment but not by English speaking adults or even by twelve months old infants raised in a non-Hindi setting (Eimas 1985, Lieberman and Blumstein 1988).

This seems to indicate that exposure to language is necessary to maintain discrimination ability and that as the child develops and is exposed to a specific language with its characteristic sound pattern the child's perceptual horizon narrows. The child seems to retain and probably sharpens perception of certain sounds, that is, those of its native language, and loses others. In addition there is some evidence that children acquire certain phonemic contrasts by being exposed to them. Lieberman (1984) refers to comparisons between Spanish and English infants showing that the former, but not the latter were sensitive to certain sounds of Spanish.

Here, although we have an innate ability of perceiving sounds seemingly uniquely specialized to human language, but not species-specific, the environment seems to have a great deal of influence on what the child eventually perceives and discriminates. This genetically determined ability for speech perception enables children to benefit from experience which in its turn greatly modifies future perceptions. The fact that the building blocks of speech perception are present at birth, or very soon after, but are very sensitive to experience, fits with the view of the developing brain as plastic. Experience helps form and structure neural substrata. According to Eimas (1985) this ability is not totally lost in an adult but can be recovered after long exposure to to an unfamiliar language, for example, after extensive experience of English Japanese adults can distinguish "r" and "l" almost as well as English speakers.

Turning to speech production we will find the same situation, that is, the production of speech sounds, although innately based, is greatly modified by experience. In looking at both speech perception and speech production and later in discussing syntactical and semantical nonlinguistic precursors of language, we are trying to identify aspects of the individual framework which allow the child to hook on to the language spoken around him or her. Let me remind the reader that this is an attempt to find an alternative to Fodor's claim that there has to be an innate language of thought just as rich as the language one is learning.

SPEECH PRODUCTION

Anatomy

Although parrots and other birds can produce speech-like sounds no other primate than humans actually can speak. The vocalization in humans seems to be a result of our unique and species-specific supralaryngal airway. This, which is also referred to as the voice box, consists of the pharynx (throat), oral and nasal cavities, lips and tongue. These, in their unique configuration, are all necessary for the "shaping" of the air escaping from the lungs via the trachea (or windpipe) through the vocal cords (Lieberman 1985, 1987; 1988, Lenneberg 1967; Laitman 1984).

All primates, including human infants younger than three months lack these anatomical features and cannot produce speech sounds, in spite of the fact that they can emit cries and other nonspeech vocalizations. When the infant's voice box starts to move back with respect to the base of the skull and into the throat and takes on adult-like structures, around three months, the first speech-like sounds like cooing occur. When the child starts to speak or at least utters recognizable word-like sounds between twelve and twenty-four months the voice box very closely resembles that of an adult (Laitman 1984). The moving of the voice box into the throat makes it impossible to breath and swallow at the same time which, of course, greatly increases the risk of choking. Thus, the adaptive value of the human voice producing anatomy must far outweigh this drawback.[20]

As the child's voice box matures, cooing, which relies mainly on the tongue and the lips to produce sounds, is succeeded around the age of six months with babbling. All children, including deaf children, babble and up to around their first birthday produce virtually the sounds of all languages. The babble of a Japanese infant is indistinguishable from an American child's (Lieberman 1984; Lenneberg 1967). After twelve months of age the deaf child ceases to babble and normal children's babbling and speech sounds show clear influence of the language surrounding it. Imitation seems to play a role in this development. For example, children early on start to imitate adult sound pattern and intonations (Lieberman 1984) but the child's mastery of speech is slow, involves years of practice and is not complete until the child is eight to ten years old (Lieberman 1988). This is not surprising since the production of speech sounds involves the voluntary control of many complex and interacting systems (respiration, larynx, etc.) and is probably one of the most complicated motor activities humans are involved in. Although Lieberman (1988) has shown in computer simulation models that chimpanzees can produce most phonemes in a nasal way it has been impossible to teach them how to speak. Chimpanzees as well as children with articulatory deficiencies and deaf children can, however, learn sign language indicating that language can be acquired without speech. The acquisition of signing seems to be easier with chimpanzees mastering a combination of ten signs at six to seven months, deaf children at nine to ten months while English speaking children produce ten different phrases between sixteen and twenty-four months (Lieberman 1984).[21]

It is clear, though, that the normal vehicle for the acquisition of language is speech, and as in the case of speech perception the building blocks of speech production seem innately determined. And as in the case of perception, production is modified and narrowed by exposure to a specific environment during childhood, but the extended use of combinations of sounds actually creates greater diversity.

Although the babble seems to contain most, if not all, speech sounds occurring in all natural languages, it is nearly impossible for an adult to acquire the sound pattern of a foreign language with native proficiency. Joseph Conrad, although he wrote perfect and exceptional English, spoke with a strong Marseillais accent and Henry Kissinger's English is marked by a strong German accent (Lieberman 1984). Both these men learned English after puberty and were able to master the syntax and semantics of English, but not its pronunciation.

It is not enough to be exposed to a language during childhood in order to acquire its characteristic phonemic structure, but it also has to be used productively in a communicative context. Snow (1977) reports that Dutch children watching German television for several hours each day did not learn German. So, the critical period in which it is possible to acquire language involves not only hearing a language but also using it in a normal communicative context.

Crying, which is present at birth and develops and is modified as the child grows, seems to have more in common with subhuman vocalizations than with speech. Such vocalizations, for example, crying, moaning, screaming, and the like, do not presuppose the human voice box and seem to have their origin in emotional and automatic parts of the brain (Ploog 1979). Although crying can have a part in language acquisition, that is, it is a way of signaling inner states to the care giver, it does not seem to be the building block of speech. Humans eventually gain some voluntary control over this type of vocalization, but even in adults their origin and function normally are different from language.

To sum up, as in the case of speech perception the building blocks of speech are present in the infant from an early stage, that is, as soon as the voice box makes it possible for the infant to produce speech sounds. The production of speech sounds seems to be genetically coded, but as in the case of perception, it is greatly modified by the experience and exercise of a specific language. As in the case of speech perception children seem eventually to produce a narrower range of phonemes, that is, only those present in their native languages.

But speaking a language is not, of course, simply producing speech sounds in any order or at any time. Instead they must be produced according to a specific syntax and semantics in a voluntary way, so along with the child's mastery of speech sounds there has to be voluntary control of when and how to produce these.

Voluntary Control and Automatization

As with the two aspects of language discussed so far, voluntary control of speech is tied to a species-specific structure of the human brain, namely Broca's area. It is located at the left frontal lobe of the cortex and was discovered by Broca in the 1860s. Trauma or lesions to this area result in expressive aphasia, where the patient has disrupted speech and writing, that is, he or she can not produce all speech sounds, is slow in producing language and has difficulty comprehending sentences of uncomplicated syntax (Lieberman 1988). The typical behavior of patients with this type of injury has led scientists to presume that the voluntary control of speech is located in Broca's area. Although primates have homologues of Broca's area (i.e., lateral frontal cortex) they are not able to voluntarily control their vocalizations, as is shown by chimpanzees, who potentially can produce many speech sounds but do not do this as a result of human training and not naturally (Lieberman 1988). Their underdeveloped counterpart to Broca's area does not seem to allow the voluntary control necessary for speech. Although voluntary control of speech can be traced to specific neural substrata, the child has to learn to say appropriate things in the appropriate way in the right context to the right people. This requires experience in a communicative context. Before turning to this problem, the acquisition of syntax and semantics, let me say something about the automatization of speech.

Another important aspect of speech production is automatization, that is, a speaker can produce correct speech sounds without having to consciously decide what to produce. Many motor activities, especially those essential for survival, such as the running of a horse or antelope, occur automatically, that is, the horse or antelope does not have to pay attention to its hoofs or legs when running away from a lion. Many automatic motor activities are learned, for example, in the case of humans bicycling, playing the violin or flying the trapeze. The building blocks of all these activities are innate motor activities but the way they are combined and refined is a result of training making these complex behaviors automatic. The same is true for speech. A fluent speaker does not have to run through all relevant phonemic or syntactical rules before saying something, on the contrary, too much attention to grammar inhibits language. This indicates that speech, like other motor activities has become automatic, and thus we can pay attention to "higher-order" aspects of what we are saying, for example, its meaning and effect on the listener. This automatization of language is not innate but acquired. I would like to argue that it is acquired through training. Just as a young child learns to play the violin or a soldier is trained to behave in combat, not by having the rules of these complex motor activities explained to them, but by performing actions over and over again under the supervision of a trainer who corrects and encourages, the language learning child has to practice its linguistic responses in a communicative context. Like Wittgenstein's builder's apprentice the child is starting with a few simple one word utterances which can be used for different linguistic tasks (i.e., "sour" to ask for a sweet and sour tasting candy, to describe a lemon or the effects of lemon juice,) which gradually are expanded and combined with other sounds according to the nonlinguistic and communicative context the child finds itself in. The adult's role is to supervise the child so that the linguistic utterances come to be automatized in accordance with linguistic conventions.

The gradual automatization of linguistic behaviors, that is, utterances, can thus be characterized as a process of training, not as a process of hypothesis formation and testing. Without utilizing a language of thought or innate language organ, the child on the basis of innate building blocks, together with others, socially constructs complex linguistic skills.

Of course, it is not enough to be able to produce and discriminate speech sounds but one has to produce and decode them in a certain way, that is, according to syntactical rules.

Before moving on to this, I would just like to stress that although human language is clearly based in genetically given capacities and behaviors, there is so far not a trace of a language of thought in Fodor's sense, which is genetically hard-wired into our brain. Children's syntactic skills, which I will turn to presently, have been seen as indications of just such a innate language. The next challenge for the Domestication Model is thus to find nonlinguistic skills that can plausibly account for this aspects of language.

SYNTACTICAL SKILLS

Parts of this section is highly speculative in that it utilizes empirical data which are not well-confirmed and accepts an analysis of grammar, namely phrase structure grammar, which is controversial among linguists or psycholinguists. Nevertheless, although much empirical and grammatical work needs to be done, it promises an analysis of syntax in terms of motor behaviors/skills, and hence is an alternative to Chomsky's and Fodor's innate syntactical competence and their view of learning as hypothesis formation and testing. It is also related to Piaget's account of language acquisition, in that it basis purely linguistic skills in nonlinguistic skills.[22] The problem here is to be able to find motor skills which are, or rather can be, analyzed in terms of rule following.

Lieberman (1984, 1985, 1988), whose primary interest is the phylogenesis not the ontogenesis of language, argues in several articles that both phonetic and syntactical behaviors/skills may be the result of preadaptation of automatized complex goal directed orofacial motor behaviors. Relatively simple automatic motor acts of the mouth and throat, such as those involved in eating a slice of bread, involve complex goal-directed routines performed in a certain order. The routine of eating a slice of bread could, in a simplified way, be described as a set of ordered actions: (1) open the mouth, (2) place the bread on the tongue, (3) raise and lower teeth, (4) push bread towards the back of the mouth, and (5) swallow. Each of these steps can be further divided into many subroutines which ultimately apply to specific muscles. Behaviors like these, once learned, become automatic, that is, we do not have to think about or treat every instance of eating bread as a novel situation, but are free to focus on other aspects of the situation. It seems that the motor acts involved in eating show both rule-like regularity and productivity. Thus in two important aspects they are similar to language.

For all these subroutines there exist corresponding neural networks in the brain and the neural network associated with the mouth and throat are located very close to Broca's area, that is, close to what is presumably the location of speech production and control. Lieberman claims that these and other motor skills associated with the mouth, throat and face and their corresponding neural substrata are organized in a way very much like sentences, especially their phrase structure. A sentence like "The girl ate her bread" can, like the motor behavior of eating the bread, be broken down into discrete segments which are arranged in a particular order. The basic division is between the noun phrase "the girl" and the verb phrase "ate her bread." The noun phrase can be further broken down into "the" and "girl," and the verb phrase into "ate" and "her bread." This breakdown is not arbitrary but reflects the "internal logic" or syntax which enables a set of speech sounds to have meaning. Lieberman assumes that the subroutines underlying motor coordination associated especially with the mouth and throat are suited to take control over other rule governed behaviors, namely speech. Since the nonlinguistic motor skills presumably evolved earlier than language they are, if Lieberman is correct, preadaptations for syntactical skills. Of course, these suggestions have to be worked out in much more detail to provide an answer to Fodor and Chomsky, and their claim that there is a specific syntactical system hard-wired into our brains.

Clinical evidence from patients with lesions in Broca's area or with Parkinson's disease show impairment both in the production of speech sounds and in the comprehension of sentences, that is, they seem to be impaired both in phonetic and syntactical skills. Patients with Broca's aphasia not only have phonetic deficiencies but also drop endings, plural markers, articles, and prepositions and have difficulty understanding sentences of moderate syntactical complexity. This coupling of disabilities is unlikely to occur if the syntactical and production skills were not associated with the same neural mechanisms. This neural mechanism, which Lieberman, on the basis of spatial proximity and similarity in structure, claims initially were adapted to other motor skills such as eating, swallowing, and so forth, has taken on a new function.

Nonhuman primates, such as chimpanzees, lack both the anatomy (voice box) and motor-control capabilities (Broca's area) necessary for the production of speech. Speech does not, though, seem necessary for at least some primitive syntactical skills because chimpanzees can be taught to communicate with sign language. Chimpanzees have been taught ASL and can make simple descriptions and requests showing that they can utilize motor control to achieve some degree of syntactical mastery, even if they lack the special requirements for speech. This is not surprising since Lieberman's analysis of skills can be applied to many different kinds of motor behaviors. There could be other possible preadaptations for linguistic skills, not just the orofacial motor routines. The fact that chimps can be taught to use sign language and that deaf children master a greater number of manual signs than speaking children have words at the same age, indicates that speech production is more complex than the control of gross motor movements. It is also suggestive that gestures play such a great role in early language production.[23] To sum up, in Lieberman's words:

> The point I would like to make is that a neural mechanism that can represent sequences of motoric activity as context sensitive phrase structure rules, can also represent other linguistic rule governed activity, including phonologic and syntactic rules of the grammar of any human language.[24]

Applying this to the ontogenetic acquisition of language[25] we would expect that phonemic control would appear as soon as the voice box has developed and as soon as the voluntary control of motor behavior of the orofacial region has become complex enough to allow for the complexity necessary to produce contrasting phonemes. This claim needs to be empirically tested, but it appears that the child's initially instinctual control of motor behavior, like swallowing, and so on, have come more under voluntary control at least around three months. At this time it also seems to have enough complexity, because as soon as the voice box matures the child starts to babble, that is, to produce segments of contrasting phonemes. Ordering the phonemes according to human and conventional syntactical rules is, however, more complex, and is fully accomplished only after several years of practice. The child not only has to learn the specific motor routines, or, in other words, to follow the syntactical rules involved in a specific language, but also to practice these skills until they become automatic. The child's motor control must have developed a complexity which allows for this, especially in the orofacial muscles and their neural substrata but also, I suggest, it must have developed general sensorimotor and manipulative skills. The last is suggested by Sinclair's studies (1971, 1972) where children start to use syntactical ordering when they reach the last stage in the sensorimotor period. This stage is not reached by chimpanzees and their syntactical deficiencies can perhaps be traced to their inability to master certain sensorimotor or manipulative skills.[26] Further evidence for the possibility that syntactical skills are utilizing other motor routines are mentioned by P. Marks Greenfield (1978). She refers to studies by Forman (1971, 1973, 1975), who studied the child's early manipulation of its own hands as forerunners or prerequisites for syntactical rules. The early mastery of hand and other motor signals in deaf children further supports the hypothesis that there is a connection between gross motor behavior and language skills.

My claim, or hypothesis, is that phonemic contrast and syntactical rules (understood in terms of phrase structure grammar) which are both necessary, but not sufficient for meaningful speech, are a result of the combination of speech production skills (due to the anatomy of the human voice box appearing in the infant around three months of age), and automatized nonlinguistic motor skills, such as the use of orofacial muscles and manipulative skills involving other parts of the body. When the latter skills are combined with or applied to the human speech producing muscles we have syntactical speech.[27] Needless to say, the lack of empirical studies to test this hypothesis and the controversy about phrase-structure grammar (Lieberman 1984) make my suggestions highly speculative. It is though an indication that specific speech skills are not fundamentally different from other sensorimotor skills and that children can utilize these to acquire speech. We do not need to assume an innate language of thought or language organ to account for the acquisition of syntax.

Above I have focused on motor skills but it is also possible that "purely" perceptual skills, that is, the ability to focus the eyes, locate sounds, feel the texture of a surface, and so forth, play a role in language acquisition. For example, Gentner (1983) has suggested that our category of noun is drawn from perception. Our perceptions are such as to let the object stand out. Nelson (1973) reports that the most common words in the child's early vocabulary are for objects, especially objects that move. Thus, the universality of nouns in natural languages could correlate to an innate perceptual tendency. It is also true that this tendency is reinforced by adults in so-called baby language, which seems to pick out nouns by stress and intonation. Again more empirical studies are needed to establish if there is a correspondence between linguistic and nonlinguistic behaviors.

The development of syntax is, however, slow, indicating I think, that syntactical skills involve more than the transfer of orofacial motor control as is suggested by Lieberman. It involves both manipulative skills and semantic skills, which will be discussed in the next section.

But there is more to language than uttering phonemes in accordance with syntactical rules—a parrot does not have language however well it modulates and formulates its sentences. One has to say something meaningful and one has to make these sounds in varying contexts and to different people, that is, language also requires semantic and communicative skills.

SEMANTICAL SKILLS

As we have seen in earlier chapters both Fodor and Wittgenstein are concerned with the nature and acquisition of semantics, and that the difficulty here is to find an account of the framework which at the same time is language like, finite and yet allows for productivity. Wittgenstein's analysis of meaning shows that we should look for meaning, not in the individual's mental structure but in the forms of life and language game children are engaged in. Leaving the language games for now, we have to ask: What are the individual skills involved in the acquisition of semantics? Clearly the skill to speak meaningfully involves two different aspects. First the child has to master the skill to use one thing, an object or a linguistic or other sign, to stand for or represent something else. Secondly the child has to acquire the conventional meanings of the words and other linguistic symbols of his or her language. The first, I will try to show in this section, is based on two skills which have innate basis, but develop during the first year, namely imitation and play. The second is a result of these combined with the child's growing social skills which develop on basis of close and regulated interaction with care givers. This social interaction is important because it delimits idiosyncratic meanings and delimits the productivity inherent in language. Without social interaction there would be no language.[28]

The two skills I discuss in this section—imitation and play—can be described as meta-skills. They involve most of the child's sensorimotor skills employed in special ways, or one could say a skillful way of using other skills or skills applied to skills. In imitation sensorimotor skills are matched with external copies of the same behavior, in the beginning the child's own earlier behavior and later that of other persons or even objects. In play sensorimotor skills are used outside their normal context, and both imitation and play in many cases modify the "original" behavior, for example, a behavior sequence is not performed in full or is simplified. This requires or involves skills "over and above" purely sensorimotor skills. Furthermore, imitation is a prerequisite for play, especially for pretend play which has a crucial role in developing semantic skills. Both imitation and play are skillful activities that involve displacement, that is, the connection to events, objects, and so forth, not present and are the germ of the "idea" that an action, object and eventually words can signify, symbolize something other than itself.

Imitation

Imitation clearly plays a role in the skills I have discussed in the section on linguistic skills. The narrowing of the range of babbling as well as the acquisition of new sound combinations seem to some extent to be the result of the child imitating the adult. There is evidence that young infants imitate intonation (Lieberman 1984) and at three to five months they can imitate pitch (Rathus 1988). Bower (see Restak 1979) reports that children as young as six days can imitate orofacial movements of adults, that is, stick out the tongue and wiggle it. Piaget (1962) and others (e.g., Rathus 1988) argue, though, that this early imitation is reflexive. Behaviors or reflexes in the child are triggered by similar behavior or reflexes in other individuals. For example, if one child in a room with other babies starts to cry, the others will soon follow, but this does not seem to be imitation but the triggering of reflexive behavior. Piaget argues that infants at this stage, and for several months see similar actions in others as continuations of their own actions, that is, their own sound and the sound of the "model" are not distinguished. Later on children also imitate the syntax, as irregular verbs and the construction of past tense, of people around them, but most of the child's early syntactical combinations are not straightforward imitations. Children frequently say things as "bye-bye shoe" and "all gone milk" but it is unlikely that the parents, although simplifying their syntax when engaged in so-called baby talk or motherese, have provided these. Kuczaj (1982) points out that children even avoid imitating syntactical forms. In spite of this, imitation of speech sounds and syntactical structures of the child's native language is clearly a central part in explaining why French children speak French, English children speak English, and so on.

The imitation of speech sounds and syntax is different from imitations of other motor behaviors as walking or drinking in that the child can imitate the effects (sound and sentence structure) without perceiving what is producing the effects. The child as observer only sees the lips and facial movements and hears the sounds. P. Reynolds (1976) suggests that vocal behavior

> is analogous from the observer's vantage point to a hypothetical kind of object manipulation in which the object is visible but the behavior is not.[29]

This means that one would not expect imitations of speech sound, especially new combinations, to be effective until the child has reached a certain mastery in the manipulation of objects. The skill of imitating sounds is a combination of the skill of manipulating objects, where the object is visible but the behaviors concerning it are not, and motor skills for producing sounds in a structured way.

The skill of imitation does not just give the child new specific motor skills, as novel sound combinations required by its sociolinguistic environment, but it is also, when used in play situations the prerequisite for meaningful language and thought, that is, semantical skills. Piaget sees imitation as a forerunner to mental representation and this points to the most important aspect of imitation, namely, that in imitation behavior is related to something different yet similar to itself.

In this section I will only give a short description of Piaget's studies on the emergence of imitation. The point is to show that imitation is a skill that grows out of the child's sensorimotor skills, and neither the ages of the different stages of the details of each stage are important to the overall claim that the acquisition of meaning is based on skills and not on an innate and intrinsically meaningful language of thought. Piaget (1962) describes the emergence of imitation in stages. In the first stage (birth to one month) there is only pseudo-imitation of the kind mentioned above, for example, the infant reflexively cries when it hears others cry. During the next few months (one to four months) sporadic imitation occurs, for example, simple hand gestures, but the child never imitates movements or sounds which are new or not already mastered by the child. Now the child also begins or intensifies some habitual behaviors upon perceiving another person doing the same. For example, the child waves its hand, the father imitates this motion and the child waves his or her hand again. In the next stage (stage three; four to eight months) the child's imitations become more systematic and he or she imitates actions on objects (as hitting or banging an object), but still only imitates responses already mastered and only those that are visible to the child as he or she does them. Imitation of behaviors not visible is mastered in the next stage (stage four; eight to twelve months) but the child is restricted to immediate behaviors already in its repertoire, but is able to combine or correlate different behaviors in new situations. If Reynolds (1976) is correct it is first at this stage that the child can imitate speech sounds, because it now masters actions not visible to the child. According to Piaget the crucial change occurs between twelve and eighteen months when the child has gained the concept of object permanence, specifically the related idea of a permanent object distinct from the child's own action. This means that objects as well as the actions of other persons are distinguished from the child's own manipulations of the object or the child's own actions. The child can now imitate novel actions and incorporate these into existing systems of behavior. Between eighteen and twenty-four months, the last stage of imitation development according to Piaget, the child becomes capable of deferred imitation, that is, can imitate complex new models, objects as well as persons, present as well as absent. This means that behaviors can be taken out of their immediate context and exhibited in novel situations. In a sense the child can use behaviors productively because he or she can relate them to other, different contexts, situations or objects. This is the beginning of displacement and semantical skills. Behavioral patterns that are associated with one context can become symbols of that context. For example, imitation of an action as lying down, closing the eyes, and putting the head on a pillow, can stand for the behavior sequence of going to bed. Soon part of an action system can represent the whole action pattern, that is, closing the eyes represents going to sleep (Hattiangadi 1987). This partial imitation can then be combined with or exchanged for the appropriate word as "sleepy" where the word takes the place of or signifies the whole action pattern. It is interesting to note that children often use many of their first words to stand for many different aspects of the whole behavior sequence associated with the word. For example, the word sour was used by a child studied by Lieberman (1984) to stand for the lemon, the act of eating it and its taste.

To sum up, it seems that the child's skill in imitating at early stages involves the practice and combinations of already mastered motor behaviors (e.g., the production of phonemes in babbling) and it is when the child has reached a certain mastery of object manipulation (i.e., object permanence) that this skill can first be combined with other sensorimotor skills. At this stage we have real imitation of speech. The child can now distinguish between its own action and that of another. He or she can distinguish between similar yet different actions and can associate similar behaviors with different contexts, that is, the behavior is freed from its immediate context and can be exhibited or used in another, or in other words deferred imitation enables the child to engage in pretend play. Piaget (1962) argues that this is the basis for the distinction between signifier and the signified, that is, between a symbol or sign and what it stands for or refer to.[30]

It is first around this time (twelve to eighteen months) that we can expect the child to use its first words or combinations of speech sounds as signals. Imitation has enabled the child both to "tailor" its speech sounds, through practicing, to the sounds occurring in its socio-linguistic environment and to master the skill of letting behaviors and words stand for or signal something else. The child now masters signifying. When the child is able to combine the speech sounds with the semantical skill acquired in imitation, the learning of new words really takes off. Rathus (1988) reports that although the learning of words is slow in the beginning it really accelerates around the child's second birthday.

Up to eighteen months the child normally masters fifty words, but around the age of twenty-four months this has grown to two hundred words, and continues to grow rapidly.

As mentioned in passing above imitation leads to semantical skills first when it is used in so-called pretend or symbolic play, the acquisition of which I will now turn to. It is in play that imitation come to have a clear representative or semantical function.

Play

Play is found in all children and in many animals.[31] It is not only a way of getting rid of surplus energy because animals have been observed to play even in cases of extreme food shortage (Lieberman 1984). Studies of play list at least thirty different functions of play in different animals, for example, muscular development, social skills and exploration of the environment (Lieberman 1984; see also Rathus 1988). Just as diverse as the ideas on the functions of play are ideas on how it should be characterized. For the present purpose I will characterize play as behavior or a system of behavior functioning normally but which is cut loose or liberated from its normal or instrumental situational constraints or consequences. The feedback system inside the behavioral system is, however, unimpaired. In this respect P. Reynolds' (1976) comparison of play to simulation studies in science or technological contexts is helpful. For example, one can simulate the effects of a tornado on the York University campus by placing a model of the campus in a wind tunnel capable of simulating a tornado. In this model system the winds created have no effect on the actual campus but the pattern of winds and destruction to the model is restricted by the same internal feedback system as a real tornado would be. This characterization of play applies both to so-called practice play (i.e., the repetition of patterns of behavior for its own sake) and so-called pretend or symbolic play, which involves reference or a relation to something other than itself. Both are exhibited out of their normal instrumental context but with an unimpaired internal feedback system. This is true both of play such as the practice of phonemic combinations in babbling and for the child playing with dolls or with a stick as a horse.

Play behavior would be a waste of energy in an organism whose behavioral repertoire functions "perfectly" and/or could not be modified, that is, if the genes rigidly determine behavior, play seems meaningless. It is just as meaningless as going on to stage repetitions of a play that is perfectly rehearsed and cannot be changed, and it is therefore not surprising that playing is only found in animals capable of ontogenetic modification. This modificability or plasticity makes the young organism vulnerable to the environment and while the organism develops its sensorimotor behavior (in non-real or play situations where the consequences do not threaten survival) parental care and training are extremely important. As I mentioned in the section on the infant's brain above, the human infant's modifiability is extreme, especially during its first extra uterine year. It is a combination of a *nidicole* and *nidifuge*—helpless yet very sensitive to environmental stimulation. Its brain is underdeveloped, plastic, and has redundant capacity.

Play, as imitation, is a skillful way of utilizing sensorimotor skills and as imitation undergoes development from "pure" practice play in the newborn to symbolic or pretend play in the year old infant. When the child first masters pretend play, the skill of deferred imitation combined with speech production skills yields language.[32] The crucial difference between practice play (the exercise of skills for their own sake) and pretend or symbolic play is that the latter includes deferred or delayed imitation and hence presupposes the imitation of new objects and behaviors, both present and absent. Imitation does come in the service of play.

Let me expand on this by recounting in a condensed form, Piaget's stages of play development. During the first stage (birth to one month) the child engages in "empty" behaviors as sucking movements without the presence of the breast or bottle. During the next three months (stage two; one to four months) the child engages in movements of parts of its body for the sheer pleasure of doing so. Between four and eight months (stage three) the child starts to manipulate objects in varying ways. This continues in stage four (eight to twelve months) when the child is clearly seen as abandoning the end of an action to play only with the means. There are also ritualizations where the child repeats and combines whole patterns of behavior. In the fifth stage (twelve to eighteen months) we have true pretense or make believe, for example, the sight of a pillow triggers part of sleeping behavior. It is in the last two stages that one can first ascribe to the child the beginning of semantical skills. For example, one of Piaget's children on seeing her pillow (or a blanket looking like her pillow) laid down her head and closed her eyes, put the thumb in the mouth, and so forth. Here she is clearly producing an action out of context but the behaviors are only representations of themselves, that is, it is both signifier and the signified. The behavior is clearly done for fun (not instrumental), in a partially different or untypical setting (presence of the pillow but absence of things as drawn blinds, pyjamas, etc.), but the behavior of going to sleep is much the same as in the real situation. A little later the same child starts to exhibit sleep behavior but does not finish it, and only closes her eyes. The last aspect of the play situation is, according to Piaget, the beginning of a differentiation between signifier (the behavior actually made) and the signified (the whole action pattern of going to sleep). In stage six this is carried further and the behaviors are found not only out of context, and are incomplete but, are applied to new and inadequate objects. Piaget's daughter, for example, used a piece of cloth and later the tail of a play donkey as a pillow. Another example (from Vygotsky 1976) is that of a child playing with a stick as a horse, which involves deferred imitation of behaviors appropriate to a horse (feeding, riding, etc.) to the inappropriate object of a stick. The child reproduces behavior not directly related to the object at hand, the stick, but to some other object. The stick, in this sense, evokes the absent horse. The stick is quite different from a real horse or wooden horse, but it is more similar than, say, an apple or an envelope. The stick is though clearly different from what it signifies but is not yet used only on conventional grounds, as a word would be used. But the basis of semantical skill is already established and speech will be combined with this skill.

> To sever the meaning of horse from a real horse and transfer it to a stick...and really acting with the stick as if it was a horse, is a vital transitional stage in operating with meanings.[33]

Behavior related to one object is transferred or combined with another object. More or less "real" actions on inadequate objects are carried further in language where words and sentences are manipulated not as motor behaviors but as representations of these. This enables the child to plan ahead, test behaviors, and so on, without immediate and perhaps disastrous consequences. Play, and later language, liberate the child from external, immediate constraints. Piaget and Inhelder (1969) add that language enables the quick representation of long event chains and simultaneous representation of different structures.

Words and sentences are signifiers determined by social conventions. Unlike idiosyncratic signifiers, such as the stick or donkey's tail in the examples above, they have a fixity or constancy of meaning (cp. Wittgenstein's private language argument) and a generality which is broader than individual experience. Using words and later sentences presuppose that the child is capable of deferred imitation and of pretend play, and it is not surprising that the child's acquisition of words speeds up when the newly developed skill of pretend play is combined with speech production skills. But since the meaning of words are conventional the child also has to master interindividual communicative skills. This will be discussed in the next section.

Playing horse with a stick or mother with a doll not only involves symbolism, but also rules of how sensorimotor behaviors are to be combined (Vygotsky 1976), that is, the child is transferring a set of structured behaviors to a new context and an object "symbolizing" the real object. Hence pretend play also utilizes the child's object manipulative and what I have called the syntactical skills above.[34] Speaking syntactically is exhibiting structured speech behavior and, if my claim in the section on syntactical skills is correct, involves the combination of motor behavior (e.g., orofacial) and object manipulation skills combined with speech production skills. Speaking a language is just as playing in the sense that it involves combining different skills and transferring a set of structured behaviors from one context to another. It seems thus that the skill of play also has a role in syntactical development. Again, the child's first syntactical constructions, telegraphic two-word utterances start when the child masters pretend play. If the skill of playing is necessary for syntactical speech this explains the fact, that it is not enough to have orofacial and manipulative control over hands, and so on, to have syntactical speech. It explains why syntactical speech, although phonemes combinations occurs earlier, is delayed to this age or stage of the child's development.

Not only syntactical skills but also speech production skills are turned from mere sounds into language with the development of play.

Let me now try to explain how speech production develops in a way that is parallel to the development of play sketched above. Babbling, the repetition and combination of phonemes, starts around six months, and can be characterized as a motor skill without a function. It is true that the babbling gets the child more attention from adults, but children seem to babble for the pure pleasure of it,[35] and infants of deaf parents babble just as much as infants of hearing parents, at least in early stages. Hence, speech sound production seems from the beginning to be freed from instrumental restraints or a particular context—it is an example of pure practice play. Babbling is pure practice play that becomes pretend play. Both types of play are exhibited "out of context" but the latter has a semantic aspect as well, in that it is related to something other than itself. Speech sounds become instrumental when the child engages in social interaction and this becomes even more effective when hooked up with the skill of pretend or symbolic play. The fact that speech sounds have minimal instrumental value (as compared to object manipulation and perception) and can be emitted concurrent with other ongoing motor behaviors facilitates the distinction between signifier and the signified, in that the real thing (behavior) and simulation (speech sounds) are differentiated by sensory channel. Speech sound seems thus to be an ideal vehicle for symbolic manipulation.[36] Furthermore, any speech sound can be combined with any extra-linguistic situation, event, object, and hence allows for great flexibility and productivity in its use. This is shown by differences in sound in different languages and by the new use old sounds can be put to. Actually, it lends itself to too great productivity or flexibility[37] in that any sound can be a representation of anything. To achieve the "fixation" or limiting of possibilities which are necessary for communication or information gathering and planning, the child's semantical skills of using speech sounds have to be restricted by intersubjective and socially shared conventions or ways of behaving.[38] Without social training we would have idiosyncratic and inconsistent use of speech sounds and syntactical combinations. Hence, to acquire language, the child also has to master communicative and social skills, which I will now turn to.

In this section I have only dealt with speech production, but something similar is taking place in speech understanding, only here the development is earlier, due in part to the fact that auditory discriminations are developed earlier.

Let me remind the reader that discussion of play and of communicative-social skills are precursors to Wittgenstein's language games.

COMMUNICATIVE-SOCIAL SKILLS: THE ACQUISITION OF LANGUAGE GAMES

Introduction

In the section on semantical skills I have tried to show what skills underlie the child's grasp of the semantic function, that is, that an object, event, action, or word can stand for, symbolize, or represent something other than itself. I have only discussed the general semantical skill, not how children learn specific meanings. I have said nothing of how it is possible for a child to acquire specific meanings or mean the same thing or use a symbol in the same way as others; that is, to use conventional symbols in speaking to different people in different contexts. To have language is not only to speak in well-formed sentences or use words that have idiosyncratic meanings, but to be able to use language or speech in a way that meets the requirements of the sociolinguistic environment. The child has somehow to acquire signs or symbols which are fixed enough to allow communication and information gathering, and general in that they "embody" experiences that go beyond individual experience. The child has to learn to mean the same thing with its words and sentences as the rest of the socio-linguistic community. This is a communicative or social skill and to speak syntactically is also a social skill in that both are a matter of social conventions and the same is true of the pragmatics of language, that is, to adjust what one says to whom one is speaking to, in what contexts, with what purpose, and so forth. These social skills presuppose or build on the skills I have discussed above but also on some specifically social skills. It is when all these skills converge or are combined around the child's first birthday that we have language, or rather the beginning of language. It is at this time the child comes to engage in language-games, in Wittgenstein's sense.

Before I turn to the discussion and illustration of the social skills necessary for language the character of the linguistic input the child encounters has to be discussed. The linguistic input is incomplete and underdetermines what can be learned, and without the structuring the sociolinguistic community provides the child could not utilize this input. Thus, the child needs basic social skills to be able to utilize the language or rather speech she or he overhears. The child's ability to engage in social interaction is necessary to acquire the conventional skills involved in language, but also to make sense of the sociolinguistic input.

Let me explain; Chomsky (1959), in his criticism of Skinner, pointed out that the language the child hears is incomplete and faulty, which is apparent from listening to any normal conversation in a family. But the situation is even worse in that the child only encounters a limited set of examples of particular language usage. Add to this the finitism of language and the task of learning from experience seems impossible. If language and thought are inherently underdetermined or open-ended, that is, it can be used in an indefinite number of ways, just overhearing examples (often faulty) of speech, cannot by itself help the child acquire language. How, then, can the incomplete experience be structured and how are communication, objectivity, and constancy of meaning acquired? Following Wittgenstein, I will try to show that the structuring or limiting framework is found in the child's social interactions. We do not need to assume an innate language of thought to explain how the child learns from experience and furthermore, the "learning mechanism" involved is not a rational process of hypothesis formation and testing, but a process of training, which combines social with nonsocial skills.

Social interaction and the acquisition of social skills have two functions: they help the child to utilize and learn from experience and to acquire the conventions of language. The necessary structure, limitation, or interpretation of examples overheard is not provided by explanation by the adults (which presupposes what is to be learned, namely language) but through social constraints and interventions. What the child's mind is not providing, and the adult cannot provide by explanations, is provided by corrections, encouragements and other social or interpersonal techniques getting the child to conform to the standards of the sociolinguistic environment.

Symbiosis

Wittgenstein suggests that the acquisition of language is a matter of training, that is, the child learns language in the same way as a dog is trained to hunt. In training the dog, horse or circus animal the trainer is rearranging, recombining, or shaping the innate and natural behavioral systems of the animal according to standards external to the original or innate behavior. The elephant's innate motor behavior is used to get it to stand on two legs, sit on a drum, and so forth. Something similar is taking place when the child is learning language, that is, its innate motor behavior (speech production, syntactical skills, object manipulation, imitation, play, etc.) are combined to meet the standards of the sociolinguistic environment. Although language acquisition in this respect is training or domestication,[39] it is better understood in terms of symbiosis (Shotter 1974, 1976, 1978). By this I mean that the child and its care-giver stand in a symbiotic relationship where the child is dependent on the adult not only for the satisfaction of its physical needs (i.e., the adult is a physical extension of the child) but also for its social, linguistic, and mental activity. The adult not only provides examples of use, for example, in baby talk; corrects the child's own attempts to speak but also ascribes to the child meanings and thoughts based on the child's natural expressions and behaviors and later on the basis of linguistic utterances.[40]

> Parents speak for the children, as in "Is baby tired?" "Oh, we're so tired." "Does baby want to go nappy?" "We want to take our nap now, don't we?" This parent is pretending to have a two-way conversation with the child. In this way parents seem to be trying to help their children express themselves by offering children models of sentences that they can use later on.[41]

Furthermore, the adult not only ascribes meaning and thoughts to the child, but also reacts towards the child as if he or she had actually thought or meant something specific. The adult treats the child as a unity which consists of the child's actual behaviors and the interpretations the adult gives to the child's behavior. In this way the child's innate expressions of pain, behaviors, and imitations of linguistic usage are incorporated into a social and communicative context. The child becomes a rational being by being treated as such.

The dyad of the mother (or other care-giver) and the child can be viewed as one psychological or linguistic being, where the mother gives social, intersubjective or conventional meaning to what the child does naturally and instinctively without concern for others. The mother, by interpreting the child's behavior and reactions and then acting on them accordingly, coordinates her own behavior to the child's. The child's behavior and reactions are from the beginning made part of a social system which is both more stable and wider than the child's individual reactions. In the beginning the child does not make a distinction between its own actions and that of the mother (Piaget 1954), but sees it as a continuation of its own behavior. The interaction is one-sided and not really social in that the child is not an actor but a recipient. As the child grows and acquires skills as manipulating objects, true imitation, and so on, he or she starts to play an active role. Around fifteen months (Shotter 1976) the child begins to say "No!" to the mother and is able to resist the mother's interpretation of the child's behavior, wishes, and so on. The symbiotic relationship is breaking up and the child becomes a social actor in its own right.

The symbiosis has trained the child first by combining its actions with another's, then coordinating its behavior with other's in a patterned and reciprocal way, and eventually, in social play, doing this according to shared conventional rules. By participating in forms of life the child becomes prepared to participate in language games and to acquire meaning, syntax, and pragmatics of the language spoken around it.

The child is preadapted for social interaction[42] by things as reflexive crying, smiling, and selective attention to speech sounds and the human face.[43] Many of the child's early reflexive behaviors are patterned which enables the mother to relate her own actions in a systematic way to the child's, for example, smiling and talking to the infant only in pauses between sucking. There is evidence that these early interactions are patterned and stereotyped in most mother-child dyads (Richards 1974; Bower 1977a), but it should be noted that although the child's behavior is innate and reflexive the mother's interpretation (and subsequent reaction) involves cultural assumptions, and are not inevitable labeling of universal behaviors. In Western cultures crying is often seen as a sign of hunger, but for mothers among

!Kungbushmen, where the infant is carried on the mother's back most of the time, certain movements are the usual sign for hunger (Konner 1972). The same undoubtedly holds true for other things, as, for example, pain or discomfort. The ascription of meaning to different behaviors cannot, though, be completely arbitrary because the child would never be satisfied or would not even survive, but there seem to be enough variation and diversity of natural expressions to allow for cultural and contextual variation.[44] Hence, children's behaviors are from the beginning combined and coordinated with others based on social conventions. The very meaning and significance of the child's reactions are thus restricted by social conventions and so are the stimuli or input, both linguistic and nonlinguistic, that the child encounters. This social language-game is quite different from Fodor's assumptions about a solitary child forming and testing linguistic hypotheses given by the child's private language of thought, and, as should be evident, much closer to Wittgenstein's suggestions about learning.

Peekaboo

Let me now illustrate the emergence of social play with an example from Bruner (1976)[45] of the emergence of the game peekaboo.[46] He studied six infants from ten to seventeen months of age and he describes the developmental changes as an example of turning

'gut-play' into play with conventions.[47]

In the beginning the game utilizes strong preadapted response tendencies in young infants. The mothers studied by Bruner reported that "looming," in which the mother approaches or looms towards the child's face from approximately one meter and says 'Boo!', precedes the peekaboo game. If the "loom" is directly toward the face there is a reflexive avoidance reaction which seems to be innate. Hence, one of the important aspects of peekaboo, that is, disappearance or avoidance, builds on the child's reflexive responses. Furthermore, appearance and disappearance, the main aspects of the game, are aspects of object manipulations, which also are innately based (Piaget 1954). So, in the beginning and also as it becomes more structured and two-sided the game is not governed by conventional (i.e., arbitrary) rules but by strong preadapted responses in the infant. These are used by the mother in the structuring of her interactions with the infant.

All peekaboo games have the same basic structure: (1) initial contact, (2) disappearance, (3) reappearance, and (4) reestablished contact. In the looming stage this is only present in an incomplete form but it soon characterizes all peekaboo games. Initially the game involves a limited set of hiding tools, time variations, vocalizations, and so on, but as the child matures and becomes more skillful in the game, which presupposes the concept of object permanence, modifications in, for example, the hiding tool occurs, for example, a rag, a hand, even a chair can function as hiding tool depending on the context. Having reached this stage in playing the game the child seems to master not only the rules for turn taking, that is, appearance and disappearance, but also a wide range of variations inside a set of relatively fixed rules "patterned variations within constraining rules" (Bruner 1976, p. 283). As the rules become more arbitrary they also become more conventional in that anything that is agreed upon can function as a hiding tool, and so forth. Before ten to twelve months the mother controls the unmasking, timing, and so forth, but after this age the child begins to take control. A few months later (fifteen months in one of the children Bruner studied) the child invents and controls variations in the game, for example, hides behind a chair. The child has now become an actor and the mother a recipient and the symbiosis is breaking up.

Bruner also points out that vocalizations play a role in peekaboo. In the beginning they help the child localize the mother's face but soon become parts of the game, occurring concurrent with specific behaviors and responses. This and other vocalizations by the mother[48] help the child make the transition from initially nonlinguistic games to language games.

To sum up: peekaboo begins with innate reflexive avoidance responses which become more developed when combined with the child's object manipulation abilities, that is, with the acquisition of skills related to object permanence. Around the time the child masters deferred imitation the "rigid" rules of the game become varied. The child, by combining different skills in interaction with the care-giver, has developed the skill of taking turns, coordinating its own action with others, follows intersubjective or conventional rules, and mastering variation inside a set of relatively determined rules. The child has now, around twelve to fifteen months, the skills required for participating in language games, which are just other systems of conventional rules which vary to fit the context and can be changed if the change is socially accepted. The child has acquired the skill of communication and of productive use of conventional rules. This is a result of combining what I have called linguistic and semantical skills with communicative skills.

Another example of the symbiotic learning can be seen if we consider how the child learns a word like "pain."[49] The child naturally exhibits both bodily signs of harm (e.g., bleeding) and typical expressions of pain as crying.[50] The care-giver not only attends to the child, that is, stops the bleeding and feels the sore leg, but also treats and talks to the child as if it felt pain and in this way language is attached to the natural signs as crying. The child comes to imitate the word and use it as part of the natural expression (i.e., as in play when one thing is used to stand for something else), and eventually uses it instead of the natural expression. The word pain does not refer to the pain behavior or expressions but gets attached, just as crying is, to the inner sensations. The symbiotic relationships has thus helped the child to acquire a new skill and to relate it to something naturally present in the mind. As a result the child eventually can talk about its own subjective feelings. All this is possible first when the child can imitate something not present, can engage in pretend play and handle conventional rules, that is, around twelve to fifteen months.[51]

Although the symbiotic interaction seems to be breaking up around the time the child begins to speak, traces of it are important in the acquisition of language even at later stages. Many of the child's first utterances are difficult, if not impossible, to understand and later idiosyncratic use of words or grammatical constructions, even when correctly pronounced, leads to difficulties. Ryan (1979) and others report that mothers often respond to children's utterances by expanding on them, adding to or changing them. They make interpretations of what the child is saying on the basis of such things as the child's intonation pattern, accompanying actions (e.g., pointing) and the circumstances (e.g., absence of an object), and delimit the meaning more exactly. A rather elaborate example is given by Rathus (1988):

If the child says, "Baby shoe," the mother may reply, "Yes, that is your shoe. Do you want me to put it on your foot? Shall Mommy put the shoe on baby's foot?"[52]

In the same way the child's tendency to overregularization or underregularization is controlled.

Hence, by participating in language games the child becomes more and more proficient in its native language.

In these early language games and games as peekaboo which precede them, the adult has not explained what pain or "baby's shoe" means but in interactions with the child *shown* how the words are used in social interactions, and trained the child to use the words in the same way. Explanations are sometimes given by the adult, and sometimes asked for by the child (e.g., when why-questions start to appear), but it is first when the child has mastered the basics of language that explanations are effective learning tools.[53]

It is not necessary that the child's use or meaning of the words pain or baby's shoe is exactly the same as the adult's, only that both their actual usages converge sufficiently for communication. By acquiring social skills as turn-taking the child has become able to coordinate its own actions to that of others. Exposed to a limited and underdetermined set of examples of particular linguistic usage, the child is able to combine its speech production skills, imitative skills with the social skill to use the language in a systematic yet varied way. The child can communicate concepts in varying circumstances to different people.[54]

The communicative and social skills illustrated above build on the linguistic and semantical skills, yet come to control these. By this I mean that the child's aim in communicating or gathering information controls the skills used to accomplish this. In this sense the communicative or social skills are higher order skills or skills applied to skills.

The child's acquired language is a result of a social construction utilizing many different skills which have some aspects that are isomorphic with language, but not by themselves can make up language. The skills are productive, as are the underlying neural structures.

CONCLUSION

Cross-Modal Transfer of Skills

In the different sections above I have tried to show that the acquisition of language can be understood as a process of training where different skills, for example, orofacial, object manipulation, imitation, and the like, are combined and result in the beginnings of language between the child's first and second birthday. The skills not only interact and are combined but are also changed as a result. This is possible because of the plastic and redundant nervous system which allows the child to be tolerant of novel experiences, actively exploring the environment. The child's behavior is quite easily disintegrated and recombined. This process is very complex requiring many different external and internal systems of behavior or responses operating in coordination. This presupposes that there is a cross-modal transfer of skills. A skill that has been mastered in one mode, for example, orofacial, can be transferred to another, as production of sounds. Other examples of the cross-transfer of skills is from object manipulation to imitation. Cross-modal transfer or association is generally seen as a prerequisite for language and is by some considered uniquely human. Monkeys and other non-human primates are, though, capable of cross-modal transfers (Premack 1980).

Most studies of cross-modal transference or association have mainly been limited to the study of perception, that is, studies of how the child is able to recognize an object as the same using different perceptual systems (e.g., tactic visual, visual-auditory) but obviously must occur in the case of motor skills as well.[55] Piaget has, for example, studied how different skills mature or are acquired at different times in different cognitive domains. Cross-modal transfer requires that experiences in different perceptual or behavioral systems are equivalent in relevant aspects. A tentative attempt to specify the equivalences between orofacial structure and phrase structure has been done by Lieberman (1988). The same needs to be done for the different systems I discuss above. The different cross-modal transfers also have to be studied to determine which, if any, are present at birth and how they develop.

Later Learning

My account of the acquisition of language and the process of learning has been limited to very early learning, but of course much important learning takes place after this. It is both similar and in important respects different from the early training. For example, imitation skills help the child to continue to learn new words and syntactical constructions, through practice speech production improves and is adult-like first around the child's tenth birthday (Lieberman 1984), when the child's increasing skill of manipulation objects result in the use and understanding of words as "cause," "time," and so on. The child's increasing social network, in play with peers and adults, increases the child's mastery of the pragmatics of language. In addition to these continuations of skills developed before the acquisition of language, language itself adds a new and powerful skill to the child's repertoire of skills. Language can be applied to, or combined with, other skills and with itself. It sharpens the child's skills in manipulating objects[56] and enables quick representation of long chains of events as well as simultaneous representation of different structures (Piaget and Inhelder 1969). With language the child can plan ahead and "test" actions before doing them, and it makes the child radically more independent from adults. It can also influence other persons in a new way. The continued acquisition of language, and cognitive knowledge, is also enhanced by language in that the child now can benefit from explanations, especially when its meta-linguistic awareness develops in a few years time. This makes later learning quite different from the early training I have discussed above.

The same processes or mechanisms are, though, still part of learning later in life. For example, symbiotic learning is found at universities. One frequently observes how under graduates ask questions with words they do not fully understand. Very often the teacher reformulates the question in an appropriate way and answers it on basis of the reformulation. Although the subject matter is very different, the situation is not far from a mother interacting with her young child.

Language and Thought

The Domestication Model of learning has no need, as we have

seen, to postulate an innate language of thought. Learning is based on the combination of skills and social interaction. In a sense the care-giver, when interacting with the child provides an external language of thought, or at least something which partly functions to delimit and give content to what the child does. But what about the development of thought in the individual child? This question is outside the scope of this book, but let me just indicate how this problem could be approached. The child's early intelligence is shown by its actions and in this sense its "thinking" or intellectual capacity is practical. It is *knowing how* to do certain things or how to solve specific problems but not yet *knowing that* or propositional thought. The skills, as object permanence, speech production, semantical and social skills eventually lead to language. It is first now, with the event of language, that the child has the basis for propositional thought. The step from public language to internal thought is a privatization and appropriation of something public into the child's private mental sphere. How this takes place and what happens once language becomes internalized is a difficult problem which cannot be discussed here. What is clear, though, is that Domestication Model here builds on ideas from Wittgenstein and goes directly against Fodor.[57]

Concluding Remarks

The Domestication Model of language learning sees learning as a process of social construction. The learning of language is based on the child's innate behaviors and skills which are shaped by social interaction. There are two main types of skills involved in the learning of language. Firstly, linguistic skills which can be further divided into speech and syntactic skills. Speech skills are based in the innate ability to perceive and produce speech, and syntactic skills are based in different kinds of motor behavior, such as orofacial and object manipulation skills. As they develop the linguistic skills are combined with the second type of skills, namely communicative-semantic skills. Examples of semantical skills are imitation and play and the communicate skills are based in the child's natural and patterned social interactions (e.g., turn-taking). But these skills are not sufficient for the acquisition of language. The child has to use them in the context of a linguistic community in close contact with a care-giver, in, what I have called, symbiosis. The last is crucial because it is in this interaction that the natural linguistic and communicative-semantic skills are shaped, or domesticated, to the expectations of the linguistic community. Learning is, thus, the training of specific innate skills to conform to social standards. It is not a "triggering" of an innate language of thought or a process where the child forms and tests hypotheses.

This social training, shaping, and combining of skills are made possible by the plasticity and redundancy of the developing brain, the unique human ability to form speech sounds and the long childhood of humans. These may well be some of the factors responsible for the fact only humans can learn language. The Domestication Model of learning could also, as mentioned, be described as a Transactional or Tri-polar Model of leaning in that it sees the acquisition of language as the combination and coming together of many different biologically encoded skills in accordance with the demands of the socio-linguistic environment. Language is the result of a nexus of interacting skills adapted to the linguistic environment. The details of this model are of course extremely complex, even if the underlying principles are simple, and it is bound to be added too and changed by further empirical as well as a priori research. At this stage the Domestication Model should be understood as an outline for a future research program that needs to be filled out and tested on both a theoretical level and an empirical level.

In the next chapter I will show how the Model deals with the two basic problems of learning, the problem of productivity and the problem of the framework.

CHAPTER 8

Conclusion: The Framework
and Productivity of Learning

INTRODUCTION

In this chapter I will show how the Domestication Model differs
from both Fodor's and Wittgenstein's account and how it man-
ages in a more successful way to solve the two fundamental problems of learning. In chapter 1, I claimed that the two basic problems of learning were the problem of productivity and the
problem of the framework. The problem of the framework refers
to the paradox that it is impossible to learn something one does
not already know. Unless one already has a basic framework of
what one is learning, it seems to be impossible to benefit from
experience. The problem of productivity stems from the fact that
learning involves going beyond information given. Learning is to
go beyond experience or previous knowledge. I also pointed out
that these pull in different directions, one denying change and
novelty and the other affirming it. As we have seen, Fodor
attempted to solve this dilemma by making the framework, the
innate language of thought, productive in that it is made up of
recursive rules. Nevertheless, it is limiting in that all that can ever
be learned is built into the language of thought. His theory is
problematic and fails to explain what it sets out to explain, but
has made a valuable contribution to our understanding of learning in suggesting that the framework itself is productive. Wittgenstein has contributed to our understanding of language learning
by pointing out problems in accounts like Fodor's, but also by
giving us another way to understand productivity, that is, his
finitism or idea of family resemblance. In combining a reconstruction of his hints with with empirical as well as theoretical studies
of language and its acquisition the Domestication Model
emerged. The rest of this chapter will be devoted to an attempt to

show how this model can and actually avoids the problems associated with the other approaches to learning that I have discussed.

IS THE DOMESTICATION MODEL
AN IMPROVEMENT OVER OTHER THEORIES?

How then does the Domestication Model go about solving the conceptual-theoretical problems that Fodor and Wittgenstein failed to solve or solved only partially?

The Problem of Productivity

In understanding learning one of the most fundamental problems to explain is how it is possible for a helpless human infant, limited by its biological structure and confronted with limited experience in a complex social world, to acquire language. How does he or she acquire language which can be successfully used to gather information and communicate, not only in familiar situations but also when confronted with something new? As we saw in chapter 1, traditional solutions to this problem, like Plato's and Hume's, failed in this respect. Plato failed because he held that all knowledge is innate and Hume failed because he had no way of accounting for how one can learn from experience.

Chomsky and Fodor, in pointing out and stressing that learning a language involves productivity or going beyond information given, focused attention on this as one of the central problems of learning. How is it possible that the learner, based on finite innate biological structures and a finite set of experiences can handle situations never encountered before? Fodor's solution was, as we have seen, to make the underlying mental framework—the language of thought, as well as the natural language themselves—productive. Both can be characterized by transformational recursive rules which makes it possible to produce, in principle, infinite linguistic output with finite means. The problem with this solution is, as we have seen, that by assuming an innate representational system as rich as the one which is learned it fails to account for productivity. It only reproduces it on another level.

The Domestication Model adopts the same basic strategy as Fodor. What is learned (language) and that which makes this possible (the underlying framework of biological skills and structures) are themselves seen as productive. With finite means such as language heard and a limited set of skills, the child is able to go beyond information given and deal with new situations. This model rejects Fodor's solution (recursive rules) to the productivity of language and sees it, like Wittgenstein, in terms of finitism, that is, that past uses do not determine future uses. Future uses of linguistic expressions are not determined by past uses or by any rules, but can change in a contingent way depending on the context and other factors. Also, the underlying framework of language-like skills is productive. Skills like orofacial movements (e.g., chewing), manipulating an object or walking in a new environment, are all productive in that the child is able to handle new situations. In general, this kind of productivity seems to be typical of many biological structures. For example, Darwin expressed two principles underlying the emergence of new structures or behaviors.[1] One and the same organ can at the same time fulfil different functions and even take on new functions, and two different organs can also perform the same function. Biological structures seem to have a redundancy in function or multiple use. So, both what is learned and what learning is based on is productive, but productivity is not accounted for in terms of innate mental representations, thus avoiding Fodor's problem. Instead of reproducing a system just like the one to be explained, the Domestication Model subsumes linguistic productivity under a more general biological productivity. How to explain this productivity still remains, but the ability of biological structures to function in different and novel ways are common.

The Domestication Model leaves the fundamental nature of productivity unsolved, but shows that linguistic productivity is not based in a unique human mental structure, but is found throughout the biological world. In general it sees productivity as a result of many different factors—both biological and nonbiological—which themselves are flexible and when co-occurring and interacting yield something new. The combination of different factors are not seen as part of an overall predetermined design but are rather coincidences.[2]

The Problem of the Framework

"Knowing How" and "Knowing That."   The Domestication Model of learning claims that Meno's paradox, that one cannot learn what one does not already know, can be resolved by presuming that the skills that are the basis of language acquisition are in some respects isomorphic with language. For example, oro-facial motor behaviors have a structure not much different from the phrase structure of grammatical sentences. Furtermore, motor behavior is like language productive in that, just as a child can produce sentences never heard before, he or she can walk through an unfamiliar room without bumping into the furniture. Imitation and play involve representations and early social interactions involve turn-taking which are central to linguistic communication. The child can, thus, be said to know what he or she is learning, but not because he or she possesses an innate language of thought but because he or she possesses or develops skills to do a great many things relevant to language. These are then combined and modified in a social and linguistic context to yield language. The mastery of language is the result of a social construction based on biological given skills of various kinds. These skills each contributes to language acquisition, but could not on their own or in combination give language, because social and linguistic contributions are necessarily part of the constructive process of combing these individual skills into language.

The non-language skills discussed above have all been treated as instances of knowing how to do things, and I have not presumed that the child has any explicit knowledge (knowing that) of what he or she is doing, as, for example, an adult learning tennis often has. Furthermore, all skills, in that they are adapted to the physical and socio-linguistic environment, contain implicit representations of the environment.[3] Language hooks on to these when combined with the relevant skills, for example, manipulating objects, and later becomes internalized in conceptual thought.[4] Language enables us to make explicit and specific what was implicit. At first glance, this may not seem to be different from assuming an innate universal grammar or a language of thought, which presumably is not consciously present in the child's mind. But there are crucial differences, which avoid the difficulties of the innatist position—concepts, grammar, and so forth, are not innate; what is innate is specific behaviors and skills. The acquisition of conceptual thought and language is a nonrational process, that is, does not presuppose language or concepts, instead these are rather a result of a process where skills are selectively retained and combined to yield new skills.

The Evolution of Language. As we saw in chapter 3, one of the problems with Fodor's theory of an innate language of thought is that its phylogenetic origin does not seem to be accountable for in terms of evolutionary biology. It seems implausible that language could be a result of one giant mutation or even of several small ones. The question of the evolution of language is, of course, very difficult, and controversial. We do not have a clear picture of everything that is involved in language, and fossil and other evidence is scant and difficult to interpret. Nevertheless, I think, that the Domestication Model fares better than Fodor's in this respect. It suggests a picture which is compatible with evolutionary theory and perhaps even provides hypotheses about the evolution of language.

Language is, as we saw in chapter 7, unique to humans. How can such a new function arise without apparent antecedents? How is a major transition as the transition from nonverbal to verbal communication possible? I would like to claim that this can be answered in terms of an implicit principle in evolutionary theory, namely, redundancy and multiple use of biological structures. The mechanism here is one of functional shift, of one structure functioning in one way shifting to another: colloquially one could call it the "new use of old features" or "tire-to-sandals" principle (Gould 1989). Darwin in *The Origin of Species* described two aspects of biological or evolutionary redundancy:

> We should be extremely cautious in concluding that an organ could not have been formed by transitional gradations of some kind. Numerous cases could be given amongst the the lower animals of the same organ performing at the same time wholly distinct functions; thus in the larva of the dragon-fly and in the fish Cobites the alimentary canal respires, digests, and excretes.[5]

> Again, two distinct organs, or the same organ under two very different forms, may simultaneously perform in the same individual have the same function, and this is an extremely important mean of transition: to give an instance,—there are fish with gills or brachiae that breathe the air dissolved in the water, at the same time they breathe fresh air in their swim bladders....In all such cases one of the two organs might readily be modified and perfected so as to perform all the work, being aided in the process of the other organ; and then this other organ might be modified for some other and quite distinct purpose.[6]

Furthermore, the Domestication Model sees language, as we have seen, as consisting of a set of dissociable skills, each able to function on its own, as is shown by the occurrence of them in other nonspeaking primates. Language is a construction from separable units (speech production, speech perception, voluntary control, nonlinguistic motor behavior, imitation, play, turn-taking, etc.) which most likely have separate origins. This fits very well with the idea of "mosaic evolution," that is, the principle of breaking complexity into dissociable units is a precondition for evolutionary change.[7]

How can this idea be applied to the evolution of language? As we saw in chapter 7, most, but not all, skills involved in language are found to a lesser or greater degree in humans as well as in nonhuman animals. They seem, thus, to have evolved in many species, but only in one did they come to play a role in language. Hence, it does not seem that they evolved as precursors of language,[8] but rather because they had other important functions or survival value. In humans, especially with the advent of speech, they took on new functions. A skill like play, with an obvious survival value in problem solving, came to take on an additional function in language (i.e., semantical, see chapter 7 above.) Here we seem to have an example of Darwin's view of a transitional mechanism where one structure performs two different functions. But the other mechanism for transition, that is, two different organs or biological systems performing the same function also played a role in the evolution of language. Animal communication like cries, bodily movement, and the like, and speech are examples of two or more biological systems performing the same function, namely communication. Most likely they functioned side by side in early man and they still function side by side in humans, and the animal mode of communications are an important aid in language acquisition. It is not difficult to see how they also aided in the evolution of speech in early humans. More importantly, the development of the ability to produce speech sounds was crucial, I think, to the evolution of language, but could not have evolved as the only mean of communication, or even as being the superior means of communication in its early stages. Let me elaborate.

In pre-speaking humans we can assume communication to be like other primates' cries, body signs, etc. We can also suppose that these pre-speaking humans, like other mammals, could discriminate speech sounds. The animal communications were no doubt effective, but mainly limited to expressive and signaling functions. They were also slow and required, except in cries, close visual or tactile contact between the two communicators. Speech, as I have already suggested, developed as a parallel mode of communication, and slowly became superior to and taking over more and more from earlier modes of communication. But speech in the beginning of its emergence cannot have been very useful for several reasons. Given the shape of today's primates' voice box, in early humans it must have been similar and quite unlike what humans have today[9] and thus unable to produce many speech sounds. Furthermore, without a developed brain with the neurological and cognitive substrata for speech this mode of communication appears to have little advantage. But due to other evolutionary changes in humans, like upright walk, the increase in the brain's size, flexibility, and redundancy in function, as well as the long childhood, this development could be combined with the ability to produce speech sounds.

According to this picture, language evolved in a mosaic fashion from nonlinguistic antecedents through two mechanisms of transition: one biological system—several functions; two biological systems—one function. This process was enhanced by the co-evolution of a larger brain and a long childhood in humans. The development of speech sounds clearly played a crucial role here, but this raises serious problems. When the voice box changes in such a manner as to allow for speech, the risk of choking is greatly increased. Did speech in its early stages have a selective value over the risk of choking? It is hard to see how rudimentary speech, with a great risk of choking, could have any value at all, especially with a well-established nonverbal system of communication. Is there anything in speech which would make it valuable in spite of this increased risk of injury and death? Lieberman (1985) argues that speech makes possible fast communication; much can be said in a short time and can easily be committed to short-term memory. It could therefore better function as an aid to action and planning than other modes of communication. The importance of speed in communication can be illustrated by studying dyslexics. Some of these persons have a great difficulty in decoding complex sentences because they read very slowly and forget the beginning of a sentence before they get to the end. The same point can be illustrated by reading a text aloud at one-tenth the normal speed of speech. One's hearer soon fails to understand anything one is reading. Speech also has an advantage over sign language in that it leaves the hands free for doing other things, and one can talk while one walks or works. Furthermore, speech is not expressive or iconic in the way that cries or signs are and can be used in many different ways, that is, it allows flexibility. As already mentioned, it also enables quicker gathering and analysis of information and just as crying, but with much greater flexibility, it can be used to communicate to someone out of sight (anyone exposed to the frustration to try to get the attention of and "saying" something to a deaf child, knows the value of this), and so on.

Could all these advantages outweigh the risk of choking, or did the life style, diet, and so forth, change at the same time, so that the risk of choking was compensated for? Or does the evolution of the voice box in humans have nothing to do with the evolution of speech? Did it perhaps develop as a side effect to cerebral enlargement; as a way of balancing the skull better, or to facilitate mouth breathing? Is speech perhaps only a new function of an organ which once had another function? Is it another example of one of the principles of transition mentioned above? Clearly, many questions remain unanswered.

Although many details remain to be worked out, the Domestication Model in stressing that language is a composite of many different skills is not incompatible with evolutionary biology. On the contrary, it suggests that language is not without antecedents in phylogentically close species, or in our direct ancestors. The Domestication Model sees language as a result of the flexibility and productivity in the functions of biological and social systems. Just as we can use a table to sit on or a dime as a screwdriver, or float on a piece of wood as well as on an air mattress, language, both in ontogenetically and phylogenetically is a result of biological flexibility and a unique combination or mosaic of skills.

The Framework and Productivity.   It could be argued that if language as well as the skills involved in its use are productive, communication and consistent use of language seem questionable. As Munz said (see chapter 1), every use of a word describing experiences involves going beyond information given and what one already knows:

> when we want to describe them we must necessarily make use of words; and these words and the propositions they form must by the nature of the case have a meaning of a more general nature than the single and individual experiences they refer to.[10]

If this is the case there must be something which delimits "wild" productivity or arbitrary use. The Domestication Model's response to this is to claim that the necessary restrictions and guidance is imposed by social habits and customs of linguistic use as well as by the limits of the biological structures and skills. Neither of these are totally plastic and unstructured. Together they limit what can be said and what cannot be said in a given context. But these factors are contingent and change over time, thus they are in this sense indeterminate.

Can the Domestication Model be said to explain productivity as well as communication and consistency of meaning on the individual level by postulating a social framework of habits and customs which itself does not change? I think the answer to this is that the social world, which is so much a product of language, is just as the individual open to change. The limits of change in the social world are, just as in biology, contingent or relative to a particular context. But does this not lead to another problem? If the social framework itself is seen as productive how is creativity in, for example, the sciences, like discoveries, to be accounted for? They often happen simultaneously in different research groups, and not everything counts as a discovery. There is a sharp distinction between "madness" and a real discovery. Also, in mathematics what counts as a proof is restricted. Creativity and novelty, although unpredictable in terms of the particular environmental and intellectual context, are not random. They are appropriate to the context and presuppose a system of constraint. Although there clearly are biological limits as well as social pressures at play here (Kuhn 1962), there also seems to be a limitation due to the subject matter at hand. There is a limiting framework in the "objective" body of concepts and knowledge, which further delimits productivity. The same is true of language as well, we are not free to construct any new linguistic utterance we or the group we belong to would like, because language itself (although it is no more than the sum of what all speakers say) does not allow any type of changes. It is a system with limitations which itself restricts what can be said and what cannot be said. So, one could say that the framework for language acquisition really has three parts, the individual contribution or part (biological skills and limitations), the social contribution (habits and customary use of language) and the contribution of language itself.

Another example of the problem of the framework, which Chomsky and Fodor brought into focus and tried to solve with the language of thought is that experience always is limited and faulty and to benefit from it one already has to know what one is learning. The problem with this is that it seems to rule out the possibility of learning something new, or newness is, at most, comparable to working out the consequences of what is already known. The Domestication Model's answer to this dilemma is to split the framework into two interacting parts, thus avoiding to have to say that learning is really a myth. The Domestication Model says that the utilizing of experience is aided by (1) innate perceptual capacities (e.g., speech perception) and (2) social interactions which delimits and sorts out what is relevant and not so relevant in experience. In social interaction the child is given both examples to imitate and corrections and shaping of behaviors. As just mentioned the language itself also puts restrictions on what can be said. The role performed by the language of thought is split into three parts language, the social, and the individual. Their interaction results in something new. Learning is not a myth. This model does not fall into the problems that Skinner and possible Wittgenstein could be accused of, namely that anything can be learned. It also goes beyond Wittgenstein and Skinner by suggesting a more detailed and complex picture of what the learning of language entails, for example, what the social interaction involves. As the example of symbiosis shows turn-taking is two-way process, negotiated between the child and the care-giver. It is based on purely instinctive reactions of the child, who in the beginning is passive but progressively takes a more active role.

The Content of the Framework.   One of Fodor's argument against empiricist theories of learning was that one cannot learn a language unless one has a language as rich as the one which one is learning (chapter 3). He uses this argument against Vygotsky, Bruner, and Piaget to claim that they cannot explain language learning, because they claim that something new is really acquired in the sense that the child learn new and different concepts from adults, or by interacting with the environment. Does this criticism affect the Domestication Model as well? Can it be said that since an infant has only nonlinguistic skills, it cannot learn from an adult's language or even corrections because these are different from what the child itself has? As we have seen the Domestication Model does not take nonlinguistic and linguistic skills to be fundamentally different, but it is their combination, controlled by a specific sociolinguistic context, which gives us language. Furthermore, the child is not required to translate from one language to another. If this is what learning involves Fodor seems to be right, but the child in learning language does not really have to understand, and does not understand, the adult in the same way as the adult understands him- or herself. The child imitates and adapts to the adult's behavior and gradually become more and more like the adult. Eventually the child will internalize language but successful communication and other use of language does not require that we have exactly the same concepts or word meanings, but that they have to converge.[11]

Is the Domestication Model an Explanatory Theory?

As we saw in chapter 3, one of the problems with Fodor's theory is that it does not really explain language acquisition. The language of thought is only a reproduction, on a different (mental) level, of what it is supposed to explain. The language of thought-model of learning also seems to confuse the description with what it describes. The Domestication Model, by not postulating an innate language of thought with the same characteristics as that which it is supposed to explain, provides a better explanatory hypothesis. It suggests that different biological structures and behaviors, which themselves are not linguistic (although in certain respects language-like, for example, orofacial movements can be described with a phrase structure grammar), but can be used in the acquisition and use of language. It also specifies the underlying mechanism which makes this possible, that is, redundancy and cross-modal transfer.

Is the Domestication Model Only a Redescription?   Fodor argued that Wittgenstein and others, which he called ordinary language philosophers, only provide examples of language use and do not deal with the phenomena themselves, thus giving us only linguistic or necessary truths. Firstly, most of these philosophers took the analysis of language to be more than empirical semantics, that is, more than describing what people actually say. Instead they thought that this would reveal ways of thinking about and explaining nonlinguistic phenomena. By studying language or deep seated ways of thinking, ways of explaining and making sense of the world could be accessed and criticized. This is what Wittgenstein tries to do in the *Philosophical Investigations*. But this is of course not enough, and it is not enough to give general hints and suggestions as Wittgenstein does. By utilizing results in different sciences the Domestication Model tries to move beyond this and provide a detailed explanatory hypothesis.

Does the Domestication Model confuse description and explanation? Could the same criticism that I posed against Fodor in chapter 3 be applied to the Domestication Model? Can it be accused of not explaining, but only redescribing some biological phenomena in such terms so they can be used to explain the acquisition of language? I think not, because it borrows its models and accounts of both the biological aspects and the social aspects of learning from other sciences, hence are restricted by these sciences. The empirical studies and theoretical models used have also been developed independently of the Domestication Model. As long as one takes care not to deviate too far from these sciences in the direction of seeing what one is looking for, the Domestication Model can avoid this problem.

Also, if the Domestication Model is right in thinking that the psychological developments of individuals consist in the internalization of its culture especially through linguistic interaction, the resulting mental set-up reflects this. An analysis of ordinary language and folk psychology does not only give us conceptual clarifications, but also provides hypothesis about psychological phenomena.[12]

Concluding Remarks.   To conclude, the Domestication Model avoids the two serious problems of Fodor's theory, namely, an innate language of thought as rich as anything one can learn and learning as a rational process of forming and confirming hypotheses. It does this by basing language learning in different skills. Another part of the role of the language of thought is assigned not to the child but to the surrounding social community. The Domestication Model agrees with Fodor that both what is learned and that which makes this possible are productive, but accounts for productivity in a different way. In seeing language learning as a process of the progressive combination of different skills with what is experienced, the Domestication Model has an approach similar to Piaget's. Learning is a process of construction, but unlike Piaget social interaction is crucial to learning language. The stressing of this and the solution to the problem of productivity is Wittgenstein's main contribution.

CONCLUSION: GENES AND JEANS

The Domestication Model of learning can, thus, deal successfully with the basic problems of learning. Learning a language is both seen as a delimiting and as an enriching process. Its delimiting aspect can be described as selective preservation of "unfocused" or "blind" variation. Here I speak of blind not in terms of random variation because the skills underlying language are the result of a long period of evolutionary history and have thus been preadapted for language and other human activities. I use the terms blind and unfocused to indicate that some skills (e.g., orofacial) are not adapted specifically to language and that others (e.g., babbling) are not specific to any particular language. The Domestication Model, thus, gives an account of the framework in terms of innate skills or behaviors, where the skills are the same as what is learned, yet different. The socio-linguistic environment functions to select and retain only those skills (e.g., in the case of babbling the skill of producing the speech sounds of its native language) that are relevant. Learning a language is, thus, adaptation to a specific language community. The process or mechanism of learning is one of selective retention and the combination of biologically grounded behaviors. But the learning is also a enriching process in that the adaptation to the socio-linguistic environment leads to the novel combinations of skills. Experience also plays an important role, but is not the "source" of, or determines what is learned, but rather limits the possibilities. Experience of socio-linguistic contexts also gives children a new skill, language, which both utilizes and organizes the other skills. The child has acquired, or constructed together with other speakers, a new and very powerful skill. Learning a language is a matter of both "genes and jeans," that is, the child has a preadapted and genetically based skill for speaking or wearing jeans, which are formed and enhanced according to the socio-linguistic conventions or changing fashions. As we have seen in the first part of the book, Fodor stressed the "genes" (or an innate language of thought), and Wittgenstein "jeans" (social training). The Domestication Model stresses both.

NOTES

CHAPTER 1.
LEARNING: GOING BEYOND INFORMATION GIVEN

1. See J. Fodor (1979), *The Language of Thought* p. 34 for a discussion of this.

2. See L. Wittgenstein, *Philosophical Investigations* (1953), Part 2, p. 232.

3. See especially Wittgenstein (1953) and Fodor (1979).

4. The idea that the development or learning in a narrow sense is just a matter of the unfolding of predetermined structures has been influential in developmental psychology from the very beginning. See, for example, J. Morss (1990) and his discussion of the influence of pre-Darwinian conceptions of development in psychology.

5. See, for example, *Cartesian Linguistics* (1966).

6. The possibility of the other kind of creativity depends on this kind being achieved. These problems are, of course, connected. See, for example, Baker and Hacker (1984), Sternberg (1988), and Piatelli-Palmarini (1980).

7. This has been forcefully stressed by Chomsky, for example in his criticism of behaviorism. See, for example, "Review of B. F. Skinner's 'Verbal Behavior'" in *Language*, 35:26–58, 1959. Skinner answered Chomsky in a short article "A lecture on 'having' a poem" in *Cumulative Record* (1972). Here he argues that creativity or going beyond information given can be explained with his theoretical apparatus. Random changes which are selected as a result of their consequences lead to new behaviors. In appealing to evolutionary theory his views are similar to the Domestication Model of learning which will be presented in chapter 7 and 8.

8. P. Munz, "Popper and Wittgenstein" in M. Bunge, ed., *The Critical Approach to Science and Philosophy* (London, Macmillan, 1964) p. 82.

211

9. Kripke (1982) in discussing the later Wittgenstein's writings on rule following showed that this was a problem not only in scientific and other inferences, but also is a problem of meaning. See chapter 5.

10. T. Kuhn, *The Structure of Scientific Revolutions* (1961).

11. *Plato. Five Dialogues*, trans., G. M. A. Grube, 80e (1981).

12. See also Fodor, chapter 2 (1979).

13. See, for example, Associationism: Pavlov (1960), Guthrie (1935), Ebbinghaus (1912), Thorndike (1931); Gestalt Psychology: Wertheimer (1945), Koffka (1921); Behaviorism: Watson (1925), Skinner (1974); Piaget (1926, 1954); Ecological Psychology: Shaw (1977), Neisser (1976) and Cognitive Psychology: Fodor (1979) and Boden (1988).

14. Although these theoretical approaches are very different they share some fundamental biological assumptions. See Morss (1991).

15. G. M. A., Grube, trans., *Plato. Five Dialogues*, 81d (1981).

16. Which, of course, fits with the Platonic theory of Forms, where knowledge is eternal and unchanging.

17. G. M. A. Grube, trans., *Plato. Five Dialogues* (1981), 72–73.

18. Meno, 81d, in G. M. A. Grube, trans., *Plato. Five Dialogues* (1981).

19. See Putnam in Piatelli-Palmarini, *Language and Learning: The Debate Between Jean Piaget and Noam Chomsky* (1979). One of the main topics discussed in the book is the problem of creativity, and a strong contrast between Piaget and Chomsky emerges, especially on the view of the innateness of language. Nevertheless, both Chomsky and Piaget see the acquisition of language based in thought or other mental processes. So, inspite of being opposed on the issue of going beyond information given they share a basic assumption in accounting for language.

20. D. Hume, *An Inquiry Concerning Human Understanding* (1957), p. 27.

21. Ibid., chapter 7.

22. See, for example, his article "The new riddle of induction" in a collection of papers (1972). Kripke (1982) points out that yet another version of the same problem arises in a semantic context.

23. Other influential behavioristic theories were developed by, for example, Watson, Tolman, Guthrie, and Hull, who all presented slightly different theories of learning.

24. The behaviorists were not unaware of this issue and tried to deal with it. See, for example, Skinner (1972, 1974) where he suggests that new responses arise when old associations can be used in new situations, and that trial and error give rise to new responses. This, though, seems less appropriate in accounting for the child's systematic errors as in cases of "over-regularization."

25. Chomsky (1959).

26. See his *The Language of Thought* (1979), which has been influential in especially cognitive or computational psychology.

27. See especially Chomsky's and Fodor's contributions to the debate between Chomsky and Piaget in Piatelli-Palmarini (1980).

28. According to Baker and Hacker (1984) the later Wittgenstein's interest in the problem of productivity was not really new, but had engaged him already in writing the *Tractatus*. Other contemporary philosophers like Frege and Schlick were also occupied by the same problem, hence both Wittgenstein and Chomsky should be seen as two prominent and very influential thinkers among many others.

29. J. Hintikka and M. Hintikka, *Investigating Wittgenstein* (B. Blackwell, Oxford, 1986). One example of this is found in the later Wittgenstein's discussion of ostensive definition (see chapter 5).

30. For using this terminology to describe Wittgenstein's position, see Bloor (1983).

31. Here the Domestication Model is similar to Skinner.

32. Wittgenstein's ideas will be discussed in chapters 4 to 6, and chapter 7 uses much material from both psychology and biology.

33. See chapter 7 and Sinclair (1971, 1972).

34. For this aspect of Fodor see chapter 2. For Wittgenstein see, for example, chapter 6.

35. See, for example, Vygotsky (1962), Piaget (1954, 1962, 1968, 1980) and Bruner (1974, 1976, 1978, 1986).

CHAPTER 2. FODOR'S THEORY OF LEARNING

1. See section on "The Language of Thought" below.

2. See Fodor (1968).

3. My discussion of Fodor's conception of learning focus on this book. Other writings will be considered only to the extent that they elaborate and illustrate the ideas of *The Language of Thought* (1979).

4. It is debatable if behaviorism really can be described as a paradigm in Kuhn's sense. For a discussion of this see Palermo, "Is a scientific revolution taking place in psychology?" (1971).

5. Both, though, denied that they were behaviorists. See, for example, L. Wittgenstein, *Philosophical Investigations* (1953) and G. Ryle, *The Concept of Mind* (1949), and also chapter 6 for discussion of whether or not Wittgenstein was a behaviorist.

6. For a good summary of the difficulties of behaviorism see, for example, the discussion of dispositional analysis in P. Churchland, *Matter and Consciousness* (1984).

7. For a discussion of Chomsky's criticism see A. MacIntyre, "Post-Skinner and Post-Freud: Philosophical causes of scientific disagreement" (1987); and J. Fodor, *The Language of Thought* (1979).

8. *Psychological Explanation* (1968), p. ix.

9. Fodor argues that neither a rejection of dualism, the problem of other minds scepticism, nor operationalism and other methodological considerations proposed by empiricist philosophers can provide a case for behaviorism. Hence, there are no methodological or a priori arguments in favor of behaviorism.

10. *Psychological Explanation* (1968), p. 29.

11. In later works, such as *Psychosemantics* (1987), Fodor relies less on productivity to argue for the language of thought. Here he stresses more the computational nature of mental processes.

12. It is worth noticing that action, learning and perception are central to behaviorism.

13. *The Language of Thought* (1979), p. 47.

14. In this respect, that is, in denying a role to introspection, Fodor is like behaviorists, but is different in postulating mental processes to account for behavior.

15. Of course limitations of memory, attention, and so forth, limit the actual outcome. Hence speaking about an infinite outcome is an idealization. Humans do not actually produce infinite outcomes.

16. See *Psychological Explanation* (1968), *The Language of Thought* (1979) and *Representations* (1983).

17. A program in economics can, for example, simulate economic development without duplicating the actual flow of money. In the same way a Turing machine can perhaps simulate, but not actually duplicate

thinking. This argument is put forth by among others J. Searle (1984) as a way of refuting theories like Fodor's. Some issues related to this will be discussed in chapter 3.

18. See Turing (1950).

19. Of course if mental processes are formal processes they are sensitive only to the formal properties of the representations. This means that two representations, concepts or thoughts are considered identical if their formal structure is identical. See the section on "The Semantics of the Language of Thought."

20. *De Trinitate*. For a good historical overview of the language of thought hypotheses see S. J. Brison "Do we think in Mentalese?" Unpublished Ph.D. thesis, University of Toronto, 1986.

21. R. Descartes, "Meditations on First Philosophy" in E. S. Haldane and G. R. T. Ross, trans., *The Philosophical Works of Descartes*, vol. 1 (Cambridge, Cambridge University Press, 1985).

22. The clear and distinct ideas, which are the ultimate undoubtable foundation of all knowledge, are not only phenomenologically intrinsically meaningful, but they are also universal and not derived from experience of the world or from public language and hence they must be expressed in a language of thought. But not only rationalists have embraced the idea of a language of thought. John Locke, who rejected Descartes innatism, accepted the notion of a language of thought. See, for example, Brison (1986). It is also worth noticing that Locke is critical of the Aristotelian conception. See T. De Mauro, *Ludwig Wittgenstein. His Place in the Development of Semantics* (Dordrecht, Holland, Eidel, 1967). Others though, such as Hobbes, Berkeley and Hume rejected a language of thought distinct from public languages.

23. *The Language of Thought*, p. 32.

24. For a critical discussion of this view see chapter 5.

25. For a good introduction and discussion of this see, for example, I. Hacking, *Why Does Language Matter to Philosophy?* (Cambridge, Cambridge University Press, 1975).

26. See chapter 7 below.

27. Similar ideas are found in Brentano, *Psychology from an Empirical Standpoint)* (RKP, London, 1973), and B. Russell, "On Propositions," "What they are and how they mean" in R. C. Marsh, ed., *Logic and Knowledge* (New York, G. P. Putnam and Son, 1971), and Wittgenstein's *Tractatus*.

28. See also "Tom Swift and his Procedural Grandmother" in *Representations* (1983).

29. J. Fodor, *Representations* (1983).

30. "Methodological Solipsism," p. 227, 1983. Similar views are put forward by Aristotle in *De Interpretatione* (1963) and Wittgenstein in *Tractatus* (1961).

31. For a discussion of this and related problems with the computational approach see J. Searle, *Minds, Brains and Science* (Cambridge, MA, Harvard University Press, 1984).

32. Fodor does not rule out the possibility of a psychological theory which can handle perception, and so forth, but he thinks it is *very* unlikely. He bases this on the claim that naturalistic psychologies are incoherent, but as we will see in the next few chapters this can be said about Fodor's theory as well. In chapter 7 a naturalistic approach to learning will be presented and discussed.

33. To get such a theory to work he first has to show that mental states supervene on brain states and that the so-called broad account of mental content (namely, that the content of belief and meaning is dependent on something external, for example, physical or linguistic states of affairs) is mistaken. He furthermore has to deal with the problems posed by meaning holism, that is, that the content of a belief or the meaning of an expression depends on the total belief system or the whole of language. He also has to show that critical objections to causal theories can be met. So far he has only provided an inconclusive sketch, and since even a solution to all these issues leaves many of the problems of learning intact, I will not focus on this new development of Fodor's theory.

34. In this Fodor is clearly in opposition to other conceptions of the language of thought. A philosopher of psychology such as Rom Harré (1986) or a psychologist such as J. Bruner (1986) argues, inspired by Wittgenstein, that the language of thought is socially constructed and conventional, that is, not innate but learned or derived from the natural language the individual encounters.

35. See Fodor *The Language of Thought*, p. 57.

36. Ibid., p. 80.

37. See *The Language of Thought*, p. 71 and "The present status of the innateness debate" in *Representations*.

38. See, for example, D. Davidson, "Truth and meaning" (1967).

39. *The Language of Thought*, p. 59.

40. Ibid., p. 113.

41. Ibid., pp. 63–64.

42. For an interesting discussion of this issue see P. Munz, "Popper and Wittgenstein" in M. Bunge, ed., *The Critical Approach to Science and Philosophy* (London, MacMillan, 1964).

43. *The Language of Thought*, p. 64.

44. Ibid., pp. 96–97.

45. Piatelli-Palmarini, *Language and Learning: The Debate between Jean Piaget and Noam Chomsky* (Cambridge, Harvard University Press, 1980), p. 260.

46. Fodor, like some of the Presocratics, seems to operate with the idea that "like knows like." See, for example, Aristotle, *De Anima*, Book 1.

47. See "The present status of the innateness controversy" (1982).

48. Ibid.

49. Fodor in Piatelli-Palmarini, p. 260 (1980).

50. It is interesting to notice that learning a language, but not understanding a language is rational activity—a matter of hypothesis formulation and testing. It is "knowledge that" (in contrast to "knowledge how"). "What I said was that learning what a predicate means involved representing the extension of that predicate; not that understanding the predicate does. A sufficient condition for the latter might be just that one's use of the predicate is always in fact conformable with a truth rule," p. 65 in *The Language of Thought*.

51. See note 43 above.

52. Fodor is here, I think, addressing Wittgenstein's *Philosophical Investigations* section 32.

53. See note 43 above.

54. Ibid., p. 64.

55. For the same claim see D. Hamlyn, *Experience and the Growth of Understanding* (London, RKP, 1978).

56. Fodor in *Cognition* 1 (1972) (1):83–85.

57. See, for example, Vygotsky (1962), Wittgenstein (1953), Skinner (1957), and Bruner (1986).

58. See note 43 above.

59. *Psychosemantics* (1987), p. 99.

CHAPTER 3.
PROBLEMS WITH FODOR'S ACCOUNT OF LEARNING

1. See, for example, Block (1981), Piatelli-Palmarini (1980), Searle (1984), Heil (1981), and the so-called debate about narrow and broad psychology, Putnam (1975) and Fodor (1987).

2. See, for example, his book *Psychosemantics* (1987).

3. See chapter 2.

4. Adopted from M. Polanyi, *Personal Knowledge* (Chicago, University of Chicago Press, 1962), p. 49.

5. The fact that it can be argued that both the bicyclist and the planets do not exhibit productive behavior but behave in a mechanical way does not change the core of this argument.

6. See, for example, the debate between Chomsky and Quine in the journal *Synthese* (1968–70).

7. See D. Dennett, *Brainstorms* (Montgomery, Vermont, Bradford Books, 1978); H. L. Dreyfus, *What Computers Can't Do* (New York, Harper and Row, 1979); and J. Heil, "Does cognitive psychology rest on a mistake?" in *Mind* vol. 90 (1981), 321–342.

8. See note 7 above, Dreyfus, p. 168.

9. See note 7 above, Heil, p. 327.

10. Wittgenstein (1953) would argue that meaning, understanding and so forth, is not something mental (see chapters 4–6 below), explaining why mental reports are rare.

11. Something like this seems to be going on in the article "Methodological Solipsism Considered as a Research Strategy in Cognitive Psychology." If something cannot fit with his model or theory of the mind it is pushed aside and not taken as a criticism. For example, if semantics cannot be understood in terms of a computational device, then semantics cannot be part of psychology, or our attempts to understand the mind.

12. See G. Ryle, *The Concept of Mind* (London, Hutchinson, 1949), p. 33.

13. See D. Dennett, *Brainstorms* (1978), p. 95.

14. Ibid.

15. What underlies this theory in Plato and perhaps implicitly in Fodor is the idea of "like knows like" prevalent in ancient philosophy. See, for example, Heracleitus's 'Logos' and Empedocles' ideas on perception and knowledge, that is, that by earth we see earth, by water water, and by love we perceive love. See, for example, P. Wheelwright, *The Presocratics* (1966), p. 61, frag. 1 and 2; and p. 139, frag. 159.

16. See, for example, chapter 9 in Baker and Hacker (1984).

17. D. Dennett, *Brainstorms* (1978).

18. Ibid., p. 103.

19. Ibid., p. 104.

20. See D. Dennett,"Skinner Skinned" in *Brainstorms* (1978), and A. MacIntyre, "Post-Skinner and Post-Freud: Philosophical causes of scientific disagreement." in H. Engelhart, Jr., and A. Caplan, eds., *Scientific Controversies: Case Studies in the Resolution and Closure of Disputes in Science and Technology* (Cambridge, Cambridge University Press, 1987).

21. The example of the robber is my own, but it is consistent with what Skinner, in a rather general way, says. See, for example, Skinner (1957, chapter 7; 1974, chapters 6, 7).

22. The problematic nature of the relation of Fodor's theory to empirical evidence is further stressed by S. Brison. She argues that empirical results from psychological experiments in bilingualism and the integration of pictorial and linguistically encoded information does not establish a special language of thought which is distinct from natural language or from pictorial representation, unless it is interpreted in light of Fodor's assumption about the nature of language and concepts. See S. Brison, "Do we think in Mentalese? A critique of the 'Language of Thought' hypothesis." Unpublished Ph.D. thesis, University of Toronto, 1986.

23. In this case he could not refer to attempts to capture mental processes by verbal reports. See Ericsson and Simon (1984).

24. A parallel point was raised by Popper in discussing Thales' cosmology and Anaximander's attempt to improve on it. See his *Conjectures and Refutations* (London, RKP, 1963).

25. *The Language of Thought*, p. 96.

26. See Chomsky's and Fodor's contributions in Piatelli Palmarini (1980).

27. See, for example, Whorf (1956) and Wittgenstein (1953).

28. See above, chapter 2.

29. For similar claims see J. Bruner, *Actual Minds, Possible Worlds* (Cambridge, MA, Harvard University Press, 1986). Bruner claims, for example, that children have clear ideas of what goes on in the mind of adults and are able to adjust their actions accordingly (p. 60).

30. S. J. Gould, "Tires to sandals," *Natural History*, 4 (1989) and "Full of hot air," *Natural History* 10 (1989).

31. Baker and Hacker (1984), pp. 329–330.

32. P. Churchland, "Fodor on Language Learning" in *Synthese*, 38 (1978), p. 153.

33. Boden (1988), chapter 7.

34. "Critical Notes" in *Synthese*, 38 (1978), 161–67. See also G. F. Bradshaw, P. W. Langley, and H. Simon in "Studying Scientific Discovery by Computer Simulation," *Science*, 222 (1983), 971–75. In this article they discuss the program BACON, which can be used for making inductive inferences leading to scientific concepts and theories.

35. "Critical Notes" p. 164

36. Both Goodman and Putnam have argued against Chomsky's strong innatism, and their arguments apply to Fodor as well. Goodman argues that the theory is very difficult to test since it can only be tested indirectly by considering ancillary considerations and evidence, and that it is unclear exactly what is innate (ideas, dispositions, limitations or what). Putnam argues along similar lines and both claim that the strong preformism is unnecessary, because the ability to learn can be accounted for by postulating a pre-linguistic symbol system, like gestures and perceptual recognition (Goodman), or a general learning mechanism (Putnam). Neither Putman, nor Goodman give any constructive "positive" suggestions, hence they are not very helpful in solving the problem of learning. See, for example, N. Goodman, "The Epistemological Argument" in *Problems and Projects* (New York, Bobbs-Merill, 1972) and Putnam in Ned Block, ed., *Readings in the Philosophy of Psychology*, vol. 2 (London, Methuen, 1981).

37. In *Psychosemantics* (1987) he argues that mental states supervene on brain states.

38. *Mind*, vol. 90 (1981), 321–342.

39. Ibid., p. 321.

40. *The Language of Thought*, p. 30.

41. *The Language of Thought*, p. 67. The causal theory in *Psychosemantics* (1987) is a further development of this.

42. In *Psychosemantics* Fodor sticks to the idea that syntax mirrors semantics and representation is a matter of formal structure. Hence the criticism presented above is relevant for this part of the argument for a causal theory of meaning.

43. Wittgenstein (1953), p. 54.

44. Heil (1981), p. 335.

45. Baker and Hacker (1984), chapter 9.

46. Heil (1981), p. 339.

47. *Minds, Brains and Science* (Cambridge, MA, Harvard University Press, 1984). Searle's argument is an attempt to refute Turing's (1950) claim that any entity that behaves as a human being would in a similar situation can be attributed thought.

48. Ibid., p. 34.

49. For a discussion of problems with Searle's account see, for example, Boden (1988).

50. *The Language of Thought*, p. 62.

51. See, for example, chapter 1 in *The Language of Thought*.

52. See, for example, L Wittgenstein, *Philosophical Investigations* (Oxford, Basil Blackwell, 1953), para. 84–87, and Norman Malcolm "Wittgenstein: The relation of language to instinctive behavior" in *Philosophical Investigation*, 5 (1982), 1:3–22, 1982.

53. Vygotsky (1962), Bruner (1961, 1966).

54. O. J. Flanagan Jr., *The Science of Mind* (Cambridge, MA, MIT Press, 1984), pp. 137–44.

55. N. Goodman, "The epistemological argument" (1972).

56. Baker and Hacker (1984) claim that the problem of productivity has been recognized and dealt with by, for example, Schlick, Frege, and the early Wittgenstein in *Tractatus*. Chapters 4–6 deal with the later Wittgenstein's approach to this problem.

CHAPTER 4. WITTGENSTEIN 1:
BACKGROUND AND THE REJECTION
OF A LANGUAGE OF THOUGHT

1. A few exceptions are Hardwich (1971), Hallett (1977), Ross (1978), Hamlyn (1978), and Malcolm (1982).

2. W. W. Bartley III, "Theory of Language and Philosophy of Science as Instruments of Educational Reform; Wittgenstein and Popper as Austrian Schoolteachers" in *Boston Proceedings in the Philosophy of Science*, 14; and *Wittgenstein* (New York, B. Lipcott Company, 1973). Not only in Vienna (with Buhler, etc.) was there an interest in learning. Most theories of learning which still are influential, as Piaget's, Vygotsky's, and behaviorism were first developed around this time, in the 1920s and 1930s. Wittgenstein was not influenced by any of these theories, but it is an indication of the general intellectual climate.

3. See, for example, Bartely (1973), Fogelin (1976), and von Wright (1982).

4. See, for example, Baker and Hacker (1980) and Arrington (1979) for a discussion of Wittgenstein's concern with ostensive definition. Baker and Hacker (1988) also point out that ostensive definition was central to the logical positivists in Vienna.

5. *Zettel* (Z), The following abbreviations will be used; *Notebooks* (NB), *Tractatus Logicus-Philosophicus* (TLP), *Blue and Brown Books* (BB), *Philosophical Investigations* (PI), *Lectures on Culture* (LC), *On Certainty* (OC).

6. *Wittgenstein. Rules and Private Language* (1982). Kripke's interpretation of Wittgenstein is very interesting and is helpful even if one does not agree with the claim that Wittgenstein is a sceptical philosopher. The book is helpful, I find, because it brings out Wittgenstein's concern with the problem of productivity, that is, that meaning always goes beyond information given.

7. M. Hintikka and J. Hintikka, *Investigating Wittgenstein* (Oxford, Basil Blackwell, 1987).

8. W. W. Bartley III, *Wittgenstein* (New York, Lipcott Company, 1973), for setting out Kant's problem in this form.

9. For a good exposition of this, see Kripke's (1982) discussion of rules and private language. For a critical discussion of Kripke, see, for example, Shanker (1987) and Baker and Hacker (1984a).

10. See Fodor (1968) and (1979).

11. Baker and Hacker (1984, chapter 9) point out that the interest in the problem of productivity, or the creative use of language, has occupied many philosophers during this century, for example, the early Wittgenstein, Schlick, and Frege.

12. M. Hintikka, and J. Hintikka (1987), chap. 1. They refer to TLP 4.12, 3.263, 2.174, as well as to PI 120 to illustrate this. They acknowledge that "language as the universal medium" is less explicit in the later works, but many of Wittgenstein's remarks make sense if understood in this way.

13. Z 412. In the preceding sections Wittgenstein points out that doubt or reason never is the basis for learning something.

14. PI 109; see also PI 126, 496, and BB p. 125.

15. PI 109.

16. Ibid., p. 230.

17. LC; "Lectures on aesthetics" 5.

18. Kripke in his book *Wittgenstein: On Rules and Private Language* (1982) argues that the main thrust of Wittgenstein's later work is a new kind of scepticism and his contribution is mainly negative. Contrary to Kripke I would like to claim that Wittgenstein is not a sceptic and does not present a sceptical argument of the kind Kripke ascribes to him. He rejects the generalized and context free scepticism which is based only in the logical possibility of doubt. This kind of sceptical challenge is meaningless and self-refuting, because it is the result of a transgression of the limits of sense. It is a misunderstanding of what doubt, justification, and related concepts entail, and is not something one should try to answer, because it is based on misunderstanding language. Doubt always presuppose that something is taken for granted, otherwise it does not make sense (e.g., OC 24, 114, 115, 120, 369, 519, and PI 485). For a more detailed discussion see Shanker (1987) and Baker and Hacker (1984a). See also Erneling (1986).

19. It is interesting to notice that the old meaning of the English "learn" also meant to teach, and that this use is still found in modern German (e.g., Lehrer) and modern Swedish. The etymology of "learning" also seem to be that it comes from a verb meaning 'to follow in the footsteps of.'

20. My reading of Wittgenstein is similar to those of Conway (1989) and Bloor (1983) in that, like them, I try to go beyond what Wittgenstein actually said and apply his ideas in areas which he did not explicitly discuss. I also stress that his naturalism, namely, give an inter-

pretation of his views that the limits of language and thought are rooted in physical, biological, psychological, and social facts about people and the world. See chapter 6 and also Bloor (1983), Conway (1989), Pears (1971), Malcolm and Strawson in Pitcher (1968), and Jones (1976).

21. R. McDonough, *The Argument of the "Tractatus"* (Albany, State University of New York Press, 1986), and N. Malcolm, *Nothing Is Hidden: Wittgenstein's Criticism of His Earlier Views* (Oxford, Basil Blackwell, 1984). For a similar argument, see also J. Heil, "Does Cognitive Psychology rest on a mistake?" *Mind* (July 1981).

22. See Baker and Hacker (1984) for a discussion of similarities in approach between the early Wittgenstein and theories of meaning in Davidson and Chomsky, among others.

23. TLP ix.

24. Ibid., 3.1.

25. Ibid., 4.002.

26. McDonough (1986). The reason for this is that the article is an attempt by Russell to elucidate Wittgenstein (Shanker, personal communication).

27. "On propositions: What they are and how they mean" (1919).

28. Brentano's conception was very influential on the so-called act-psychology, which developed as a reaction to the failure of Wundt and his followers to find uniform mental content. This is interesting since Wittgenstein's criticism of *Tractatus* in *Philosophical Investigations* can also be read as a criticism of act-psychology. See D. Bloor, *Wittgenstein: A Social Theory of Knowledge* (New York, Columbia University Press, 1983). I will return to this in its context below.

29. This is reminiscent of Descartes' "clear and distinct ideas" and also Hume's "impressions," which are presumed to be intrinsically meaningful. I agree with Bartley that Wittgenstein in *Tractatus* is pre-Kantian. See also the closeness to Feyerabend's interpretation of Aristotle's *De Anima* in *Science in a Free Society*, 1982.

30. TLP 4.023.

31. Ibid., 4.121, see also 4.1212 and 4.022.

32. For a discussion of the similarities between Frege, the early Wittgenstein, and the Chomsky-Fodor approach to language, see Baker and Hacker (1984).

33. G. Pitcher, *The Philosophy of Wittgenstein* (Englewood Cliffs, NJ, Prentice Hall, 1964).

34. M. Black, *A Companion to Wittgenstein's 'Tractatus'* (Ithaca, NY, Cornell University Press, 1964).

35. NB 82 (12.9.16).

36. Ibid., 130 (19.8.19).

37. PI 4. 1121; McDonough (1986), argues that thoughts are logical entities and Kenny in the article "Wittgenstein's early philosophy of mind" (1981) claims that meaning in *Tractatus* is seen as located in the transcendental self.

38. Russell p. 302 (1919).

39. Augustine has no explicit theory of learning, but what he says implies certain assumptions about learning.

40. PI 1.

41. G. P. Baker and P. M. Hacker, *Wittgenstein: Understanding and Meaning* (Chicago, University of Chicago Press, 1980). Although Wittgenstein explicitly mentions Augustine here, it is clear that he is attacking an archetypical picture of language, which Augustine as well as himself had adopted.

42. Wittgenstein never directly refers to these schools of psychology, but he was familiar with some of their writings through some works by Russell and Wundt, and he also met Buhler. See Bloor (1983) and the section on "Criticism of image- and act-psychology."

43. See note 40 above.

44. TLP 3.202.

45. Ibid., 3.203.

46. PI 27.

47. TLP 2.02.

48. Ibid., 3.23.

49. PI 47.

50. Ibid., 48.

51. See my discussion of Heil in chapter 3.

52. PI 257.

53. See chapter 5 for a more detailed discussion of this argument. See also Hacker (1986).

54. Shanker (1987) rejects Kripke's reading and argues that Wittgenstein's argument is not sceptical but a *reductio ad absurdum* argument.

55. PI 693.

56. See, for example, Humphery (1951).

57. See, for example, BB pp. 155–56, PI 175–78, 330, 332. Wittgenstein's use of introspection does not mean he endorsed it as a method in psychology or philosophy; to claim that would be to accept the view he is rejecting.

58. PI 33.

59. Ibid., 34.

CHAPTER 5. WITTGENSTEIN 2: LEARNING IS NOT BASED ON THE LANGUAGE OF THOUGHT

1. PI 30.

2. Ibid., 28.

3. Ibid.

4. Ibid., 31.

5. Ibid., 1.

6. See Baker and Hacker (1980) for a comprehensive discussion of this.

7. BB p. 5.

8. PI 156.

9. Ibid., 1.

10. Ibid., 257, 243.

11. Ibid., 257.

12. Ibid., 258, cp. 259, 262, 265, and 202.

13. Like, for example, W. James and Russell.

14. PI 329.

15. Ibid., 330.

16. Ibid., 351, cp. 352.

17. TLP 3.1.

18. PI 341.

19. BB p. 42.

20. PI 322.

21. Ibid., 347.

22. Ibid., 344, cp. PI 361.

23. Ibid., 201.

24. Kripke (1982) p. 9.

25. Since Fodor appeals to internal rules and representations to explain a person's cognitive conduct, this criticism seems to destroy his position that human behavior can be understood in terms of rules in the mind.

26. Kripke (1982) p. 89.

27. This account of rule following is not without problems, but a discussion of this is beyond the scope of this book.

CHAPTER 6. WITTGENSTEIN 3: RECONSTRUCTING A WITTGENSTEINIAN ACCOUNT OF LEARNING

1. See chapter 2.

2. The terms "accommodating" and "assimilating" are borrowed from Piaget, but are here used in a much "looser" sense and without their strong ties to biology Piaget gives them. See Piaget (1926, 1954, 1980).

3. See section "The Limits of Learning" below.

4. PI 1.

5. See previous chapters.

6. PI 66.

7. Ibid., 67.

8. Bloor (1983) p. 25.

9. See S. Toulmin, *Foresight and Understanding: An Inquiry into the Aims of Science* (New York, Harper and Row, 1961). He argues that science takes certain aspects of reality as unproblematic or natural;

and explanation, theory development, and so forth, only deals with what deviates from the perceived natural order. In Wittgenstein's case the "natural order" seems to be the open-endedness of language.

10. This is also related to Wittgenstein's rejection of essentialism, that is, of fixed and absolute meanings.

11. See chapter 4.

12. TLP 4.1212.

13. A. Janik and S. Toulmin, *Wittgenstein's Vienna* (New York, Simon and Schuster, 1973).

14. Plato's account of primary education of the guardians, whose moral training consists of censored examples of brave and high-spirited behavior, comes to mind here.

15. As an example, see *Short Stories*, vol. 2 (1965), which contain stories written between 1872 and 1911. Wittgenstein is reputed to have said that Tolstoy impressed him much more when he told a story than when he tried to explain something to the reader. He said "It seems that his philosophy is most true when *latent* in the story." N. Malcolm, *Wittgenstein: A Memoir* (London, Oxford University Press, 1969).

16. TLP 3.262.

17. Ibid., 3.263.

18. The German word translated as 'elucidations,' *Erlauterung*, means according to my German dictionary elucidation by exemplification or illustration.

19. I think Tolstoy was an important influence on Wittgenstein's later conception of language. I have been trying to trace a reference in Vygotsky from Tolstoy (see Vygotsky 1962, pp. 83–84). For example, Vygotsky quotes Tolstoy and he clearly expresses ideas very similar to the ones later developed by Wittgenstein. Vygotsky's is clearly influenced by Tolstoy's ideas on language and it is reasonable to assume that the similarities one finds between Wittgenstein and Vygotsky can be explained, at least partly, by their common admiration for Tolstoy. This seems to me a more likely explanation than assuming that Wittgenstein was familiar with Vygotsky.

20. Z 116.

21. PI 71, cp. PI 75.

22. Ibid., 133.

23. See, for example, TLP 3.363 "So they can only be understood if the meanings of those signs are already known."

24. PI 5.

25. See chapter 4 on language as universal medium. Of course there are such things as explicit or contextual definitions, but these can only function in learning if the child has the rudiments of language.

26. T. Kuhn, "The function of dogma in scientific research" in A. C. Crombie, ed., *Scientific Change* (New York, Basic Books, 1963), p. 351.

27. For comparison see Z 410, OC 139, 140, 141, 143, 144, 160, 161, 170, 204, 263, 283, 343, 473, 476, 603, 612. Although these sections deal with many different issues they all express the attitude that learning is typically a matter of being trained to conform to standards the learner is in no position to contest.

28. T. Kuhn, "Second thoughts on paradigms" in *The Essential Tension* (University of Chicago Press, 1977), pp. 239–319.

29. This question will be discussed later in the chapter.

30. See chapter 4 above.

31. PI 208, compare PI 211, 212 and BB pp. 89–90. See "Was Wittgenstein a Behaviorist?" below for a discussion of whether or not Wittgenstein was a behaviorist.

32. New York, Appleton-Century (1957).

33. *Verbal Behavior* (1957), p. 52.

34. Ibid., p. 31.

35. Ibid., pp. 29–30.

36. Although Wittgenstein mentions the importance of rewards in shaping behavior (BB pp. 89–90) he never develops this aspect of learning. This is clearly a weakness. Would he accept Skinner's account or does he have something else in mind?

37. PI 244.

38. B. F. Skinner, "Operational analysis of psychological terms" in H. Feigl and M. Broadbeck, eds., *Readings in the Philosophy of Science* (Appelton-Century Crofts Inc., 1959), pp. 585–95. D. Bloor in *Wittgenstein: A Social Theory of Knowledge* (Columbia University Press, New York, 1983), drew my attention to these similarities between Skinner and Wittgenstein.

39. See note 37 above.

40. The question whether or not Wittgenstein was a behaviorist

has puzzled many commentators. For example, it has been argued that he presented something very close to behaviorism (Klemke 1971) or operant conditioning (Harwick 1971); that there is some textual evidence in favor of a behavioristic reading of Wittgenstein (Hallett 1967, Fogelin 1976); that the textual evidence is inconclusive (Ayer 1988); that Wittgenstein only agreed with the behaviorists in stressing the importance of behavior in understanding mental concepts (Bolton 1979, Hacker 1972, Kenny 1973, Pears 1988) but that ascribing mental events to someone is not to ascribe behavior to them. Most commentators agree, though, that he was not a behaviorist, even if some things pointed in that direction. Finch (1977), Baker and Hacker (1980). Malcolm (1977) on the other hand uses Wittgenstein to argue against Skinner.

41. Skinner's account of creativity (e.g., 1972) indicates that he took his behaviorism to be less deterministic in the sense that behaviors and responses were always changing.

42. For a discussion of this in a different context see see Bloor (1983), chapter 8.

43. He is not denying the existence of mental entities (ontological behaviorism), nor is he saying that the studying of behavior is the only legitimate method in psychology.

44. PI 293.

45. Ibid., 308.

46. New York, Random House, 1974.

47. Wittgenstein's account of learning is also very close to the account given by Quine. But if Kripke is correct Quine's dispositional analysis would be rejected by Wittgenstein.

48. Fodor and Chihara (1968) argues that Wittgenstein was a logical behaviorist. Although Wittgenstein in some works preceeding the *Philosophical Investigations* sometimes says things that sound like he was a logical behaviorist, it is clear that he did not express any such views in *Philosophical Investigations*.

49. Here I am following Bloor (1983).

50. OC 359.

51. PI 2 p. 226.

52. Conway (1989) rightly remarks that very little has been written on the concept of 'forms of life' in Wittgenstein and adds that the interpretations given vary widely. She describes four common interpre-

tations; language-game and form of life are equated; cultural system and language-game are equated; human nature is a form of life; and form of life is conceived in terms of an organism. I, like Conway, find these unsatisfactory. Forms of life encompass both natural and social factors, and are therefore constantly changing.

53. This is mentioned in "Cause and Effect: Intuitive Awareness" published in *Philosophia*, 6:3–4, pp. 391–408, (1976).

54. PI 244.

55. Z 532, compare Z 533–34.

56. Ibid., 540.

57. Ibid., 541.

58. Ibid., 545.

59. PI 2, p. 223.

60. L. Wittgenstein, "Remarks on Frazer's *Golden Bough*" in C. G. Luckhardt, ed., *Wittgenstein. Sources and Perspectives* (Hassocks, Sussex, Harvester Press, 1979). From this it is clear that Wittgenstein did not endorse cultural solipsism any more than he endorsed individual solipsism (PI 206, BB p. 103).

61. *Remarks of the Philosophy of Psychology* 1, 664.

62. See, for example, Piaget (1926, 1954, and 1980).

63. Kripke (1982), chapter 2.

64. OC 476.

65. This point is from I. Scheffler, *The Language of Education* (Springfield, IL, Charles Thones Books, 1965).

66. BB p. 81

67. Hamlyn makes this the central point in his reconstruction of Wittgenstein's theory of learning. See his *Experience and the Growth of Understanding* (London, RKP, 1978).

68. See Vygotsky (1962).

69. See, for example, Kuhn (1962).

70. See Harré (1986).

71. PI 2, p. 232

72. See my remarks on behaviorism above.

CHAPTER 7. THE DOMESTICATION MODEL
OF LANGUAGE ACQUISITION

1. PI 309.

2. Bloor (1983), p. 5.

3. See Harré (1986).

4. For suggestions along these lines see P. Churchland (1986), Piaget (1926, 1954, 1980), and Hattiangadi (1987).

5. Some argue that it is a mistake to compare the chimpanzee's ability to that of human children. According to the leading proponent of this view Terrace (1979), there is no difference between the signing chimpanzee and the horse "Clever Hans" who seemed to be able to count but on closer inspection only reacted to unconscious promptings (twitching of an eyebrow) of his trainer. Although prompting probably plays a role in the animals' behavior, as it does in children's, the chimpanzees are less tied to prompting than the horse—which is not surprising given their higher intelligence.

6. This is Lenneberg's estimate (1967) but according to Gould (1973) it is 40%. It is notable that there is such a wide difference in different estimates. Variation in estimates of brain weight seem to be the rule and not the exception.

7. See Fishbein (1984), J. Vaclair, K. Bark (1983), and others.

8. See Gibson (1985).

9. For a discussion of how how to best measure and compare the relative weight of brains in different species see Gould (1973).

10. They are also known as bird-head dwarfs and reach the average height of two and a half feet but have the bodily proportions of an adult.

11. Again estimates vary. Rathaus (1988) claims that the brain develops from 23% to 70% in the first year.

12. The location where the signals from one nerve cell pass to another, that is, from axon to dendrite.

13. Nerve-cell process conducting nervous impulses.

14. Snow and Hoefnagel (1978) found that Dutch adults and teenagers learned faster than three to five year olds. This throws doubt on the claim that there is a sensitive period for language learning. It is still agreed, though, that children never exposed to language fail to learn, even when exposed to language later in life.

15. A typical example of a *nidifuge* is reptiles, while mammals and birds are combinations of *nidifuge* and *nidicole*.

16. de Waele and Harré, p. 201.

17. Lenneberg argues that this pattern is not only a slow down of a general primate pattern but is unique to humans. Whether or not this slowing of development results in neoteny, that is, the retention of juvenile characters in adulthood is debatable. Gould (1973) argues that this is the case but Lieberman (1984) think there are very few juvenile characteristics in an adult human. This issue is not important to my general argument.

18. See Walker (1981). Also, many other aspects of the developing brain, as myelination, is important for the acquisition of language. For example, the myelination of auditory neurons occurs earlier in gestation and is completed, after birth, earlier than for visual neurons. See Rathus (1988).

19. The difference between so-called retroflex and dental stops. These have to do with ways of curling the tongue, for example, in dental stops to produce the sound "t." Retroflex stops are not found in English.

20. This fact is a challenge to theories of the evolution, as Lieberman's (1984), which sees the development of speech as crucial for the evolution of language. Did language in early humans outweigh the risk of choking? See chapter 8.

21. Children exposed early to ASL perform just as well as hearing children. Learning ASL can even facilitate language acquisition in hearing children (Rathus 1988).

22. See, for example, Piaget (1926, 1968, 1980).

23. D. Kimura (1979).

24. Lieberman (1985), p. 662.

25. I am not claiming that ontogenesis recapitulates phylogenesis, but that Lieberman's analysis can be applied to ontogenesis as well.

26. Gibson (1985) reports that the chimpanzees she studied didn't show object-to-object manipulations or sequential manipulations. The chimpanzees were reared in a home and treated as children yet failed to develop these skills.

27. Chimpanzees lack most of these specializations and can only learn the rudiments of sign language.

28. See chapter 5.

29. Reynolds (1976), p. 631.

30. Behavior is seen as different and yet as similar to itself. P. Marks Greenfield (1978), suggests that this starts already when the child starts to play with its hands. The two hands are different yet move in a similar way, reflecting each other. This is like Piaget, who sees sensorimotor action as the basis of signification.

31. This section utilizes the analysises and empirical observations of Piaget (1962), Vygotsky (1976), P. Reynolds (1976), V. Reynolds (1978), Lieberman (1984), Hattiangadi (1988).

32. In the next section I will discuss communicative or social skills which also are necessary for language.

33. Vygotsky (1976), p. 548.

34. In this context it is interesting to note that Gibson (1985) reports that the chimpanzee she studied exhibited maternal behavior to a baby chimp but not to a doll.

35. See Lorenz (1966) for a discussion of the importance of Funktionslust.

36. Deaf children and chimpanzees obviously master manual signs earlier and quicker than speaking children, but I think that this can be explained by the fact that speech motor control is more complex than manual manipulation, hence it takes longer time to develop.

In this context it could be interesting to speculate on the fact that chimpanzees and other primates do not babble. Can it be that babble, which is ideally suited for the practice of speech sounds, also is ideally suited for representation and semantics? Does this explain why it is so difficult to teach primates more than the rudiments of language? This obviously cannot be the only thing distinguishing nonhuman primates since deaf children and children with articulatory problems learn language.

37. See Wittgenstein and Kripke's explication of his argument.

38. See chapters on Wittgenstein.

39. See Harré (1976).

40. This fact is, I think, the source of our anthropomorphic ascriptions to children; we teach them by treating them as already having what we are teaching them.

41. Rathus (1988), p. 276.

42. Its helplessness due to the underdeveloped nervous system, and so forth, makes social interaction a necessity.

43. Much of the basis of symbiosis has been explored in so-called attachment studies beginning with Bowlby; see Richards (1974).

44. Eible-Eibesfeldt (1970) claims that, for example, the smile has a universal meaning.

45. See also Lock (1978), Gray (1978), and Newson (1978) for other examples, for example, the emergence of pointing from reaching gestures; raising of arms as anticipating and signaling a wish to be lifted and development of object exchange.

46. Peekaboo seems to be a universal game: *Eckergiek* (German), *tittut* (Swedish), *kurkistus-lekki* (Finnish), *coucou* (French), *cucú* (Spanish), and *nascondino* (Italian).

47. Bruner (1976), p. 284.

48. See Newson (1978).

49. See chapter 6 and Wittgenstein (1953) for a discussion of the difficulties involved in accounting for the acquisition of words like "pain."

50. These signs are given different interpretations in different cultures.

51. A similar, but more complicated, account can be given for the acquisition of the concept of 'self.' With 'self' I am referring to the unifying and organizing principle of perception, action, and emotion. The adult treats the child and speaks too it as if it had a self. Certain behaviors are reacted to and described as if they originated from a self. The self as an organizing principle originates from these public descriptions and reactions and the adult help the child to connect language and concepts with its natural behaviors. For a discussion of this, see Harré (1986).

52. Rathus (1988), p. 276.

53. See the chapters on Wittgenstein above.

54. The social interaction between mother and her infant is not uniquely human, it is seen in other primates, as well. See, for example, Premack (1980).

55. For a review of the literature see Rose and Rurr (1987).

56. See, for example, Vygotsky's discussion of children engaging in so-called egocentric speech, that is, talk aloud to themselves when encountering a difficult problem (Vygotsky 1962).

57. See Harré (1986) and Vygotsky (1962) for a discussion of these issues along the lines indicated.

CHAPTER 8. CONCLUSION:
THE FRAMEWORK AND PRODUCTIVITY OF LEARNING

1. See the section on the evolution of language below.

2. For a similar view of scientific and artistic creativity see Feldman (1988).

3. See Hattiangadi (1987), Bartley (1987), and Campbell (1987).

4. Vygotsky (1962). See also Lakoff and Johnson (1980) for a discussion of how the metaphorical nature of our concepts can be linked with object manipulations skills.

5. Darwin (1859, 1958), p. 172.

6. See note 5 above.

7. See Darwin (1872, 1965) and Gould (1992).

8. Seeing certain skills in this way is teleological and close to creationism.

9. .See Lieberman (1985) for a discussion of the fossil evidence.

10. Munz (1964), p. 82. See also the discussion of Wittgenstein's private language argument.

11. How can the Domestication Model explain that several different linguistic expressions express the same proposition? Quine (1970) addresses this issue by saying that of course we take some linguistic expressions to say the same thing, for example, "Es regnet" and "It is raining," because the understanding of one (the German) is a result of translating from the other (English). The meaning of the English is carried over into German because we can not transcend English when translating. Another answer, which is closer to Wittgenstein and the idea of flexibility of language and skills, is that it does not matter if they express the same proposition or not. It only matters that they function in a similar way in similar contexts. The search for the *same* only leads one to look for essences where there are none.

12. See Harré (1986) for discussion of this.

BIBLIOGRAPHY

Ackermann, R. *Wittgenstein's City.* Amherst, MA, University of Massachusetts Press, 1988.

Anscombe, G. E. M. *An Introduction to Wittgenstein's Tractatus.* Philadelphia, University of Pennsylvania Press, 1971.

Aristotle "De Anima" in *Aristotle: Selected Works.* Translated by H. G. Apostle and P. P. Gerson. Ginnell, Iowa, The Peripathetic Press, 1982.

―――. "De Interpretatione" in *Aristotle's Categories and De Interpretatione.* Translated by J. L. Ackrill. Oxford, Oxford University Press, 1963.

Arrington, R. L. "Mechanism and calculus: Wittgenstein on Augustine's theory of ostension" in C. Luckhardt, ed., *Wittgenstein: Sources and Perspectives.* Hassocks, Sussex, Harvester Press, 1979.

Augustine, Saint. *Confessions.* Translated by A. N. Menston. England, Scholarship Press, 1972.

―――. "De Trinitate" in R. A. Markus, ed., *Augustine.* New York, Anchor, 1972.

Ayer, A. *Wittgenstein.* London, Weidenfeld and Nicolson, 1985.

Baker, G. and P. Hacker. *Wittgenstein. Understanding and Meaning.* Chicago, University of Chicago Press, 1980.

―――. *Language, Sense and Nonsense.* Oxford, Basil Blackwell, 1984.

―――. *Scepticism, Rules and Language.* Oxford, Basil Blackwell, 1984 (1984a).

―――. *Wittgenstein, Frege and the Vienna Circle.* Oxford, Basil Blackwell, 1988.

Barnes, B. *T. S. Kuhn and Social Science.* London, Macmillan, 1982.

Bartley III, W. W. "Theory of language and philosophy of science as instruments of educational reform; Wittgenstein and Popper as Austrian schoolteachers." In *Boston Proceedings in the Philosophy of Science*, 14. New York, B. Lipcott Company, 1973.

————. *Wittgenstein*. New York, Lipcott Company, 1973.

————. "Philosophy of biology versus philosophy of physics" in W. W. Bartley III, ed., *Evolutionary Epistemology, Theory of Rationality, and the Sociology of Knowledge*. La Salle, IL, Open Court, 1987.

Black, M. *A Companion to Wittgenstein's Tractatus*. Ithaca, NY, Cornell University Press, 1964.

Block, I., ed. *Perspectives on the Philosophy of Wittgenstein*. Oxford, Basil Blackwell, 1981.

Block, N. ed. *Readings in the Philosophy of Psychology, Vol. 2*. London, Methuen, 1981.

Bloor, D. *Wittgenstein: A Social Theory of Knowledge*. New York, Columbia University Press, 1983.

Boden, M. *Computer Models of Mind*. Cambridge, Cambridge University Press, 1988.

Bolton, N. *Philosophical Problems in Psychology*. London, Methuen, 1979.

Bower, T. G. R. *The Perceptual World of the Child*. Cambridge, MA, Harvard University Press, 1977.

————. *A Primer of Infant Development*. San Franscico, W. H. Freeman, 1977 (1977a).

Bradshaw, G. F., P. W. Langley, and H. Simon. "Studing scientific discovery by computer simulation." In *Science*, 22, 971–975, 1983.

Brentano, F. *Psychology from an Empirical Standpoint*. London, RKP, 1973.

Brinkley, J. *Wittgenstein's Language*. The Hague, Martinus Nijhoff, 1973.

Brison, S. "Do we think in Mentalese? A Critique of the 'Language of Thought Hypothesis.'" Unpublished Ph.D. thesis, University of Toronto, 1986.

Bruner, J. S., and J. Goodman. *A Study of Thinking*. New York, Wiley, 1961.

Bruner, J. S., R. Oliver, P. Greenfield, and others. *Studies in Cognitive Growth: A Collaboration at the Center for Cognitive Studies*. New York, Wiley, 1966.

Bruner, J. S., "The organization of early skilled action." In M. Richards, ed., *The Integration of a Child Into a Social World.* Cambridge, Cambridge University Press, 1974.

———. "Peekaboo and the learning of rule structures." In J. S. Bruner, A. Jolly, and K. Sylvia, eds., *Play: Its Role in Development and Evolution.* Harmondsworth, Penguin, 1976.

———. "Learning how to do things with words." In J. S. Bruner and A. Garton eds., *Human Growth and Development: Wolfson Lectures 1976.* Oxford, Clarendon, 1978.

———. *Actual Minds, Possible Worlds.* Cambridge, MA, Harvard University Press, 1986.

Campbell, D. "Blind variation and selective retention in creative thought as in other knowledge processes." In W. W. Bartley III, ed., *Evolutionary Epistemology, Theory of Rationality, and the Sociology of Knowledge.* La Salle, IL, Open Court, 1987.

Canfield, J. *Wittgenstein: Language and the World.* Amherst, MA, University of Massachusetts Press, 1981.

Cavell, S. *Must We Mean What We Say?* New York, Cambridge University Press, 1969.

Changeux, J-P. "Genetic determination and epigenesis of the neural network: Is there a biological compromise between Chomsky and Piaget?" In M. Piatelli-Palmarini, ed., *Language and Learning: The Debate Between Jean Piaget and Noam Chomsky.* Cambridge, MA, Harvard University Press, 1980.

———. *Neural Man.* New York, Pantheon, 1985.

Chomsky, N. "Review of B. F. Skinner's 'Verbal Behavior.'" In *Language*, 35:26–58, 1959.

———. *Cartesian Linguistics.* New York, Harper and Row, 1966.

———. *Language and Mind.* New York, Harcourt, Brace and Jovanovich, 1972.

———. *Rules and Representations.* New York, Columbia Press, 1980.

Churchland, P. M. *Matter and Consciousness.* Cambridge, MA, MIT Press, 1984.

Churchland, P. S. "Fodor on language learning." In *Synthese*, 38:149–159, 1978.

———. *Neurophilosophy.* Bradford, MIT Press, 1986.

Conway, G. *Wittgenstein on Foundations*. Atlantic Highlands, NJ, Humanities Press, 1989.

Darwin, C. *The Origin of Species*. (1859), New York, Mentor, 1958.

———. *The Expression of Emotion in Man and Animal*. (1872), Chicago, University of Chicago Press, 1965.

Davidson, D. "Truth and meaning." In *Synthese*, 304–23, 1976.

———. "The very idea of a conceptual scheme." In Krausz and J. Meiland eds., *Realtivism: Cognitive and Moral*. London, Notre Dame, 1982.

De Mauro, T. *Ludwig Wittgenstein: His Place in the Development of Semantics*. Dortrecht, Holland, Eidel, 1967.

Dennett, D. *Brainstorms* Montgomery, VT, Bradford Books, 1978.

Descartes, R. "Meditations on First Philosophy." In E. S. Haldane and G. R. T. Ross, trans., *The Philosophical Works of Descartes, Vol 1*. Cambridge, University of Cambridge Press, 1985.

Dreyfus, H. L. *What Computers Can't Do*. New York, Harper and Row, 1979.

Ebbinghaus, H. *The Principles of Psychology*. 1902.

Edwards, J. *Ethics without Philosophy: Wittgenstein and Moral Life*. Tampa, University of South Florida Press, 1982.

Eibl-Eibesfeldt, I. E. *Ethology: The Biology of Behavior*. New York, Holt, Rinehart and Winston, 1970.

Eimas, P. D. "The perception of speech in early infancy." In *Scientific American*, 46–52, January 1985.

Ericsson, K. and H. Simon. *Protocol Analysis Data: Verbal Reports as Data*. Cambridge, MA, MIT Press, 1984.

Erneling, C. "On Language Acquisition," MA thesis, SUNY Binghamton, 1983.

———. "Kripke, Wittgenstein and Scepticism." Unpublished paper, 1986.

Feldman, D. "Creativity, dreams, insights and transformations." In R. Sternberg, ed., *The Nature of Creativity*. Cambridge University Press, Cambridge, 1988.

Feyerabend, P. *Science in a Free Society*. London, Verso, 1982.

Finch, H. *Wittgenstein—The Later Philosophy*. Atlantic Highlands, NJ, Humanities Press, 1977.

Fishbein, H. D. *The Psychology of Infancy and Childhood: Evolutionary and Cross-cultural Perspectives*. Hillsdale, NJ, Lawrence Erlbaum, 1984.

Flanagan, Jr., O. *The Science of Mind*. Cambridge, MA, MIT Press, 1984.

Fodor, J. *Psychological Explanation*. New York, Random House, 1968.

———. "Some reflections on L. S. Vygotsky's Language and Thought." In *Cognition*, 1:83–85, 1972.

———. *The Language of Thought*. Cambridge, MA, Harvard University Press, 1979.

———. "The present status of the innateness controversy." In *Representations*. Cambridge, MA, MIT Press, 1982.

———. *Representations*. Cambridge, MA, MIT Press, 1982.

———. *The Modularity of Mind: An Essay in Faculty Psychology*. Cambridge, MA, MIT Press, 1983.

———. *Psychosemantics*. Cambridge, MA, MIT Press, 1987.

——— and C. S. Chihara. "Operationalism and ordinary language." In G. Pitcher, ed., *Wittgenstein: The Philosophical Investigations*. Notre Dame, University of Notre Dame, 1968.

Fogelin, R. *Wittgenstein*. London, RKP, 1976.

Forman, G. E. "Scattered thoughts on the origin of similarity with focus on motor pattern as constrained by bilateral symmetry in human anatomy." Unpublished manuscript, 1971.

———, Langlin, F. and M. Sweeney. "The development of jigsaw puzzle solving in preschool children: an information processing report." In *Paper and Reports*, 5:8, 1973.

———, Kuschew, D. and J. Dempsy. "Transformation in the manipulations and productions with geometric objects: an early system of logic in children." Center for Early Childhood Education, University of Massachusetts at Amherst, 1975.

Geach, P. *Wittgenstein's Lectures on Philosophical Psychology, 1946–47*. New York, Harvester, 1988.

Gentner, D. "Why nouns are learned before words: Linguistic relativity vs. natural partitioning." In C. Kuczaj, ed., *Language, Thought and Culture*. Hillsdale, NJ, Lawrence Erlbaum, 1983.

Gibson, K. "Challenging chimpanzees." Interview in *Equinox*, July–August, 17–18, 1985.

Goodman, N. "The epistemological argument." In *Problems and Projects*. New York, Bobbs-Merill, 1972.

———. "The new riddle of induction." In *Problems and Projects*. New York, Bobbs-Merill, 1972.

Gould, S. J. *Ever since Darwin*. New York, Norton, 1977.

———. "Tire to sandals." In *Natural History*, 4:8–15, 1989.

———. "Full of hot air." In *Natural History*, 10:28–38, 1989.

———. "Mozart and modularity." In *Natural History*, 9:8–16, 1992.

Gray, H. "Learning to take an object from the mother." In A. Lock, ed., *Action, Gesture and Symbol: The Emergence of Language*. New York, Academic Press, 1978.

Grayling, A. *Wittgenstein*. Oxford, Oxford University Press, 1988.

Greenfield, P. M. "Structural parallels between language and action in development." In A. Lock, ed., *Action, Gesture and Symbol: The Emergence of Language*. New York, Academic Press, 1978.

Gruber, H. E., J. Girus, and A. Banuazizi. "The development of object permanence in the cat." In *Developmental Psychology*, 4:9–15, 1971.

Guthrie, E. *Psychology of Learning*. New York, Harper and Row, 1935.

Hacker, P. M. S. *Insight and Illusion*. Oxford University Press, 1972.

———. *Insight and Illusion*. 2nd edition. New York, Clarendon, 1986.

Hacking, I. *Why Does Language Matter to Philosophy?* New York, Cambridge University Press, 1975.

Hallett, G. *Wittgenstein's Definition of Meaning*. New York, Fordham University Press, 1967.

———. *A Companion to Wittgenstein's "Philosophical Investigations."* Ithaca, NY, Cornell University Press, 1977.

Hamlyn, D. *Understanding and the Growth of Knowledge*. London, RKP, 1978.

Hardwick, C. *Language Learning in the Later Wittgenstein*. The Hague, Mouton, 1971.

Harré, R. *Personal Being: A Theory for Individual Psychology*. Cambridge, MA, Harvard University Press, 1986.

Hattiangadi, J. N. *How Is Language Possible?* LaSalle, IL, Open Court, 1987.

Heil, J. "Does cognitive psychology rest on a mistake?" In *Mind*, 90:321–342, 1981.

Hilmy, S. *The Later Wittgenstein: The Emergence of a New Philosophical Method.* Oxford, Basil Blackwell, 1987.

Hintikka, M. and J. Hintikka. *Investigating Wittgenstein.* Oxford, Basil Blackwell, 1987.

Hofstadter, D. R. and D. C. Dennett eds., *The Mind's I.* New York, Bantam Books, 1981.

Holtzman, S. and C. Leich eds., *Wittgenstein: To Follow a Rule.* London, RKP, 1981.

Hull, C. *Principles of Behavior.* New York, Appleton Century-Crofts, 1943.

Hume, D. *An Inquiry into Human Understanding.* London, Macmillan, 1986.

Humphery, G. *Thinking: An Introduction to Its Experimental Psychology.* London, Methuen, 1951.

Janik, A. and S. Toulmin. *Wittgenstein's Vienna.* New York, Simon and Schuster, 1973.

Jones, P. "Strains in Hume and Wittgenstein." In D. Livingstone and J. King, eds., *Hume: A Re-evaluation.* New York, Fordham University Press, 1976.

Kenny, A. *Wittgenstein.* Middlesex, Penguin, 1973.

———. "Wittgenstein's early philosophy of mind." In I. Block, ed., *Perspectives on the Philosophy of Wittgenstein.* Oxford, Basil Blackwell, 1981.

Kimura, D. "Neuromotor mechanisms in the evolution of human communication." In H. D. Steklis, ed., *Neurobiology of Social Communication in Primates.* New York, Academic Press, 1979.

Klemke, E., ed., *Essays on Wittgenstein.* Urbana, IL, University of Illinois Press, 1971.

Koffka, K. *The Growth of the Mind.* New York, Harcourt, Brace & World, 1921.

Konner, M. J. "Aspects of the developmental ethology of a foraging people." In N. J. Blurton Jones, ed., *Ethological Studies of Child Behavior.* London, Cambridge University Press, 1972.

———. "The long haul." In *The New York Times*, 55–56, July 9, 1989.

Kripke, S. *Wittgenstein on Rules and the Private Language.* Cambridge, MA, 1982.

Kuczaj II, S. A. "On the nature of syntactic development." In S. A. Kuczaj II, ed., *Language Development: Vol 1. Syntax and Semantics.* Hillsdale, NJ, Erlbaum, 1982.

Kuhn, T. *The Structure of Scientific Revolutions.* Chicago, University of Chicago Press, 1962.

——. "The function of dogma in scientific research." In A. Crombie, ed., *Scientific Change.* New York, Basic Books, 1963.

——. "Second thoughts on paradigms." In *The Essential Tension.* Chicago, University of Chicago Press, 1977.

Lakoff, G. and M. Johnson. *Metaphors We Live By.* Chicago, University of Chicago Press, 1980.

Lenneberg, E. H. *The Biological Foundations of Language.* New York, J. Wiley, 1967.

Lieberman, P. *The Biology and Evolution of Language.* Cambridge, MA, Harvard University Press, 1984.

——. "On the evolution of human syntactic ability: Its preadaptive bases—Motor control and speech." In *Journal of Human Evolution,* 14:657–668, 1985.

——. "Voice in the wilderness: How humans acquired the power of speech." In *The Sciences,* July/August, 23–29, 1988.

—— and S. E. Blumstein. *Speech Production, Speech Perception and Acoustic Phonetics.* Cambridge, Cambridge University Press, 1988.

Lober, J. "Is your brain really necessary?" In *Science,* December, 1232–34, 1980.

Lorenz, K. *On Agression.* Translated by M. Kerr Wilson. New York, Harcourt, Brace and World, 1966.

MacIntyre, A. "Post-Skinner and post-Freud: Philosophical causes of scientific disagreement." In H. Engelhart, Jr., and A. Caplan eds., *Scientific Controversies: Case Studies in the Resolution and Closure of Disputes in Science and Technology.* Cambridge, Cambridge University Press, 1987.

Malcolm, N. "Wittgenstein's *Philosophical Investigations.*" In G. Pitcher, ed., *Wittgenstein: The Philosophical Investigations.* London, MacMillan, 1968.

———. *Wittgenstein: A Memoir*. London, Oxford University Press, 1969.

———. *Thought and Knowledge*. Ithaca, Cornell University Press, 1977.

———. "Wittgenstein: The relation of language to instinctive behavior." In *Philosophical Investigation*, 5, 1, 3–22, 1982.

———. *Nothing is Hidden: Wittgenstein's Criticisms of His Earlier Views*. Oxford, Basil Blackwell, 1984.

McDonough, R. *The Argument of the Tractatus*, Albany, NY, SUNY Press, 1986.

McGinn, C. *Wittgenstein on Meaning*. Oxford, Basil Blackwell, 1984.

McGuiness, B., ed., *Wittgenstein and His Times*. Chicago, University of Chicago Press, 1982.

Morss, J. *The Biologising of Childhood: Development Psychology and the Darwinian Myth*. Hillsdale, NJ, Erlbaum, 1990.

Munz, P. "Popper and Wittgenstein." In M. Bunge, ed., *The Critical Approach to Science and Philosophy*. London, MacMillan, 1964.

Nelson, K. "Structure and strategy in learning to talk." In *Monographs of the Society of Research in Child Development*, 149, 1973.

Newson, J. "Dialogue and development." In A. Lock, ed., *Action, Gesture and Symbol: The Emergence of Language*. New York, Academic Press, 1978.

Palermo, D. S. "Is a scientific revolution taking place in psychology?" In *Science Studies*, 11:135–155, 1971.

Pavlov, I. P. *Conditioned Reflexes*. New York, Dover Publications, 1960.

Pears, D. *Wittgenstein*. London, Fontana, 1971.

———. *The False Prison: A Study of the Development of Wittgenstein's Philosophy*. Vol 1. Oxford, Clarendon, 1987.

———. *The False Prison: A Study of the Development of Wittgenstein's Philosophy*. Vol 2., Oxford, Clarendon, 1988.

Piaget, J. *The Language and Thought of the Child*. Translated by M. Gabin. New York, Meridian, 1926.

———. *The Child's Construction of Reality*. Translated by M. Cook. New York, Basic Books, 1954.

————. *Play, Dreams and Imagination in Childhood*. Translated by C. Gattengo and F. M. Hodgson. New York, W. W. Norton, 1962.

————. *On the Development of Memory and Identity*. Translated by E. Duckworth. Worcester, MA, Clark University Press, 1968.

————. "Language within cognition." In M. Piatelli-Palmarini, ed., *Language and Learning: The Debate Between Jean Piaget and Noam Chomsky*. Cambridge, MA, Harvard University Press, 1980.

———— and B. Inhelder. *The Psychology of the Child*. London, RKP, 1969.

Piatelli-Palmarini, M., ed., *Language and Learning: The Debate Between Jean Piaget and Noam Chomsky*. Cambridge, MA, Harvard University Press, 1980.

Pitcher, G. *The Philosophy of Wittgenstein*. Englewood Cliffs, NJ, Prentice-Hall, 1964.

Plato. *Dialogues by Plato*. Translated by B. Jowett. Oxford, Oxford University Press, 1924.

————. *The Republic*. Translated by G. M. A. Grube. Indianapolis, Hackett, 1974.

————. *Plato. Five Dialogues*. Translated by G. M. A. Grube. Indianapolis, Hackett, 1981.

Ploog, D. "Phonation, emotion, cognition with reference to the brain mechanisms involved." Ciba Foundation Symposium 1969, in *Brain and Mind*, 79–98, 1979.

Polanyi, M. *Personal Knowledge*. Chicago, University of Chicago Press, 1962.

Popper, K. *Conjectures and Refutations*. London, RKP, 1963.

Premack, D. "Representational capacity and accessibility of knowledge: The case of chimpanzees." In M. Piatelli-Palmarini, ed., *Language and Learning: The Debate Between Jean Piaget and Noam Chomsky*. Cambridge, MA, Harvard University Press, 1980.

Putnam, H. "The meaning of 'meaning'." In *Mind, Language and Reality: Collected Papers*. New York, Cambridge University Press, 1975.

————. "What is innate and why: Comments on the debate." In M. Piatelli-Palmarino, ed., *Language and Learning: The Debate Between Jean Piaget and Noam Chomsky*. Cambridge, MA, Harvard University Press, 1980.

Quine, W. "Methodological reflections on current linguistic theory." In *Synthese*, 21:386–398, 1970.

Rathus, S. A. *Understanding Child Development*. New York, Holt, Rinehart and Winston, 1988.

Restak, R. M. *The Brain: The Last Frontier*. Garden City, NJ, Doubleday and Company, 1979.

Reynolds, P. C. "Play, language and human evolution." In J. S. Bruner, A. Jolly, and K. Sylva, eds., *Play: Its Role in Development and Evolution*. Harmondsworth, Penguin, 1976.

Reynolds, V. *The Biology of Human Action*. Reading, W. H. Freeman, 1976.

Richards, M. "First steps in becoming social." In M. Richards, ed., *The Integration of a Child into a Social World*. Cambridge, Cambridge University Press, 1974.

Rose, S. A. and H. A. Ruff. "Cross-modal abilities in human infants." In J. D. Osofsky, ed., *Handbook of Infant Development*. New York, Wiley, 1987.

Ross, J. J. "Ludwig Wittgenstein and the learning of language." In E. Leinfellner et al., eds., *Wittgenstein and his Impact on Contemporary Thought*. Vienna, 1978.

Russell, B. "On propositions: What they are and what they mean." In C. Marsh, ed., *Logic and Knowledge*. New York, G. P. Putnam's Sons, 1971.

Ryan, J. "Early language development: Towards a communicational analysis." In M. Richards, ed., *The Integration of a Child into a Social World*. Cambridge, Cambridge University Press, 1974.

Ryle, G. *The Concept of Mind*. London, Hutchinson, 1949.

Scheffler, I. *The Language of Education*. Springfield, IL, Charles Thones Books, 1965.

Searle, J. *Minds, Brains and Science*. Cambridge, MA, Harvard University Press, 1984.

Shanker, S. *Wittgenstein and the Turning-Point in the Philosophy of Mathematics*. London, Croon Helm, 1987.

Shotter, J. "The development of personal powers." In M. Richards, ed., *The Integration of a Child into a Social World*. Cambridge, Cambridge University Press, 1974.

————. "Acquired powers: The transformation of natural into social powers." In R. Harré, ed., *Personality*. Totowa, NJ, Rowman and Littlefield, 1976.

Sinclair, H. "Sensorimotor action pattern as a condition for the acquisition of syntax." In E. Ingram and R. Huxley, eds., *Language Acquisition: Models and Methods*. New York, Academic Press, 1971.

————. "A study in developmental psycholinguistics." In *Journal of Experimental Child Psychology*, 14:328–348, 1972.

Sinnott, J. M., D. B. Pison, and R. N. Askin. "A comparison of pure auditory thresholds in human infants and adults." In *Infant Behavior and Development*, 6:3–18, 1983.

Skinner, B. F. *Verbal Behavior*. New York, Appleton Century-Crofts, 1957.

————. "Operational analysis of psychological terms." In H. Feigl and M. Broadbeck, eds., *Readings in Philosophy of Science*. New York, Appelton Century-Crofts, 1959.

————. "A lecture on 'having' a poem." In B. F. Skinner, *Cumulative Record. A Selection of Papers*. New York, Meredith, 1972.

————. *About Behaviorism*. New York, Random House, 1974.

Snow, C. E. "Mother's speech research: from input to interaction." In C. E. Snow and C. A. Ferguson, eds., *Talking to Children: Language Input and Acquisition*. Cambridge, Cambridge University Press, 1977.

————, and M. Hoefnagel-Hohle. "The critical period of language acquisition: Evidence from second language learning." In *Child Development*, 54:227–232, 1978.

Stenlund, S. *Det osägbara*. Stockholm, Nordstedts, 1980.

Sternberg, R., ed. *The Nature of Creativity*. Cambridge, Cambridge University Press, 1988.

Strawson, P. "Review of Wittgenstein's 'Philosophical Investigations'," In G. Pitcher, ed., *Wittgenstein: The Philosophical Investigations*. London, Macmillan, 1968.

Terrace, H., et al. "Can an ape create sentences?" In *Science,* 206: 891–902, 1979.

Thorndike, E. *Human Learning*. New York, Appleton Century-Crofts, 1931.

Tolman, E. *Purposive Behavior in Animal and Man.* New York, Century, 1932.

Tolstoy, L. *Short Stories.* Vol. 2, 1965.

Toulmin, S. *Foresight and Understanding: An Inquiry into the Aims of Science.* New York, Harper and Row, 1961.

Turing, A. "Computing Machinery and Intelligence." In *Mind*, 433–460, 1950.

Vauclair, J. and K. A. Bard. "Development of manipulations with objects in ape and human infants." In *Journal of Human Evolution*, 12:631–645, 1983.

Vohra, A. *Wittgenstein's Philosophy of Mind.* La Salle, IL, Open Court, 1987.

von Wright, G. H. *Wittgenstein.* Oxford, Basil Blackwell, 1982.

Vygotsky, L. S. *Thought and Language.* Translated by E. Hofmann and G. Vakar. Cambridge, MA, MIT Press, 1962.

————. "Play and its role in mental development of the child." In J. Bruner, A. Jolly, and K. Sylva, eds., *Play: Its Role in Development and Evolution.* Harmondsworth, Penguin, 1976.

Waele, J-P. and R. Harré. "The personality of individuals." In R. Harré, ed., *Personality.* Totowa, NJ, Rowman and Littlefield, 1976.

Walker, L. C. "The ontogeny of neural substrate for language." In *Journal of Human Evolution*, 10:429–441, 1981.

Walker, S. "The evolution and dissolution of language." In A. W. Ellis, ed., *Progress in Psychology of Language, Vol. 3.* Hillsdale, NJ, Lawrence Erlbaum, 1987.

Wasow, T. "Critical notes." In *Synthese*, 38:161–167, 1978.

Watson, J. *Behaviorism.* New York, Norton, 1925.

Wertheimer, M. *Productive Thinking.* New York, Harper and Row, 1945.

Wheelwright, P. *The Presocratics*, Indianapolis, Bobbs-Merill, 1966.

Whorf, B. *Language, Thought and Reality.* Edited by J. B. Carroll. Cambridge, MA, MIT Press, 1956.

Winch, P. *The Idea of a Social Science and Its Relation to Philosophy.* London, RKP, 1958.

Wittgenstein, L. *Philosophical Investigations.* Translated by G. E. M. Anscombe. Oxford, Basil Blackwell, 1953.

———. *On Certainty.* Edited by G. E. M. Anscombe and G. H. von Wright. Translated by D. Paul and G. E. M. Anscombe. New York, Harper and Row, 1958.

———. *The Blue and Brown Books.* New York, Harper and Row, 1958.

———. *Notebooks 1914–1919.* Edited by G. H. von Wright and G. E. M. Anscombe. Translated by G. E. M. Anscombe. Oxford, Basil Blackwell, 1961.

———. *Tractatus Logico-Philosophicus.* Translated by D. Pears and B. McGuinness. New York, Humanities Press, 1961.

———. *Lectures and Conversations on Aesthetics, Psychology and Religious Belief.* Edited by C. Barrett. Berkeley, University of California Press, 1967.

———. *Zettel.* Edited by G. E. M. Anscombe and G. H. von Wright. Translated by G. E. M. Anscombe. Oxford, Basil Blackwell, 1967.

———. *Philosophical Grammar.* Translated by A. Kenny. Oxford, Basil Blackwell, 1974.

———. *Philosophical Remarks.* Edited by R. Rhees. Translated by R. Hardgreaves and R. White. Oxford, Basil Blackwell, 1975.

———. "Cause and effect." In *Philosophia*, 6:3–4, 391–408, 1976.

———. "Remarks on Frazer's *Golden Bough*." In C. G. Luckhart, ed., *Wittgenstein: Sources and Perspectives.* Hassocks, Sussex, Harvester Press, 1979.

———. *Remarks on the Philosophy of Psychology, Vol. 1.* Edited by G. E. M. Anscombe and G. H. von Wright. Translated by G. E. M. Anscombe. Chicago, University of Chicago Press, 1980.

———. *Remarks on the Philosophy of Psychology, Vol 2.* Edited by G. E. M Anscombe and G. H. von Wright. Translated by G. E. M. Anscombe. Chicago, University of Chicago Press, 1980.

INDEX